D0081241

THE SWORD
IN
ANGLO-SAXON ENGLAND

THE SWORD
IN
ANGLO-SAXON ENGLAND

Its Archaeology and Literature

HILDA ELLIS DAVIDSON

Illustrated by Ewart Oakeshott

THE BOYDELL PRESS

Copyright © Hilda Ellis Davidson 1962

All Rights Reserved. Except as permitted under current legislation
no part of this work may be photocopied, stored in a retrieval system,
published, performed in public, adapted, broadcast,
transmitted, recorded or reproduced in any form or by any means,
without the prior permission of the copyright owner

First published 1962
Corrected reprint 1994 by
The Boydell Press, Woodbridge

ISBN 0 85115 355 0

The Boydell Press is an imprint of Boydell & Brewer Ltd
PO Box 9, Woodbridge, Suffolk IP12 3DF, UK
and of Boydell & Brewer Inc.
PO Box 41026, Rochester, NY 14604–4126, USA

British Library Cataloguing-in-Publication Data
Davidson, Hilda Ellis
  Sword in Anglo-Saxon England: Its
  Archaeology and Literature. – New ed
  I. Title
  942.01
  ISBN 0–85115–355–0

Library of Congress Cataloging-in-Publication Data applied for

Printed in the United States of America

PREFACE

THE beginning of this book can be traced to a lecture given
to English students at Bedford College about ten years ago.
At that time there was much interest among archaeologists
in the patterns on sword blades used by the Anglo-Saxons and
Vikings, since X-ray photography was now revealing how many of
these had survived in our museums. There was much speculation
also about various theories put forward in England, France, and
Scandinavia to account for these complex patterns. As our knowledge of this skill increased, so did our respect for the old sword-
smiths, and so also, it seemed to me, did our understanding of the
descriptions of fine swords in Anglo-Saxon poetry and the Old
Norse sagas. The keen interest of the students and the questions
which they asked prompted me to begin a short article on this
subject, but it was never completed, for in the course of the next
few years it stubbornly persisted in growing into a book. From the
early literature of north-western Europe, I gradually became aware
of the supreme importance of the sword in the Anglo-Saxon
period, first as a weapon and secondly as a symbol. I came to
realize too what a wonderful collection of swords existed in the
museums of this country, and how little known it was, both at
home and abroad. In this book I have given an account of part of
my discoveries, although a study of sword names in detail and of
the significance of the sword as a poetic image yet remains to
be completed.

With the help of archaeology we can learn something of the
practical basis underlying the rich and romantic traditions sur-
rounding the weapons of the past. Thus we gain a new understanding of the minds of men in the Anglo-Saxon period, whose
craftsmanship and skill in making and using weapons must other-
wise be lost to this modern age. It is a very serious loss, inasmuch
as the weapons on which the survival not only of individuals but
of families and communities depended were of paramount

importance, and no serious picture of their world is complete
without them. If students and teachers of our early literature will
only avail themselves of the help given by archaeological research
at home and abroad, this more than anything else will, I believe,
keep such studies alive, and give them permanent value outside
the narrow bounds of the specialist's study and the examination
syllabus.

I have called this book a study of the sword in Anglo-Saxon England because the archaeological section is primarily based on the
material in our own museums; since I have not included the enormous field of Scandinavian and Continental material, to add the
term 'Viking' to the title would be presumptuous. But the Anglo-
Saxon period continued until 1066, and the Viking invasions,
which left many fine swords resting in graves or river-beds in this
country, are included in it. Since a large part of England was held
from time to time by Viking rulers and peopled by Scandinavian
colonists, I have felt that it was reasonable to include the evidence
of Old Norse literature for information about the swords of the
period. Certainly I have not restricted myself wholly to Anglo-
Saxon weapons, since it is not possible to view these in isolation.
The story of the making and using of swords from the close of
the Roman period to the Norman Conquest takes us far beyond
the bounds of our own islands, and the rich mixture of weapons
which resulted from battles, trade, and gifts between the various
peoples of western Europe is mirrored by the rich mixture of
literary traditions which the Anglo-Saxons enjoyed.

In writing this kind of book, subject to many different disciplines,
one becomes more than usually conscious of the problems of
spelling. I have followed what seems to me the sensible custom
of Scandinavian scholars and have simplified the spelling of
personal names and the names of swords, only keeping the Old
Icelandic form in the names of sources or unsimplifiable sword
names given in italics. For the sake of readers unfamiliar with Old
Norse I have also tried to avoid the initial β as far as possible and
have substituted *Th* for it. Since consistency in these matters is
wellnigh unattainable it seemed better to avoid undue pedantry

in a book which is bound to include so many specialized and technical terms. I can only hope that I have not merely succeeded in offending language specialists without making for greater all-round understanding.

The book has taken a long time to write, the more so because it has grown up along with my own family. But I do not regret the years spent on it, for it has led to new friendships and I think more stimulating discussions than any other subject which I have studied. The sword both catches men's imaginations and teases their curiosity, and my meetings with Ewart Oakeshott, the illustrator of this book, who collects medieval swords and handles them with love and knowledge, and with John Anstee, who arrived one day with a pattern-welded sword of his own making strapped on under his coat, have taught me more than many books could do. I should also like to express here my warm gratitude for the kindness which I have received from the curators of many museums, who have allowed me free access to the swords in their possession and given me much help from their records. In particular, Mr. R. L. S. Bruce-Mitford, Keeper of British and Medieval Antiquities in the British Museum, has been unfailingly generous with help, advice, and information, particularly in the early stages of the book. I am grateful also to Mr. David Wilson, the Assistant Keeper, for his kind assistance in tracking down swords in the British Museum and elsewhere. Out of many enjoyable visits to museums, I must recall with pleasure two days at Dublin, where Mr. Joseph Raftery, Keeper of Irish Antiquities in the National Museum of Ireland, made me free of the splendid collection of Viking swords, some housed in cases in the Museum and many more in strange subterranean depths below, and sent me away with a fine hoard of photographs. I am glad too to make acknowledgement here to those who have helped me on the scientific and technical side— the most thorny one for me—and especially to Mr. Leo Biek of the Ancient Monuments Laboratory of the Ministry of Works.

It is a great pleasure also to express my thanks here to many generous and busy people—the busier they are, it seems, the more prompt to reply—who have responded to my cries for assistance and have answered my queries or read and criticized parts of this book. From them I must single out Mrs. Sonia Hawkes and Miss Rosemary Cramp, who gave help on the archaeological and Anglo-Saxon sections, Professor G. D. Willcock and Mr. Mathison Cain, on the literary side, Professor A. T. Hatto, who read the section on the use of the sword, Mr. R. D. V. Elliott, who gave help with the runes, and Professor Jocelyn Toynbee, who helped with the Latin of Cassiodorus. There are many others whom I remember with gratitude, and who are mentioned in footnotes.

Many prefaces end with appreciation of the help given by patient wives; I must here add one to the group of rarer tributes to long-suffering husbands. Mine has done much more than suffer in silence the domestic disruptions that the writing of books of this kind by wives and mothers involves. He has tried to enlighten my ignorance of scientific matters, he has helped in proof-reading, and amiably convicted me of not a few errors of logic, grammar, and style, and above all he has been the ideal person on whom to try out new ideas. Finally I must thank the Secretary and Staff of the Clarendon Press for setting me a standard in the preparing and correcting of manuscripts towards which to work in future, and for the help which they have given me throughout.

HILDA R. ELLIS DAVIDSON

CONTENTS

x CONTENTS

LIST OF ILLUSTRATIONS

(*at end*)

PLATES

ACKNOWLEDGEMENTS

I AM indebted to the following for permission to publish photographs or drawings of objects in their possession:

The Trustees of the British Museum (photographs of the Sutton Hoo and Fetter Lane hilts, and figs. 16, 17, 18, 19, 23, 27, 30, 37, 38, 46, 49, 54a, 63, 64, 69, 84, 91, 93, 101, 103, 107, also fig. 108, from MS. Tib. C. VI, fol. 10; fig. 109, from MS. Tib. C. VI, fol. 9; and fig. 110, from MS. Harley 603, fol. 8; also fig. 20 from their *Catalogue of Anglo-Saxon Coins*); the National Museum of Ireland (photographs of Ballinderry and Kilmainham hilts, and figs. 70, 77, 78, 79, 82, 85, 104); the Victoria and Albert Museum (photograph of damascened blade); the National Museum, Copenhagen (photographs of blades from Nydam and Kragehul); the Cambridge University Museum of Archaeology and Ethnology (photograph of the Ely Fields sword and fig. 21); the Maidstone Museum (photograph of Bifrons hilt and figs. 44, 45, 51, 52, 53, 55, 92); the Liverpool Public Museums (photograph of Gilton pommel and fig. 50); the London Museum (fig. 73); the Wallace Collection (fig. 87); the Ministry of Works (fig. 76); the Ashmolean Museum (figs. 48, 67, 100, and also fig. 97 from publication on the Abingdon Cemetery); the South Shields Museum (fig. 15a); Reading Museum and the Thames Conservancy Board (fig. 25, and drawing in Appendix B); Wisbech Museum (fig. 31); Salisbury Museum (fig. 36); Norwich Castle Museum (fig. 40); Saffron Walden Museum (fig. 65); Sheffield Museum (fig. 66); Dorchester Museum (fig. 74); the Universitet Institutionen för nordisk Fornkunskap, Uppsala (fig. 54b); the Universitets Oldsaksamling, Oslo (fig. 89); the Rheinisches Landesmuseum, Bonn (fig. 90).

Drawings have also been made from published material as follows: from J. Brøndsted, *Danmarks Oldtid*, iii, Copenhagen, 1940 (fig. 1); J. Engelhardt, *Vimosefundet*, Copenhagen, 1869 (fig. 2), and *Nydam Mosefund*, Copenhagen, 1859–63 (figs. 3, 4); W. Krause, *Runeninschriften im älteren Futhark*, Halle, 1937 (fig. 5); E. Behmer, *Das zweischneidige Schwert der germanischen Völkerwanderungszeit*, Stockholm, 1939 (figs. 6, 7, 14, 33, 56, 57, 60, 61, 96); J. Petersen, *De norske Vikingesverd*, Oslo, 1919 (figs. 34, 35, 39, 80, 86); L. Jacobsen and E. Moltke, *Danmarks Runeindskrifter* (Atlas), Copenhagen, 1942 (fig. 105); M. Olsen, *Norges Indskrifter med de ældre Runer*, iii, Oslo, 1942 (fig. 15*b*); H. Arntz and H. Zeiss, *Die einheimischen Runendenkmäler des Festlandes*, Leipzig, 1939 (fig. 22); A. L. Lorange, *Den yngre Jernalders Sværd*, Bergens Museum, 1889 (fig. 32); H. Stolpe and T. J. Arne, *La Nécropole de Vendel*, Stockholm, 1927 (figs. 59, 106); G. Arwidsson, *Valsgärde 8*, Uppsala, 1954 (fig. 62); Sir G. Laking, *A Record of European Arms and Armour*, i, London, 1920 (fig. 75); O. Klindt-Jensen, *The Vikings in England*, Gyldendalske Boghandel Nordisk Forlag, Copenhagen, 1948 (fig. 83); J. Werner, *Das alamannische Gräberfeld von Bülach*, Basel, 1953 (figs. 94, 95, 102); E. Salin, *La Civilisation mérovingienne*, iii, Paris, 1957 (fig. 99); R. L. S. Bruce-Mitford, paper on 'Late Saxon Disc-brooches' in *Dark Age Britain*, London, 1956; also from the following publications of the Society of Antiquaries: *Proceedings*, iv, 1868 (fig. 26); xvi, 1897 (fig. 68); xxviii, 1916 (fig. 71); *Antiquaries Journal*, xviii, 1938 (fig. 115); xxxviii, 1958 (fig. 43); also from the *Transactions* of the Cumberland and Westmorland Antiquarian and Archaeological Society, xxxiv (N.S.), 1934 (figs. 24, 47, 72); from *Viking* (Norsk Arkeologisk Selskap, Oslo) xvi, 1952 (fig. 8); from the *Bonner Jahrbücher* (Rheinisches Landesmuseum, Bonn), cxlviii, 1948 (fig. 9); cxlix, 1949 (fig. 58); from *Gallia* (Comité technique de la recherche archéologique), xiv, 1956 (fig. 10); from *IPEK* (Walter de Gruyter and Co., Berlin), xii, 1938 (fig. 11); from *Préhistoire* (Presses Universitaires de France), xx, iv (fig. 12); from *Germania* (Deutsches archäologisches Institut), xx, 1936 (fig. 13); xxi, 1937 (fig. 98); from *Mannus* (Reichbund für deutsche Vorgeschichte), xxi, 1929 (figs. 81, 88); from *Archaeologia Geographica*, i, a map by H. Jankuhn, with additions (fig. 28). Fig. 111 is from a reproduction of the Lothair Gospels, in the Bibliothèque Nationale, Paris. Fig. 112 is from a facsimile of the Utrecht Psalter, in the University Library, Utrecht, and figs. 113 and 116 are from reproductions of scenes from the Bayeux Tapestry. R. E. Oakeshott has contributed the map, fig. 29, and the drawing, fig. 114, is his own. John Anstee has provided the photograph of the sword made by him. Mrs. S. Gardner, of the Maidstone Museum, has supplied the design included in fig. 45.

SWORDS IN MUSEUMS
IN THE BRITISH ISLES

This list is not a complete one, but gives the most important swords
or parts of swords mentioned in this book.

Cambridge University Museum of Archaeology and Ethnology:
Lark, sword with boar stamps, found in river.

Carlisle, Tullie House Museum:
Hesket, Cumberland, sword from cremation grave.
Thames, sword with inscribed blade, from river.

Dagenham, Valence House Museum:
Rainham, Essex, pattern-welded sword fragments from cemetery.

Dorchester Museum:
Wareham, Dorset, sword from River Frome, found in gravel.

Dublin, National Museum of Ireland:
Askeaton, Co. Limerick, sword found near Askeaton, in river.
Ballinderry, Co. West Meath, sword with inscribed hilt and blade,
from crannog.
Bann, sword with inlaid pattern, from river.
Galway, sword found in Galway.
Greenmount, Co. Louth, scabbard-mount with runes found in Nor-
man motte.
Kilmainham (and Islandbridge), Dublin, many swords, one with
inscribed hilt, from large Viking cemetery.
Wicklow, ornamented sword-guard found near Wicklow.

Hull, Mortimer Museum of Prehistoric Archaeology:
Acklam, sword of unusual length.

Liverpool Public Museums:
Gilton, Kent, ringed sword-hilt, pommel with runic inscription;
both from cemetery.

London, British Museum:
Battersea, London, knife with runic alphabet from River Thames.
Broomfield, Essex, sword from burial mound.

London, British Museum (*cont.*):

Canwick Common, Lincoln, sword with inscribed blade.

Chessel Down, Isle of Wight, seven swords (one with runes on scabbard) from cemetery.

Crundale Down, Kent, two swords from cemetery.

Cumberland, sword with horn hilt.

Droxford, Hants, six swords from cemetery.

Edmonton, Essex, sword from old bed of River Lea.

Exeter, pommel-bar with Latin inscription.

Faversham, Kent, several swords (two with ringed hilts) from cemetery.

Fetter Lane, London, hilt of sword, incomplete.

Howletts, Kent, eight swords (two pattern-welded) from cemetery.

Ingleton, Yorks., pommel from Scalesmoor.

Little Bealings, Suffolk, short sword found near ford.

Longbridge, Warwickshire, sword with pyramid from cemetery.

Lough Gur, Ireland, short sword with smith's marks, from crannog.

Seine, pommel from river at Paris.

Sittingbourne, Kent, knife with Anglo-Saxon inscription found at house-site.

Sutton Hoo, near Woodbridge, sword from ship burial in tumulus.

Taplow, Bucks., sword from burial mound.

Temple, London, sword inscribed *Ingelrii*, from River Thames at the Temple.

Temple, London, sword reputed to come from Earl of Pembroke's tomb in the Temple Church.

Thames, sword with coin stamps found in river.

Waterbeach, Cambs., sword with pattern-welded blade.

Westminster, sword from the River Thames.

Windsor, sword from the River Thames.

Witham, sword inscribed *Leutlrit* from river at Monks Abbey, Lincoln.

London, Jewel House, Westminster:

Westminster, sword found in the Palace.

London Museum, Kensington Palace:

Mitcham, Surrey, sword from cemetery.

Sherborne Lane, London, decorated bronze guard of sword.

Thames, many one-edged swords and knives of various types from the river, also several Viking swords.
Walthamstow, Essex, sword with grooved blade.

London, Wallace Collection, Hertford House, Manchester Square: sword with inscribed hilt, provenance unknown.

Maidstone Museum:
Bifrons, Kent, several swords (two with ringed hilts) from cemetery.
Holborough, Kent, two swords, pattern-welded, from cemetery.
Lower Shorne, Kent, sword-pommel.
Sarre, Kent, many swords from cemetery.

Norwich Castle Museum:
sword-pommel, bronze, provenance unknown.

Ospringe, Museum of Ministry of Works:
Finglesham, Kent, sword from cemetery.

Oxford, Ashmolean Museum:
Abingdon, Berks., two swords from cemetery; one sword from Bog Mill (formerly known as the Wallingford sword).
Brighthampton, Oxon., three swords from cemetery.
Fairford, Glos., two swords from cemetery.
Windsor, Berks., pommel from sword or dagger.

Reading Municipal Museum:
Shifford, sword inscribed *Ulfberht*, found in River Thames.

Reading University Museum:
Lowbury Hill, Berks., sword from burial mound in Roman fort.

Rochester Museum:
Rochester, Kent, sword with pattern-welded blade.

Saffron Walden Museum:
Coombe, Kent, sword reputed to come from cremation grave.

Salisbury, South Wilts. and Blackmore Museum:
Petersfinger, Hants, three swords from cemetery.

Sheffield City Museum:
Brushfield, Derbyshire, sword, with pattern-welded blade, from burial mound.
Witham, sword from river, found at Lincoln.

South Shields Museum:

South Shields, sword fragments, pattern-welded and one with inlaid figure, from Roman fort.

Wisbech Museum:

Nene, sword, inscribed *Ingelrii* (?), from bed of old river, Raven's Willow, Peterborough.

In private possession:

Wensley, Yorks., sword from churchyard.

Westminster, London, sword from River Thames.

Location unknown:

Battersea, sword from River Thames.

Caenby, Lincs., sword from burial mound.

Reading, sword from ballast pit in bank of Thames.

LIST OF ABBREVIATIONS

A.A.	*Acta Archaeologica* (Copenhagen).
A.C.	*Archaeologia Cantiana* (Kent Archaeological Society Transactions).
A.n.O.H.	*Aarbøger for nordisk Oldkyndighed og Historie* (Copenhagen).
A.J.	*Antiquaries Journal* (Society of Antiquaries, London).
Akerman	J. Y. Akerman, *Remains of Pagan Saxondom*, 1855.
Arbman 1	H. Arbman, 'Les Épees du tombeau de Childeric', *Bulletin de la Société Royale des Lettres de Lund*, 1947–8, pp. 7 f.
Arbman 2	H. Arbman, *Schweden und das karolingische Reich*, Stockholm, 1937.
Arch.	*Archaeologia* (Society of Antiquaries, London).
Arch. J.	*Archaeological Journal* (Archaeological Institute, London).
Arch. Soc.	Reports of meetings of architectural societies.
Arntz and Zeiss	H. Arntz and H. Zeiss, *Die einheimischen Runendenkmäler des Festlandes*, Leipzig, 1939.
Arwidsson 1	G. Arwidsson, *Valsgärde 6*, Uppsala, 1942.
Arwidsson 2	G. Arwidsson, *Valsgärde 8*, Uppsala, 1954.
Atkinson	R. J. C. Atkinson, 'Technical Notes on the Construction of the Swords at Petersfinger' (in Leeds and Shortt, *Anglo-Saxon Cemetery at Petersfinger*, Salisbury, 1953).
Baldwin Brown	G. Baldwin Brown, *Arts in Early England* (6 vols.), London, 1903–37.
Beck	L. Beck, *Die Geschichte des Eisens*, vol. i, Brunswick, 1884.
Behmer	E. Behmer, *Das zweischneidige Schwert der germanischen Völkerwanderungszeit*, Stockholm, 1939.
Belaiev	N. T. Belaiev, '"Damascene" Steel', *J.I.S.I.* xcviii, 1918, pp. 417 f.
Beow.	*Beowulf.*
Beowulf	*Beowulf and the Fight at Finnsburg*, edited F. Klaeber, (3rd edn. with supplement), New York and London, 1941.
B.J.	*Bonner Jahrbücher* (Bonn).

B.M. Guide   *British Museum Guide to Anglo-Saxon Antiquities*,
                  R. A. Smith, 1923.

Böhner 1   K. Böhner, 'Das Langschwert des Frankenkönigs
                  Childerich', *B.J.* cxlviii, 1948, pp. 219 f.

Böhner 2   K. Böhner, 'Die fränkischen Gräber von Orsoy',
                  B.J. cxlix, 1949, pp. 164 f.

Bosworth and   *Anglo-Saxon Dictionary* (with supplement), Oxford,
  Toller   1882–98, 1908–21.

Bruce-Mitford   R. L. S. Bruce-Mitford, 'The Sutton Hoo Ship
                  Burial', *Proceedings of the Suffolk Institute of Archaeo-*
                  logy, xxv, 1949.

Brøgger   A. W. Brøgger, 'Rolvøyætten', *Bergens Museums*
                  Aarbog (Hist.-Antik.), 1920–1, pp. 14 f.

Brøndsted   J. Brøndsted, *Danmarks Oldtid* (3 vols.), Copenhagen,
                  1938.

B.W.S.A.   *Bury and West Suffolk Archaeological Proceedings*
                  (Ipswich). Later published as *Proceedings of the*
                  Suffolk Institute of Archaeology and History.

C.A.S.   *Cambridge Antiquarian Society Proceedings* (Cam-
                  bridge).

Chambers   R. W. Chambers, *Beowulf, an Introduction*, Cam-
                  bridge, 1921.

Chenet   G. Chenet, 'La Tombe 319 et la buire chrétien du
                  cimetière mérovingien de Lavoye (Meuse)', *Pré-*
                  histoire, iv, pp. 34 f.

Coffey and   G. Coffey and E. C. R. Armstrong, 'Scandinavian
  Armstrong   Objects found at Islandbridge and Kilmainham',
                  P.R.I.A. xii (xxviii), 1910, p. 111.

Coghlan   H. H. Coghlan, *Notes on Prehistoric and Early Iron*
                  in the New World, Pitt Rivers Museum (Occasional
                  Papers on Technology, 8), Oxford, 1956.

Coll. Antiq.   *Collectanea Antiqua*, C. Roach Smith (7 vols.),
                  1848–80.

Cowen   J. D. Cowen, 'Catalogue of Objects of the Late
                  Viking Period in the Tullie House Museum, Car-
                  lisle', *C.W.A.A.S.* xxxiv (N.S.), 1934, pp. 180 f.

Cramp   R. J. Cramp, '*Beowulf* and Archaeology', *M.A.* i,
                  1957, p. 57.

C.W.A.A.S.   *Cumberland and Westmorland Antiquarian and*
                  Archaeological Society Transactions (Kendal).

D.D.A.S.   *Dartford and District Antiquarian Society Transactions*
                  (Dartford, Kent).

De Vries   J. de Vries, *Altgermanische Religionsgeschichte* (Grund-
                  riss XII, 2nd edn., 2 vols.), Berlin and Leipzig,
                  1956–7.

E.H.D.   *English Historical Documents*, edited D. C. Douglas,
                  vol. i (edited and translated Whitelock), London,
                  1955.

Elliott   R. W. V. Elliott, 'Two Neglected English Runic In-
                  scriptions: Gilton and Overchurch', *Mélanges de lin-
                  guistique et de philologie in memoriam Fernand Mossé*.

Ellis   H. R. Ellis, *The Road to Hel*, Cambridge, 1943.

Engelhardt 1   C. Engelhardt, *Vimosefundet*, Copenhagen, 1869.

Engelhardt 2   C. Engelhardt, *Nydam Mosefund*, Copenhagen,
                  1859–63.

Evison 1   V. Evison, 'Anglo-Saxon Finds near Rainham,
                  Essex', *Arch.* xcvi, 1955, pp. 159 f.

Evison 2   V. Evison, 'Anglo-Saxon Cemetery at Holborough,
                  Kent', *A.C.* lxx, 1956, pp. 84 f.

Falk   H. Falk, *Altnordische Waffenkunde*, Kristiania, 1914
                  (Videnskaps Skrifter, ii, Hist.-Filos., 6).

Faussett   B. Faussett, *Inventorium Sepulchrale*, London, 1856.

Forbes   R. J. Forbes, *Metallurgy in Antiquity*, Leiden, 1950.

France-Lanord 1   A. France-Lanord, 'La Fabrication des épées dama-
                  sées aux époques mérovingiennes et carolingiennes',
                  Pays gaumais, 1949.

France-Lanord 2   A. France-Lanord, 'Communication présentée aux
                  Journées métallurgiques', *Revue de métallurgie*, xlix,
                  1952, pp. 411 f.

Garscha   F. Garscha, 'Das völkerwanderungszeitliche Fürsten-
                  grab von Altlussheim', *Germ.* xx, 1936, pp. 19 f.

Germ.   *Germania* (Deutsch archäolog. Inst., Bamberg).

Gessler   E. A. Gessler, *Die Trutzwaffen der Karolingerzeit*,
                  Basel, 1908.

Gordon   E. V. Gordon, *Introduction to Old Norse* (2nd edn.),
                  Oxford, 1957.

Gowland   W. Gowland, 'The Early Metallurgy of Copper,
                  Tin and Iron in Europe', *Arch.* lvi, 1899, pp. 268 f.

Grönbech   W. Grönbech, *The Culture of the Teutons* (3 vols.),
                  translated Worster, Copenhagen, 1931.

Grove   L. R. A. Grove, 'Five Viking Period Swords', *Arch. J.*
                  xviii, 1938, pp. 251 f.

H. of T.	*History of Technology*, edited Singer and others, vol. ii, Oxford, 1956.
Harmer	F. Harmer, *Select English Historical Documents of the 9th and 10th Centuries*, Cambridge, 1914.
Hatto	A. T. Hatto, 'Snake-swords and Boar-helmets in *Beowulf*', *English Studies*, xxxviii, 1957, pp. 145 f.
Hillier	G. Hillier, *History and Antiquities of the Isle of Wight*, London, 1885.
Hoffmeyer	A. B. Hoffmeyer, *Middelalderens Tveæggede Sværd*, Copenhagen, 1954.
IPEK	*Jahrbuch für prähistorische und ethnographische Kunst* (Berlin).
Ís. Forn.	*Íslensk Fornrit* (12 vols.), Reykjavik.
Jacobsen and Moltke	L. Jacobsen and E. Moltke, *Danmarks Runeindskrifter* (3 vols.), Copenhagen, 1941–2.
Jankuhn	H. Jankuhn, 'Ein Ulfberht-Schwert aus der Elbe bei Hamburg', *Festschrift für Gustav Schwantes*, Neumünster, 1951, pp. 212 f.
Janssens	M. Janssens, 'Essai de reconstitution d'un procédé de fabrication des lames d'épées damassées', *Studies in Conservation*, iii. 3, 1958, pp. 93 f.
J.B.A.A.	*Journal of the British Archaeological Association* (London).
Jessup	R. Jessup, *Anglo-Saxon Jewellery*, London, 1950.
J.I.S.I.	*Journal of the Iron and Steel Institute*, (London).
Jones	Gwyn Jones, 'Some Characteristics of the Icelandic *Hólmganga*', *Journal of English and Germanic Philology*, xxxii, 1933, pp. 203 f.
J.R.A.I.	*Journal of the Royal Anthropological Institute* (London).
Keller	M. L. Keller, *The Anglo-Saxon Weapon Names*, Heidelberg, 1906 (Anglistische Forschungen, xv).
Kendrick	Sir T. D. Kendrick, 'Some Types of Ornamentation on Late Saxon and Viking Period Weapons in England', *Eurasia Septentrionalis Antiqua* (Helsinki), ix, 1934, pp. 392 f.
Kershaw	N. Kershaw, *Anglo-Saxon and Norse Poems*, Cambridge, 1922.
Klaeber	See *Beowulf*.
Klindt-Jensen	O. Klindt-Jensen, 'Keltisk Tradition i Romersk Jernalder', *A.n.O.H.* 1952, pp. 199 f.

Kirby	W. E. Kirby, *The Hero of Estonia* (2 vols.), London, 1895.
Kossinna	G. Kossinna, 'Die Griffe der Wikingschwerter', *Mannus*, xi, 1929, pp. 300 f.
Krause	W. Krause, *Runeninschriften im älteren Futhark*, Halle, 1937.
L.A.A.S.	*Leicestershire Architectural and Archaeological Society Transactions* (Leicester).
Laking	Sir G. Laking, *A Record of European Armour and Arms through Seven Centuries*, London, 1920–2.
Landnámabók	*Landnámabók Íslands*, Kong. Nord. Oldskriftsselskab, Copenhagen, 1900.
Larson	L. M. Larson, 'The Household of the Norwegian Kings', *American Historical Review*, xiii, 1908, pp. 4 f.
Laur-Belart	R. Laur-Belart, 'Eine alamannische Goldgriffspatha aus Klein-Hüningen bei Basel', *IPEK* xii, 1938, pp. 126 f.
Leeds and Harden	E. T. Leeds and D. B. Harden, *The Anglo-Saxon Cemetery at Abingdon, Berkshire*, Oxford, 1936.
Leeds and Shortt	E. T. Leeds and H. de S. Shortt, *The Anglo-Saxon Cemetery at Petersfinger*, Salisbury Museum, 1953.
Lethbridge 1	T. Lethbridge, 'A Sword from the River Lark', *C.A.S.* xxxii, 1936, p. 64.
Lethbridge 2	T. Lethbridge, *Merlin's Island*, London, 1948.
Liestøl	A. Liestøl, 'Blodrefill og mal', *Viking*, xv, 1951, p. 71.
Lindenschmidt	L. Lindenschmidt, *Die Alterthümer unserer heidnischen Vorzeit*, Mainz, 1864–1911.
Lorange	A. L. Lorange, *Den yngre Jernalders Sværd*, Bergens Museum, 1889.
M.A.	*Medieval Archaeology* (Society for Medieval Archaeology, London).
Marstrander	C. J. S. Marstrander, 'De nordiske Runeinskrifter i eldre Alfabet', *Viking*, xvi, 1953, p. 1.
Maryon 1	H. Maryon, 'A Sword of the Nydam Type from Ely Fields Farm', *C.A.S.* xli, 1947, p. 73.
Meissner	R. Meissner, *Die Kenningar der Skalden*, Bonn und Leipzig, 1921.
M.L.R.	*Modern Language Review* (Cambridge).
Montelius	O. Montelius, 'Ringsvärd och narstäender Typer', *Antikvarisk Tidsskrift för Sverige*, xxii. 5, 1924, p. 1.
	F. Morawe, 'Hiltipreht', *Mannus*, xxi, 1929, p. 298.

Neumann	B. Neumann, 'Romanischer Damaststahl', *Archiv f. d. Eisenhüttenwesen* (Düsseldorf), i, 1927–8, p. 24.
N.I.S.	*Den Norsk-Islendzk Skjaldedigtning* (2 vols.), edited F. Jónsson, Copenhagen, Kristiania, 1912–15.
Oakeshott 1	R. E. Oakeshott, 'Some Medieval Sword-Pommels', *J.B.A.A.* xiv, 1951, p. 47.
Oakeshott 2	R. E. Oakeshott, 'An *Ingelri* Sword in the British Museum', *A.J.* xxxi, 1951, p. 69.
Olrik	A. Olrik, *Heroic Legends of Denmark*, translated Hollander, New York, 1919.
Oman	C. Oman, *The History of the Art of War in the Middle Ages*, vol. i (2nd edn.), 1923.
Petersen	J. Petersen, *De Norske Vikingesverd*, Oslo, 1919 (Videnskaps Skrifter, ii, Hist.-Filos. 1).
T. Petersen	T. Petersen, 'Gravfundene paa Flemma i Tingvoll', *Aarsskrift f. Nordmör historielag*, 1925, p. 31 (Abb., p. 37).
P.M.L.A.	*Publications of the Modern Languages Association of America* (Baltimore).
P.R.I.A.	*Proceedings of the Royal Irish Academy* (Dublin).
P.S.A.	*Proceedings of the Society of Antiquaries*, London.
Richardson	H. C. Richardson, 'Iron Prehistoric and Ancient', *American Journal of Archaeology* (2nd series), xxxviii, 1934, p. 363.
Robinson	B. W. Robinson, 'The Sword of Islam', *Apollo Annual*, 1949, p. 58.
S.A.C.	*Surrey Archaeological Collections* (London).
Salin	E. Salin, *La Civilisation mérovingienne* (3 vols.), Paris, 1949–57.
Salin and France-Lanord	E. Salin and A. France-Lanord, 'Sur le trésor barbare de Pouan', *Gallia*, xiv, 1956, pp. 65 f.
Saxo	*The First Nine Books of the Danish History of Saxo Grammaticus*, translated Elton, Folk-Lore Soc. xxxiii, 1893.
Scheurer and Lablotier	F. Scheurer and A. Lablotier, *Fouilles du cimetière barbare de Bourogne*, 1914.
Schubert	H. R. Schubert, *History of the British Iron and Steel Industry*, London, 1957.
Shetelig and Falk	H. Shetelig and H. Falk, *Scandinavian Archaeology*, translated Gordon, Oxford, 1937.

Smith   C. S. Smith, 'Decorative Etching and the Science of Metals', *Endeavour*, xvi (64), 1957, p. 199.

Stephens   G. Stephens, *The Old-Northern Runic Monuments of Scandinavia and England* (4 vols.), 1866–1901.

Stolpe and Arne   H. Stolpe and T. J. Arne, *La Nécropole de Vendel*, Stockholm, 1927.

Sturlunga Saga   *Sturlunga Saga*, Kongelige Nordiske Oldskrifts-selskab Copenhagen–Kristiania, 1905–11.

Sutton Hoo   *The Sutton Hoo Ship Burial*, British Museum Provisional Guide, 19.

Sussex A.C.   *Sussex Archaeological Collections* (London).

Thiðriks Saga   *Þiðriks Saga af Bern*, edited H. Bertelsen (2 vols.), Copenhagen, 1905–11.

V.A.   *Viking Antiquities in Great Britain and Ireland* (8 vols.), edited H. Shetelig.

V.C.H.   *Victoria County History.*

Veeck   W. Veeck, *Die Alamannen im Württemberg*, Berlin, Leipzig, 1931.

Vígfusson   *An Icelandic-English Dictionary*, by R. Cleasby and G. Vígfusson, Oxford, 1874.

Wagner   F. Wagner, 'L'Organisation du combat singulier au moyen âge dans les états scandinaves et dans l'ancienne république islandaise', *Revue de synthèse*, xi (Hist.), vi, 1936, p. 41.

Werner   J. Werner, *Das alamannische Gräberfeld vom Bülach*, Basel, 1953.

Wheeler 1   R. E. M. Wheeler, *London and the Saxons*, London Museum Catalogue, 6, 1925.

Wheeler 2   R. E. M. Wheeler, *London and the Vikings*, London Museum Catalogue, 1, 1927.

Whitelock   D. Whitelock, *Anglo-Saxon Wills*, Cambridge Studies in Legal History, 1930.

Wrenn   *Beowulf*, edited C. L. Wrenn, London, 1953.

Z.f.d.A.   *Zeitschrift für deutsches Altertum* (Leipzig).

Z.f.h.W.   *Zeitschrift für historische Waffenkunde* (Dresden).

Zeki Validi   A. Zeki Validi, 'Die Schwerter der Germanen, nach arabischen Berichten des 9–11. Jahrhunderts', *Zeitschrift d. deutschen morgenländischen Gesellschaft*, xc, 1936, p. 19.

Zenetti   P. Zenetti, 'Das Ringschwert von Schnetzheim', *Mannus*, xxxii, 1940, p. 275.

INTRODUCTION

... Precious swords, rusty and eaten away, since there
for a thousand winters they had rested in the earth's
embrace. *Beowulf* 3048–50.

A STUDY of the swords of Anglo-Saxon times must begin with
the practical questions: What were the swords like, and how
were they made? It would be unprofitable to work on the
evidence from literary sources without first finding out all we can
from the swords which survive into our own day, and it is fortunate that our knowledge of early weapons has increased greatly of
recent years. Archaeological finds have added to their number,
while work in museum laboratories in England and abroad has
ensured the preservation of these finds, and shown also that there
is far more to wonder at in the early weapons than had been
realized.

It is not easy for the student of early literature to find out quickly
what is known of the swords which the heroes of poetry and saga
use so enthusiastically. The evidence is scattered; much of it is
couched in technical language, almost as intimidating to literary
specialists as Anglo-Saxon to a scientist. Some of it lurks in
scientific journals outside the ken of the literary man, housed
in libraries which he is unaccustomed to enter. Nevertheless it
proves most relevant for the better understanding of early literature, and most rewarding. The first section of this book, therefore,
is a survey of what is known of the making of swords in Anglo-
Saxon times and of their appearance and qualities. It is by no
means an exhaustive treatise on early swords; such a treatise would
necessitate detailed knowledge of the weapons in many scores
of museums in Europe and would require far more space than is
given to it here. It is impossible to consider the finds from the
British Isles in isolation, for reasons which should become clear in
the course of this chapter, and outstanding evidence from abroad
is introduced when it appears necessary. But the main object is to

present clearly and briefly the essential evidence for the origin and development of the swords used by Anglo-Saxons and Vikings in Britain, giving some idea of what archaeology and science have revealed of the appearance and the worth of the finest of these weapons. All too many of the swords which are to be seen in our museums are rusty, pathetic survivals of a lost past, and arouse little interest or respect in the chance observer. But in justice to the warriors who treasured them and the poets who praised them, we must remember that the weapons which they saw and handled were as different from these as is the rusted chassis of a derelict car or the decaying wreck of a yacht from the new and shining creation which left factory or shipyard fresh from the makers' hands.

The two main works classifying the swords of this period are Elis Behmer's careful and beautifully illustrated study, *Das zweischneidige Schwert der germanischen Völkerwanderungszeit* (1939), which traces the sword's development to the seventh century A.D., and Jan Petersen's work, *De norske Vikingesverd* (1919), dealing with swords of the Viking Age in Scandinavia. Apart from these two, there is no major work on the swords of these periods. Information must therefore be sought in journals published in England, France, Germany, Italy, and Scandinavia, and it is necessary to see and handle the many swords in our own museums to gain an idea of the wealth of material available. The swords have come from three main sources: from the peat bogs of Denmark, from lakes and rivers, and from graves, and of these more will be said below.

The second section of this book deals with the literary evidence for the appearance and use of the sword. This, like the archaeological evidence, must be sought in varied and scattered sources, and much of it is relatively late in date. The warriors who used the swords from the bog-finds before the break-up of the Roman Empire and those who took part in the Anglo-Saxon settlement remain inarticulate, for to our misfortune they have left no literature behind them. We have to rely on chance comments from outsiders, on what appear to be early heroic traditions preserved in poetry and saga, and on allusions to swords in Latin chronicles and histories, as well as on a few valuable references to swords in early wills. Sometimes the information given by outsiders is most illuminating: there is, for example, the fifth-century letter describing some Teutonic swords sent to Theodoric, and again there are detailed descriptions by intelligent Arab scholars of swords used by their Viking neighbours. The chroniclers and antiquarians can help us too, but the fact that these are trying to instruct rather than to entertain does not necessarily mean that their statements about swords are wholly reliable, for the atmosphere of the monastery and the library is not the most promising for our purpose. To my mind, more valuable evidence is likely to be gained from the poets and the story-tellers, working to satisfy an audience trained from youth to the use of the sword, and bound to prove severe critics of inaccuracy. This is what Hewitt felt when he remarked in his work on *Ancient Armour and Weapons*[1] that 'a simile or an epithet lets in more light than all the limners and all the historians', and that therefore 'the best testimony we obtain is that of the poets'.

Although the small amount of Anglo-Saxon heroic poetry which we possess was written down, together with much religious material, about the year A.D. 1000, there are two points to reassure us, should this seem late in comparison with the archaeological evidence: first, at this time the sword was still an essential and valued weapon, and therefore there was less chance of men misunderstanding earlier traditions concerning it; secondly, it is certain that much earlier material—opinions differ as to how much—has been preserved in the heroic poetry dealing with heroes of the Migration period. The only long poem in the heroic tradition which has survived in entirety is *Beowulf*, and it is from this that much of the literary evidence about swords has been taken. At about the same time as *Beowulf* was recorded, Icelandic poets like Egill and Kormak were composing their vigorous, complex verses in the skaldic tradition. These form valuable evidence,

[1] J. Hewitt, *Ancient Armour and Weapons in Europe*, London and Oxford, 1855, p. 61.

since not only are we helped by knowing the names of the poets and the dates at which they lived, but we know too that many of these men were skilled in the use of the sword, and knew what it was to defend their lives with it. Not only early skaldic verse but evidence to do with the sword from Old Norse literature as a whole has been included in this study, for it proves a most profitable field of investigation. From the ninth century onwards a history of Anglo-Saxon England must include that of the Viking adventurers who fought and settled there, and the relationship between Anglo-Saxons and Vikings, while often hostile, was close. The Vikings left their swords in many parts of the British Isles. A considerable number, recovered from rivers and graves, may be seen in the museums of London and Dublin, while there are isolated examples from many regions of northern and eastern England. We need to turn to the literature of the Vikings, then, to supplement evidence from other sources. While most Old Norse literature was recorded late, in the twelfth or thirteenth centuries, it contains much concerning the appearance and the use of the sword in the Viking Age. We have the advantage, moreover, that we are able to use the abundant evidence of Viking Age archaeology as a check on our reading.

Indeed on such a subject the bringing together of archaeological and literary evidence is essential, if real progress is to be made. The comment of poet or chronicler may explain what is obscure in material discovered in the graves, and it may confirm the guesses of the archaeologist and correct his sense of values. Conversely the student of literature needs to be ready to profit from anything which the archaeologist can offer—laboratory reports, photographic records, anything which can throw light upon the many technical terms and metaphors with which descriptions of weapons in early poetry abound.

The possibilities of setting different kinds of evidence for weapons side by side were shown in Hermann Falk's work, *Altnordische Waffenkunde* (1914–16), to which all interested in Viking sword terms and names must be greatly indebted. May Keller attempted something of the same kind for Anglo-Saxon sword terms in 1906, but her book, *Anglo-Saxon Weapon Names*, was written at a time when comparatively little was known about swords of the Anglo-Saxon period. Another early explorer in the field was Gessler, who utilized material from Latin writers in a study of swords in German and Swiss museums published in 1908. But now the tendency is for ever-increasing specialization, and the gap between the archaeologist and the student of literature is widening as the field of knowledge increases, until a certain diffidence is felt in viewing a subject from more than one direction. Because of this, we run the risk of missing much of the enjoyment to be gained from early literature, which was composed by men knowing no such artificial barrier between the practical world of the makers and users of weapons and the imaginative world of poets and story-tellers. This search for the sword will have been worth while if by it other students of Anglo-Saxon and Old Norse literature are saved time and effort, and gain a glimpse into the heroic world of weapons which the makers of that literature inherited as their natural birthright, but which is now lost to us.

Before beginning on the evidence for the making of the sword, it is necessary to give a brief survey of the conditions under which swords have been found. From it something may be learnt concerning the ownership of the sword, and the way in which it was regarded by its possessors, which will be relevant for the detailed study of the sword which follows.

The first group of sword-finds comes from the peat bogs of Denmark and presents us with a strange phenomenon, believed to have arisen out of the religious practices of the Teutonic peoples, which has proved most profitable for our knowledge of these early times. Collections of different objects, dating from the second to the sixth century A.D., have been found at various sites, apparently left as a sacrificial rite after they had been taken from the dead and vanquished at the close of a battle. These include a large number of weapons as well as clothes and ornaments, tools, farming implements, pottery, and animal and occasionally human bones. Some of the objects were deliberately burned, torn, bent, or cut in pieces, and many of the sword-blades bent in such a way as to render them virtually useless. The objects at first appeared to lie at random, but closer investigation showed signs of deliberate placing: for instance, certain things like mail-coats and bows had been set out in groups, others were in bundles and had even been tied with rope, and sometimes stones or small objects had been forced inside vessels. There can be no question here of goods abandoned after battle; rather it seems that they were laid out in a special holy place, and in some cases there were signs of a fence or boundary of some kind marking off this area. Although the objects were sunk into the bog, it was evident from wormholes and marks of insects on some of them that the ground was less boggy when they were placed there, and in some cases at least they probably lay in the open air for a long period before they sank into the peat.

The evidence from the four main finds—Thorsbjerg, Vimose, Nydam, Kragehul—collected and discussed by Brøndsted in *Danmarks Oldtid*,[1] indicates that the ancient practice in Denmark and north Germany was to make repeated offerings in a holy place. This is exactly what Caesar reported[2] as a practice of the Gauls in the first century before Christ, when he described piles of booty taken in war left on consecrated ground, none daring to remove anything from them because such a crime would be punished by a terrible death. There is no doubt that the Teutonic peoples made similar sacrifices to the gods of battle, and from Orosius[3] we have an account of the Kimbri in 106 B.C. wildly destroying all they had captured, throwing gold and silver into the river, hacking breast-plates to pieces, tearing up clothing, and killing horses and men. It is to such practices that we owe much of our knowledge of the swords of the Migration period in northern Europe.

The finds from Thorsbjerg, Vimose, and Nydam range in date from about A.D. 100 to 500, and those from Kragehul are probably late fifth or early sixth century. In 1950 a fifth deposit of weapons was found in a marsh at Illerup in Jutland, where many objects

---

[1] Brøndsted, iii, pp. 201 f.   *Gallic War*, vi. 9.
[3] *History of the World*, v .16.

had been thrown into a deep pool; this has been dated about A.D. 400, and thought to have been the result of one complete sacrifice after a great battle.[1] There are also a number of smaller finds, which again are likely to represent booty captured on one occasion only. Swords are numerous in these finds, which include a number with patterned blades and some in scabbards with runic inscriptions. Spears are even more plentiful, and were found in hundreds at Thorsbjerg, Vimose, and Nydam, while arrows, axes, shields, and mail-coats were also found, so that a vivid picture is given us of the methods of battle at this period. At Thorsbjerg the swords had suffered from the acid soil, and fragments only survive, but at Vimose they were well preserved, and about eighty were recovered.[2] The greatest number came from Nydam, nearly all long swords with patterned blades, many of which had been deliberately bent. The lake sacrifice at Illerup included the weapons and equipment of about sixty warriors, including fifty-six long two-edged swords; each of these had been bent and twisted, and they had apparently been collected and burned on a pyre after battle and then carried some distance and thrown into the lake. In the later finds swords were rarer, and since more chapes and scabbard-mounts were found it is possible that it had become customary to substitute part of a scabbard or hilt for the whole weapon.

The question of who were the owners of these swords is not altogether easy to answer. The objects in the finds resemble those from Danish graves of the same period, and there are no striking differences between weapons of any one class such as would suggest that widely different cultural groups were represented. At Thorsbjerg and Vimose many objects of Roman provincial manufacture were found, as might be expected at that date, and objects more typically German in type at Nydam and Kragehul. Behmer (pp. 50, 107) has tried to associate the different types of hilt with

---

[1] A brief account appeared in the *Illustrated London News*, 10 Jan. 1953, and a fuller account in *Kuml*, 1951, pp. 9 f. (H. Andersen, 'Det femte store Mosefund'). I should like to express gratitude to Mr. T. G. Bibby, of the Institute of Prehistoric Archaeology, Aarhus University, for information given in a letter.

[2] Klindt-Jensen, p. 199.

different warring tribes likely to have been found in this region. But in a time of rapid movement and many battles swords must frequently have changed hands, since not all booty is likely to have been sacrificed (particularly in the later Migration period) and many warriors no doubt were proud to carry captured weapons. The fact that runic inscriptions were found on some scabbard-mounts, however, confirms the idea that these weapons were owned by Teutonic peoples.

Besides the swords from the bogs, there are a number of fine weapons in English and continental museums which have been dredged up from rivers, many of them dating from the Viking period. It is generally assumed that these were lost in battle or dropped at a ford, but the possibility of deliberate sacrifice, as at Illerup, must be borne in mind. Several fine swords have been taken from the Thames, while in Lincoln Museum there is a good collection dating from the ninth century onwards recovered from the River Witham. A Viking sword from this river was examined at the British Museum, and the conclusion reached was that it 'fell, or was thrown, into a fresh-water pond in the marsh'.[1] So many weapons have been taken from rivers, indeed, that Lethbridge (2, p. 25) suggested that this is a valuable source of evidence for reconstructing the campaigns of the Viking Age. A rather surprising result of immersion for centuries is that in general a sword taken from the water is in a better condition when recovered than one which has been buried. Swords taken from graves have frequently rusted into their scabbards, so that it is impossible to examine the blade, but those from rivers can be cleaned and polished with excellent results, as can be seen from the beautiful sword recently recovered from the River Witham by a boy who was out fishing, and now in Sheffield Museum.

By far the greatest number of swords from Anglo-Saxon and Viking times, however, have been taken from graves where they have been buried with their owners. The sword is comparatively rare among weapons buried with the dead, but it is found in rich graves, like those of Sutton Hoo, Taplow, Broomfield, Caenby,

[1] *A.J.* xxx, 1951, p. 177.

and Lowbury Hill, which were within great burial mounds and are presumed to be the burial-places of men of some importance, perhaps of royal rank. In Anglo-Saxon cemeteries the common weapon is the spear, and Lethbridge (2, p. 69) reckoned that the number of swords in men's graves is less than one to every twenty burials. However, in a number of cemeteries a larger proportion of fighting men possessed swords, as will be seen if the graves of women and children are discounted in making the reckoning. At Sarre, Kent, for instance, there were about 272 graves recorded,[1] but only 66 graves contained weapons of any kind. Out of these 27 men had swords (including one grave holding a sword-pommel, one part of a hilt, and one part of a scabbard). In this case at least it would seem that nearly half the armed men in that particular community bore swords. Other cemeteries in Kent and elsewhere in southern England have a high proportion.[2] On the other hand, the cemetery at Abingdon, Berkshire, had only two swords out of a total of 82 cremation graves and 119 burials;[3] and at Bidford-on-Avon, a rich cemetery where at least 26 men were buried with weapons, no swords were found.[4] Thus the distribution of swords among Anglo-Saxon cemeteries appears to be uneven, but in some districts the number of warriors who owned them is comparable with that of sword-warriors in the early Alamannic cemeteries, which are especially rich in swords.

The large number of swords in certain Anglo-Saxon cemeteries cannot be accounted for by the use of the sword as a cavalry

---

[1] *A.C.* v, 1864, pp. 305 f.; vi, pp. 157 f.; vii, pp. 307 f.

[2] For example, Gilton, 1 in 10 (106 graves, 49 with weapons, 5 with swords), Faussett, pp. 1 f.; Horton Kirby, over half (115 graves, 10 with weapons, 6 with swords), *D.D.A.S.* viii, 1938; Alfriston, Sussex, over a quarter (151 graves, 38 with weapons, 9 with swords), *Sussex A.C.* lvi, 1914, pp. 16 f.; lvii, 1918, pp. 197 f.; Petersfinger, Hants, a quarter (64 graves, 12 with weapons, 3 with swords), Leeds and Shortt, p. 53; Brighthampton, Oxon., half (54 graves, 6 with weapons, 3 with swords), *Arch.* xxxvii, 1857, pp. 391 f.; xxxviii, 1860, pp. 84 f.; Droxford, Hants, not fully recorded, but about a fifth (at least 32 spears and 6 swords), *P.S.A.* xix, 1903, p. 127.

[3] Leeds and Harden, p. 59.

[4] *Arch.* lxxiii, 1923, p. 89; lxxiv, 1924, p. 271. With this may be compared Sleaford, Lincs., with no swords in 241 graves, *Arch.* l, 1887, p. 386; Frilford, Berks., *Arch.* xlii, 1869, pp. 481 f.; *A.J.* i, 1921, pp. 87 f.; and Marston St. Lawrence, Northants., *Arch.* xlviii, 1885, p. 327.

weapon, as has been suggested was the case among the Alamanni, since the Anglo-Saxons never developed the art of fighting on horseback, and the men at Sarre could hardly have been more accustomed to this type of warfare than those at Sleaford. This question will be discussed further below (p. 189). Factors which may be taken into account are the different burial customs prevailing in different localities, and the ease with which new swords could be obtained;[1] two points about which we know all too little. The general assumption is that a man buried with a sword is likely to have been one of rank and wealth, while the spear and shield without a sword mark the less distinguished follower. Veeck (p. 129) noted that in Alamannic cemeteries in general the arrangement of the graves represented a patriarchal society, with two rich graves of a man and woman, the heads of the family, forming the centre, and poorer graves, presumably of the household, arranged around them. The rich man's grave always held a sword.

In a few cases blades in the graves were deliberately damaged, as in the bog-finds. At Sarre two swords were broken, perhaps in battle, but in a third case fragments of the sword were scattered through the grave.[2] Lorange shows illustrations of several Viking swords from Norway which have been bent, and there are other examples from the Kilmainham cemetery, Dublin.[3] At the Alamannic cemetery at Lezéville a sword was found in fragments,[4] while in the Burgundian cemetery at Bourogne one scramasax was broken in two and another heated and bent before being laid on the body.[5] The occasional destruction of weapons in this way before laying them in the grave is often accounted for by the desire to 'kill' the object, and so prepare it for the use of the dead in the next life. The burning of possessions at a cremation might be similarly explained, and one of the few examples of the deliberate destruction

[1] Leeds and Shortt (p. 53) suggest that the presence of swords in a cemetery indicates that there was strong native opposition to the Anglo-Saxon invaders, but surely this would only apply if many swords were found with young warriors. One might indeed argue that in times of constant fighting swords were less likely to be buried with the dead, since they would be so necessary to the living.

[2] See above, graves 8, 54, and 3.   [3] Coffey and Armstrong, p. 110.

[4] E. Salin, *Le Cimetière barbare de Lezéville*, 1922, p. 12, grave 104.

[5] Scheurer and Lablotier, nos. 51, 106.

of a Viking Age sword in this country comes from the Hesket cremation burial, objects from which may be seen in the Tullie House Museum, Carlisle. A cairn of stones held cremated remains together with the sword, which appeared to have been subjected to great heat and then vigorously bent, and one spearhead had been similarly treated.[1] But ideas about grave-goods can seldom have been clear-cut and consistent, since unburnt objects are often deposited with burnt remains. Swords have rarely been found in Anglo-Saxon cremation graves;[2] in one grave from Coombe, Kent, two were said to have been placed beside a bowl containing human ashes, and to have been wrapped in cloth.[3] Another idea which might lie behind the destruction of weapons, however, is the desire to make a complete sacrifice by rendering them useless. This seems to have been the motive in some at least of the bog-finds, and may also explain the fact that the helmet in the Sutton Hoo grave had had a deliberate spear-thrust made through it before burial. Since there was the chance of the grave being disturbed if a valuable weapon was known to lie there, an additional reason for the destruction of a sword might be to prevent it falling into the hands of robbers. The famous Icelandic sword Skofnung was said to have been taken from a Danish burial mound (pp. 172 f. below), while Paul the Deacon in his *History of the Lombards*[4] refers to a sword being removed from the tomb of Alboin in his own day (the eighth century). According to an Arab writer, the Moslems used to disturb the graves of Scandinavian settlers in Russia to get their swords (p. 117 below).

In general, however, great care was taken to preserve the sword within the grave. In fourteen cases at Sarre swords were laid unbroken with the dead, in contrast to the three examples of broken

---

[1] Cowen, p. 174.

[2] Akerman (p. 35) gives an example from near Rugby, but this rests only on the testimony of workmen. A shield-boss with decayed wood inside was mistaken for a bowl of ashes at Oxton, Notts., *V.C.H.* i, p. 198.

[3] There is no reliable account of this excavation, and while objects said to have been found with the sword are Roman, the sword itself can hardly be earlier than the seventh century (p. 68 below). The account of the find is in *B.W.S.A.* i, p. 27. Objects from the grave and one sword are in the museum at Saffron Walden, but I have been unable to trace the second. [4] ii. 28.

ones from the same cemetery. The sword generally rested at the side of the dead, a favourite position being on the left, perhaps because it was generally worn on that side. But the right side was by no means an uncommon position, and there are examples of both from Kentish cemeteries (see p. 95 below). Sometimes it was placed higher in the grave, beside the warrior's shoulder or head,[1] and in other cases laid diagonally across the body.[2] When there was a coffin, the sword would rest inside;[3] when no trace of the body was found, as in a grave on Salisbury racecourse[4] and in the royal grave at Sutton Hoo, the sword was laid in an honourable position near the centre, where the body would be expected to lie. In the barrow at Lowbury Hill it was placed along the centre of the body, the top of the hilt up to the breast-bone and the point to-wards the feet.[5] These positions can all be paralleled from conti-nental graves. The cemetery at Selzen, of which careful drawings were made by the Lindenschmidt brothers,[6] shows the sword in a number of different positions in a small group of graves.

In some cases the sword seems to have been worn by the dead man in the grave (p. 96 below), but this was not the general rule. It was almost invariably in its scabbard. It seems probable that the sword buried with the warrior was the one which he had been accustomed to use in life, but two customs would tend to prevent this: one was that of handing down a valuable sword from father to son through several generations, for which there is plenty of evidence in the literature (p. 171 below), and the other was that of the *heriot*, by which the sword received from a man's overlord

[1] For example, Taplow, according to the best plan of the contents (Bruce-Mitford, pl. xv); Mitcham (*S.A.C.* xxi, 1908, pp. 6, 14); Petersfinger (Leeds and Shortt, pp. 7 f., graves xx, xxi); Finglesham, grave G2, where the sword was placed on the right side, pommel almost in line with shoulder, and apparently on its edge, propped up against the body (information from Sonia Chadwick; pub-lished account, *A.C.* xli, 1929, p. 123).
[2] For example, Mitcham (op. cit., grave 65); Coulsdon (*S.A.C.* vi, 1874, p. 111, grave 12); Sarre (*A.C.* vi, no. 12); Ozingell (*Coll. Antiq.* iii, 1854, p. 1); N. Luffenham (*Arch. Soc. Leicester*, xxvi, 1902, pp. 246 f.).
[3] As in several Kentish graves recorded by Faussett (e.g. pp. 7, 20).
[4] R. Colt Hoare, *Ancient Wiltshire* (Roman Æra, 1821), p. 26.
[5] D. Atkinson, *The Romano-British Site on Lowbury Hill, Berks.*, Univ. College, Reading, 1916, p. 16.
[6] *Das germanische Todtenlager bei Selzen*, Mainz, 1848.

when he entered his service was handed back to him after the man's death.[1] Unfortunately, we know less than we should like about the condition of swords when they were laid in the grave, but a number of surviving ones were clearly most valuable weapons, and were buried in excellent condition, like the sword from Sutton Hoo, which was perfect when laid in the burial mound.[2] However, it may be noticed that in the Swedish ship-grave no. 6 at Valsgärde, where the dead man was laid in a bed within the ship with many belongings, one of the two swords at his side was found to be an old weapon roughly repaired by having a piece from a second sword fastened to it.[3] It was thought that a man of rich family was buried here, but that the weapons given to him at his funeral were ancient ones no longer usable, perhaps collected from store-room or armoury. Since other objects in this particular grave were old and worn, it is possible that the rather mean policy of one family is represented here, and that the case is exceptional. But the natural tendency to replace swords by chapes or fragments of weapons, noted in the bog-finds, would lead one to expect that some at any rate of the weapons in the graves would not be of first-class quality and condition. A find of a different kind is that in a mound near Ringerike in Norway mentioned by Engelhardt (1, pp. 18 f.), where a sword and two spears appeared not to be fully finished. The sword edges had been filed but not sharpened, and there was a smith's mark on the tang. This suggests weapons made specially for the funeral, but again the case seems to be an exceptional one. It may be noted that it is rare to find more than one sword in a man's grave, although the evidence of the Anglo-Saxon wills reminds us that a rich man would certainly own several; an Anglo-Saxon prince in the eleventh century left as many as twelve swords to kinsmen and followers.[4] Exceptions to this rule are sometimes found: for instance, a grave at Oberflacht[5] which held three

---

[1] See Brunner, *Forschungen zur Geschichte des deutschen und französischen Rechtes*, Stuttgart, 1894, pp. 22 f.; F. W. Maitland, *Domesday Book and Beyond*, p. 298; and Whitelock, p. 100.
[2] I owe this information to Mr. Bruce-Mitford.
[3] Arwidsson 1, p. 47.
[4] Whitelock, pp. 56 f. See p. 120 below.　　　[5] *Arch.* xxxvi, 1854, p. 134.

I

THE MAKING OF THE SWORD

Assuredly the work of Weland will not fail any man
who can wield keen Mimming.   *Waldere*

I. IRON FOR THE BLADE

TO the warrior the essential part of the sword must be the blade;
and the sword-blades of the Anglo-Saxon and Viking periods
provide a fascinating study. It has been known for a long time
that many of the blades used by Teutonic and Viking warriors
were of a special kind, often described as 'damascened'. It is easy
to find illustrations of these blades, with zigzag and wavy patterns
running up their centres, but anyone who has tried to discover
their precise nature will know how elusive is the information. In
1899 Lorange in a study of Norwegian swords, *Den Yngre Jernalders Sværd*, showed that the true 'damask' or 'damascened' blades
produced by Oriental smiths and deriving their name from
Damascus were quite different from the blades of western Europe,
whose patterns were produced by a different process to which he
gave the name 'false damascening'. But he made no attempt to define
the two processes, and indeed could not have done so at that time.

The question is further complicated by the fact that the term
'damascened' is also correctly used to describe processes in which
an ornamental effect on the blades of knives or swords is produced
by an inlay of one or more metals. Kendrick (pp. 302 f.) uses it in
this way, and prefers the term *Samé* or *Bulat* for the watered effects
on Eastern sword-blades. It is clear then that the term 'damascening' must not be loosely employed, and since 'true' and 'false'
damascening are terms which may also be used of two different
methods of inlay ornamentation, it is not surprising that confusion
has arisen.

Neumann (pp. 241 f.), writing in 1927 about the blades of swords from Nydam, some fragments of which he had examined, recognized that their patterns were caused by a welding process and not by inlay or the methods of Eastern damascening. He was interested in them as examples of Roman workmanship, and appeared to be unaware that the process continued to be used for sword-blades until the Viking Age. The distinction between Eastern damascening and these welded patterns long remained something of a mystery, but recent work done in archaeology and metallurgy has now made it possible to be more precise.

The metal iron may be produced from iron ore by heating to a temperature of over 500° C.[1] with charcoal, in a furnace into which air is blown, either by a natural draught or by bellows. The furnaces of early times were not adequate to allow contact with carbon for a long time at a very high temperature, as in a modern blast furnace into which hot air is forced, so that little absorption of carbon with the formation of iron carbide took place, and the product was a spongy mass of iron mixed with slag.[2] This could be worked when hot so as to squeeze out most of the slag; such a product is therefore known as 'wrought' iron. But good steely iron could not be produced in this way, and unless exceptionally good ores were used, the metal obtained was not hard and springy and would not be suitable for a good sword-blade.

Many early furnaces were of clay, destroyed after each operation.[3] The remains of simple stone ones, suitable for producing wrought iron, are known in this country from the Roman period, but there were others more elaborate, like the welding furnace at Corstopitum and the shaft furnace near Ely in Glamorgan. In places where good ores could be obtained, as at Petleywood in Sussex, hard steely iron was produced, and elaborate smelting and refining works were excavated near Warrington early in this century.[4]

[1] To give good iron, however, a temperature of over 1,100° C. is desirable. See Coghlan, pp. 38–40.

[2] Although it is possible that slivers of a fairly high carbon steel were occasionally formed on furnace walls (Gowland, p. 321).

[3] Gowland, p. 308, and Coghlan, pp. 86 f.

[4] Thomas May, *Warrington's Roman Remains*, Warrington, 1904.

A good account of the wide scope of the iron industry in Roman Britain is given in H. R. Schubert's recent survey.[1] The most important areas for iron-production in Roman times, however, important enough to be government-controlled, were on the Continent: at Noricum on the Danube, the Sana valley in Bosnia, Carinthia in Spain, and Aude in Gaul.

With fine-quality ores it was possible by careful heating and hammering to produce blades of good steely iron. The ores from Noricum gave excellent results because they contained an unusually high proportion of manganese and titanium and were relatively free from the common impurities of phosphorus, arsenic, and sulphur. Celtic smiths were probably using these ores as early as 500 B.C. But when the Roman Empire declined there was no longer central control of the mines, and for hundreds of years the smiths had to be satisfied with surface ores and old workings. Not until the ninth century did conditions become more settled so that new mines and smelting sites could be established, and it was at this time that the *Ulfberht* blades were produced, probably by use of superior ores and efficient furnaces.

Thus the smiths in north-west Europe who worked on swords from the fifth century onwards had to make use of impure bog ores (limonite).[2] Such ores had a high phosphorus content; this meant that they could be reduced at a comparatively low temperature, but the resulting product was a soft, impure iron, by no means suitable for sword-blades. A successful sword-smith had not only to find his ores, but also to show his skill in recognizing good nodules in the spongy mass obtained from the furnace and knowing what to reject. One simple practical method of selecting material is that which Diodorus the Sicilian (v. 33) tells us was practised by the Iberian Celts. They would bury pieces of iron in the earth before reforging it, so that the softest parts would be eaten away

---

[1] H. R. Schubert, *History of the British Iron and Steel Industry*, London, 1957, pp. 34 f.; cf. L. Beck, *Die Geschichte des Eisens*, Brunswick, 1884 (an old but valuable account); Forbes, *History of Technology*, ii (ed. Singer and others), 1957, pp. 55 f.; and Coghlan, *Notes on Prehistoric and Early Iron*, pp. 21 f.

[2] This is found in irregular sheets on lake bottoms and in marsh lands. See Coghlan, p. 15.

by rust and the harder iron be left to be worked anew by the smith. Beck (pp. 651 f.) and Forbes (p. 412) confirm this as a reasonable procedure.

The difference between wrought iron and steel is essentially one of carbon content. Steel which contains 0·7 per cent. of carbon can, if properly worked, be rendered hard and flexible as a sword-blade needs to be. If, however, it absorbs as much as 1 per cent. of carbon it becomes extremely hard, and further increase of carbon produces still greater hardness and also brittleness. Hard brittle iron of this kind is known as 'cast' iron, because the increase of carbon lowers the melting-point so that it can be melted and cast. It is a debatable point whether cast iron was ever deliberately produced in Roman times; May believed that he found traces of it at Warrington, but it seems probable that in ancient times cast iron was known but regarded as a waste product, obtained accidentally.[1]

A weapon of good steely iron could be made harder and at the same time more flexible by quenching and tempering. It was first heated, and then *quenched*, or cooled down very rapidly; then it was again heated to a lower temperature which the experienced smith could gauge from the colour, and cooled again either rapidly or relatively slowly. The rapid cooling of the blade by quenching caused it to become very hard but not flexible, and flexibility could be regained with no great loss of hardness by the tempering process. The hardness first produced is due to cementite being stabilized in the blade, and the first cooling must be rapid, since slow cooling at this stage would allow the breaking down of the cementite into carbon and iron. Quenching causes the cementite to crystallize out into layers, while the second heating and cooling disperses these into a less regular arrangement of crystals, so that brittleness is lost and there is increase of flexibility. The process of reducing brittleness by heating steel to a red heat and cooling slowly without quenching is known as *annealing*.

Water is not altogether effective for the sudden quenching of steel, since it boils at a low temperature and forms a steam barrier to the passage of heat, and in modern processes liquids such as oil

[1] Forbes, pp. 407 f.; Coghlan, pp. 75 f.

or molten lead are used. The ancient writers believed that the water of certain rivers was of special value for quenching weapons, but this may have been a mere piece of folk-belief fostered by the smiths who liked to keep their techniques secret. It was known in early times that oil and honey could be used, and honey is mentioned in the Finnish *Kalavala* (p. 169 below). No doubt much experimenting went on to find the ideal liquid for quenching, and early works on metallurgy[1] suggest the urine of a goat or of a red-headed boy, and the juice of radishes mixed with sliced earthworms. Solids may also be used, and Neumann mentioned moist clay as a possibility in the case of the Nydam blades. It is hardly surprising that legends grew up around the quenching of swords, for it must have seemed a mysterious process. It was known in Egypt many centuries before Christ, perhaps as early as 900 B.C.,[2] but the art of tempering was probably a Roman invention, although it seems likely that the process was seldom used and not fully understood in Roman times.[3]

It was only possible to quench and temper a blade successfully, however, if the carbon content was sufficiently high. The problem which faced the sword-smith of the Dark Ages, working with a small furnace and with ores of indifferent quality, was how to turn his iron into steel by absorption of the correct amount of carbon. He needed also to find some method to ensure even distribution of carbon in the product; for examination of early sword-blades shows that the carbon content often varied greatly in different parts of the blade, so that some parts were weak and soft and others hard and tough. There are various solutions to be found to these problems, and the two to be considered here in detail are, first, that adopted in the East by the makers of damascened blades, and secondly, the technique of pattern-welding practised in western Europe.

[1] For example, *Mappae Clavicula* and *Fons Memorabilium*, Forbes, p. 378; cf. p. 413.

[2] Carpenter and Robertson, 'The Metallurgy of Some Ancient Egyptian Implements', *J.I.S.I.* cxxi, 1930, pp. 417 f.

[3] Pearson and Smythe, *Proc. Univ. Durham Philosophical Soc.* ix, 1934, p. 141: report on a Roman chisel which shows signs of quenching and tempering. Cf. Schubert, pp. 55 f.; Richardson, p. 579; and H. Coghlan, 'A Note upon Iron as a Material for the Celtic Sword', *Sibrium*, iii, 1956-7, p. 133.

2. EASTERN SWORD-BLADES

The Romans imported their best steel from the East, not in the form of blades but in cakes of steely iron (later known as *wootz*) manufactured in the Hyderabad region of India. The earliest known examples of this date from about the sixth century B.C., and by the first century A.D. Indian smiths were very skilled in its manipulation. It reached the Romans through Abyssinia, and was generally believed to come from China, as the real place of origin seems to have been kept a trade secret. The Romans knew it as Seric Iron.[1] Parthian steel, made in Persia by a somewhat similar method, was also highly valued and widely exported.

The Indian method was to heat black magnetite ore in the presence of carbon in a sealed clay crucible inside a charcoal furnace.[2] An alternative to this was to smelt the ore first to give wrought iron, which was heated and hammered to free it from slag and broken up into small pieces, while the Persians generally used iron bars, heated with charcoal or plumbago. The carbon was obtained by the Indian smiths from bamboo and the leaves of certain plants, and the crucible was piled up with a number of others and heated in a furnace in a blast of air for about two-and-a-half hours. The ore was reduced to iron, which then began to absorb carbon; when it had absorbed 3 or 4 per cent., the melting-point was lowered sufficiently for the iron to melt, just as the addition of salt lowers the melting-point of ice.[3] The molten iron fused into a 'button' of metal, which according to some accounts was heated and cooled again four or five times, and according to others was left in the furnace and allowed to cool down with it

[1] The name Seric arose from a confusion between the *Chera* kingdom of South India and *Seres*, 'Chinese'. See Warmington, *The Commerce between the Roman Empire and India*, Cambridge, 1928, pp. 37, 71, 257–8.

[2] Accounts of the making of wootz are given by W. H. Schoff, 'Eastern Iron Trade of the Roman Empire', *Journal American Oriental Soc.* xxxv, 1915, pp. 233 f.; and H. C. Richardson, 'Iron Prehistoric and Ancient', *American Journal of Archaeology* (2nd series), xxxviii, 1934, p. 580. Cf. Forbes, pp. 410, 437 f.; *H. of T.*, ii, p. 57; Coghlan, pp. 156 f.

[3] In some cases, as Smith points out, *Endeavour*, xvi, 1957, (p. 201), the process was not carried to the point of complete fusion, and plates of wrought iron seem to have been merely carburized and 'brazed' together with white cast iron.

very slowly over a period of days. At the end of the process a round cake of metal was obtained, about 5 inches in diameter and 2 lb. in weight, sufficient for two sword-blades. Although with such a high carbon content one would expect the metal to be equivalent to cast iron, very hard and brittle, the slow cooling caused chemical and physical changes to occur in the form of the carbon present, and it was possible to work the iron so as to produce weapons of excellent steely quality.[1] The 'wootz' was usually marketed in circular form, or in short, stout bars.

Eastern steel was much valued by European smiths in Roman times. It was not easy to forge, but a skilled smith working with extreme care could avoid cracking in the initial forging process, since the brittle material was no longer in continuous planes of weakness (as in cast iron) but dispersed in tiny dots.[2] It was the working of this discontinuous material which produced the characteristic watered pattern running over the whole surface of damask sword-blades, giving the appearance of watered silk or *moiré* ribbon. As a result of forging, the material lost the tendency to crack and became tough and steely, and successful working produced weapons of extreme flexibility and great hardness, which would take a perfect cutting edge. Methods of working varied: one was by flowing the metal in two or more directions by hammer blows, followed by prolonged annealing and quenching, while another was to work the steel at dark red heat without quenching. The carbon content of good damascened blades was usually between 0·7 and 1·5 per cent., so there was evidently considerable loss of carbon during the forging process.

The pattern on the blade was brought out by polishing and etching, and this also necessitated long and careful work. A mineral called *zag* was used in solution, which Smith believes to have been a natural ferric sulphate.

The quality of the completed sword would be judged by its

---

[1] In the production of modern cast steel, a similar result is obtained by inclusion of an additive which has a dispersing effect on the carbon.

[2] Smith outlines some of the difficulties: the temperature must be kept low enough to avoid re-solution of the carbon, and the structure of the ingot must not be too distorted, or the pattern is lost (p. 201).

pattern, and the smith aimed at creating contour lines in various directions along the blade, the most coveted pattern being known as 'Mahomet's Ladder', because it had horizontal bands running across it at regular intervals, a most difficult effect to produce (Plate I*a*). The darkness of the background and the golden lustre of the shining metal were also important features of the best swords.

Such a process must depend on the skill and experience of the individual smith, and was bound to be slow and difficult. It is interesting, though hardly profitable, to speculate on the origin of so elaborate a technique; Forbes suggested that the damask patterns might have been inspired by meteorites, which are covered by a thin film of iron oxide and when forged at low temperatures produce a distinct pattern.[1] The best blades were forged in Persia from Indian steel, and although they took their name 'damascened' from Damascus, this does not appear to have been the most renowned centre for fine swords.[2] There is some difference of opinion as to the date at which these patterned blades were first produced, but Smith quotes lines from an Arab poet, Imru'ul-Qais, who died in A.D. 540, which describe a sword-blade as having wavy marks like the tracks of ants, and another reference to a sword-blade from a slightly later poet, Aus ibn Ḥajar, which has 'a water whose wavy streaks are glistening'.[3] In the nineteenth century French and Russian metallurgists worked hard to discover the lost secret of damascened steel, and finally succeeded in producing fine-quality blades by modern scientific methods. The fascinating story of this rediscovery has been outlined by Colonel Belaiev, on whose description of the process I have drawn for parts of the account given above.[4]

---

[1] For the use of meteoric iron, see Coghlan, pp. 13 f.; Smith (fig. 3) shows a photograph of an etched meteorite.

[2] B. W. Robinson, 'The Sword of Islam', *Apollo Annual*, 1949, pp. 58–59.

[3] Smith, p. 200. The comparison with ant-tracks later became a cliché among Arab poets.

[4] N. Belaiev, 'Damascene Steel', *J.I.S.I.* xcvii, 1918, pp. 417 f. Cf. Belaiev, *Crystallisation of Metals*, London, 1923, pp. 137 f., and 'Sur le damas oriental et les lames damassées', *Métaux et civilisations*, 1945, 1, pp. 10 f.

3. PATTERN-WELDED BLADES

Damascened blades of the Eastern type do not appear to have been made in Europe in Roman times and the Migration period, for there the smiths had quite a different method of hardening their swords. They may have adopted it in their efforts to deal with the impure bog ores which formed their main source of iron, and then continued to use it in a deliberate attempt to develop and elaborate the fine decorative patterns which their methods produced. Baldwin Brown (iii, p. 214) pointed out long ago that this method has nothing to do with the art of inlay or plating, any more than has the Eastern one; but the definition which he gave, that it was a process of welding wires or strips of iron of varying quality together to form patterns, needs further explanation. The main difference from Eastern damascening is that the necessary carbon was introduced not by heating the iron in a crucible, but by causing it to be absorbed into the surface of the solid metal. The problem was to do this in such a way that the carbon was distributed evenly throughout the blade, and the Western solution to this was, like damascening, slow and laborious, a process of trial and error depending on the skill and experience of the individual craftsman.

When Neumann examined the Nydam swords (Plate I*b* and p. 6 above), he distinguished three types of pattern, which he called *streifendamast*, *winkeldamast*, and *rosendamast* (pp. 241 f.). Convenient English equivalents for these terms are 'straight', 'herring-bone', and 'curving', and these are the ones I shall employ. They were not, as he thought, produced by different processes, and they are somewhat arbitrary divisions, but this has only been realized in the light of later work. He believed that the straight patterns on the central part of the blade were produced by welding together layers of steel of high and low carbon content, before welding on the cutting edges separately. A piece of straight-patterned steel twisted in one direction like a barber's pole and then hammered out and welded on to a piece twisted in the opposite direction would, he thought, give a herring-bone pattern. But how the curving pattern was produced he found himself unable to say.

In 1947 Herbert Maryon[1] published a description of a sword from an Anglo-Saxon grave of the pagan period near Ely which aroused much interest. This sword has a band of pattern running down the centre of its blade which is alternately straight and herring-bone in type (Plate I*c*). Maryon suggested that the process by which this effect was produced was as follows: the core of the blade was built up from four bundles, each formed of five very narrow metal strips about one-hundredth of an inch thick. The bundles were first allowed to run straight and then twisted; this was done at regular intervals down the blade until the four zones of pattern were produced. After the welding was completed the sword was ground down and polished, and as much as two-fifths of the outer surface removed to give a flat finish. Maryon hoped to have this process copied by a modern welding firm, but the manipulation of the tiny strips of metal proved too delicate to be carried out. It is indeed difficult to see how such a process could be managed effectively. It is to Maryon that we owe the convenient term 'pattern-welding' for this type of work.

The next attempt to show how the different patterns were produced was made by Albert France-Lanord, who in 1948 published a report on a sword from the Musée Historique Lorrain, Nancy.[2] The selected sword came from the Alamannic cemetery of Vieil-Aître; sections were cut from its blade in the laboratory, and the surface etched and polished and examined under high and low magnification, so as to reveal the general structure, lines of welding, and nature of the metal employed. From this France-Lanord presented his theory of how the patterned blades were produced, illustrating it by models in coloured wax. A later account published in 1952 gives his conclusions after further work.[3]

[1] *C.A.S.* xli, 1946–7, pp. 73 f.

[2] A. France-Lanord, 'La Fabrication des épées damassées aux époques mérovingienne et carolingienne', *Le Pays gaumais*, 1949, pp. 1–27.

[3] *Revue de Métallurgie*, xlix, 1952, pp. 411 f. See also the account by E. Salin (in collaboration with France-Lanord) in *La Civilisation mérovingienne*, iii, 1957 (chap. 25, esp. pp. 58 f.).

In Norway work on similar lines was done by Aslak Liestøl and published in 1951.[1] He took sections from a Viking sword with a patterned blade, and his results were illustrated by excellent photographs and diagrams, based on models in plasticine which he claimed made more allowance for pattern variation than did France-Lanord's first series.

These explanations throw much light on the problem of the patterns, but they remain theoretical. It has been left to an English investigator, John Anstee, to produce single-handed a pattern-welded blade (Plate Id), working in a small forge and using the technique of a primitive smith. His work shows that the most complex patterns can be produced by simple direct methods, that there was nothing miraculous about them, and no need for excessively complex theories of manufacture. A full account of his work will be found in the appendix.[2]

To understand these accounts it must be remembered that the essential difference between the Eastern and Western methods of producing patterns was the way in which the carbon was introduced into the iron to harden it. Instead of heating the ore with carbon in a crucible, the Western smiths used the method of case-hardening. The best method of doing this was to beat the iron into narrow bars, which were tightly packed with crushed charcoal in an iron box and then kept at red heat for a long time in the forge,[3] but a similar effect could be brought about by repeated heating in a charcoal fire. The result was a bar of hard steely iron on the outside and soft malleable iron within. Since the iron did not melt, the amount of carbon absorbed was considerably less than in the crucible process, and remained under 1 per cent. The ninth-century sword from the Palace at Westminster, which was cleaned and examined by Anstee and Biek, and which had a pattern-welded blade, contained about 0·2 per cent. of carbon. Similarly the carbon content was relatively low in a number of pattern-

---

[1] 'Blodrefill og mål', *Viking*, xv, 1951, pp. 77 f.

[2] The first account was published in *Nature*, clxxviii, 1956, pp. 1430 f. (Summary of papers given at the 1956 Meeting of the British Association at Sheffield).

[3] A process known probably as early as 600 B.C. See E. M. Burgess, 'The Mailmaker's Technique', *A.J.* xxxiii, 1953, p. 52.

welded blades examined by Salin,[1] although that of the cutting edges might be as high as 0·4 or 0·6 per cent.

The process outlined by France-Lanord and Liestøl begins with the production of a bar of case-hardened iron. From this a long narrow strip was built up, the length of the sword to be, of alternate layers of light steely iron containing carbon and dark soft iron without carbon, so that the result was like a multiple sandwich. The Viking sword examined by Liestøl was based on a three-decker sandwich of three dark and four light stripes, and this seems to have been the most popular combination, although others are found. The long bar was then cut longitudinally into four narrower strips, and each of these twisted, cut in half to give eight pieces, and then welded together with the new faces upward. When the composite bar which resulted was filed and polished, Liestøl claimed that the pattern would be identical with that of the Viking blade which he had examined.

In his second paper France-Lanord distinguished between different methods of treating the case-hardened bar. It might be twisted to give an effect like a barber's pole, or for more elaborate patterns it could be bent up in a series of 'accordion' pleats and these then welded together in a continuous process like the making of puff pastry.[2] At the end of this process the bar would be fairly thick, but could be considerably reduced by beating and filing down. There is no doubt that filing played a great part in the making of these blades, and France-Lanord pointed out how this could give variety to the patterns.

Anstee and Biek, however, have now shown that it is possible to produce blades showing all variations of pattern in a comparatively simple way, and without case-hardening. They have shown that there is no difference in structure between a blade showing herring-bone and one showing curving patterns; for if the curving pattern is eaten away by rust, a herring-bone effect will result. Anstee's work was done in a small forge, using a Chinese-type box bellows, hammer, tongs, vice, and a crude anvil; at first he used

[1] Salin, iii, p. 66.
[2] For other suggestions of rolling round a core, see Janssens, pp. 99 f.

home-made charcoal, but had to resort to coke because it took as much as 2 cwt. to make one sword. Instead of a 'sandwich' bar of case-hardened metal, he began with three rods of good Victorian wrought iron, which he forged into strips with a ratio of width to thickness of 9 to 1. These strips were then laid flat on one another and forge-twisted into a screw, while two 'filler rods' of square section were incorporated at the same time. On either side of this bar two more composite bars of opposite twist were placed, with straight 'packing rods' in between them. This assembly of three bars was then welded together, using a sliding wire-clip and heating an inch at a time. The result was a triple band of characteristic herringbone pattern, with each of the three twisted units tapering to a point at one end where the tongs had gripped it; this effect had been noted on patterned blades of this type, but no explanation of it had been found. Another unfinished sword, forged in the same way with one twisted unit only, was virtually free from carbon, but the blade carried slag inclusions which accounted for the pattern seen on the surface after it had been etched and polished.

Thus such patterns can be produced even when there is no alternate layering of wrought iron and steel, and the most complex ones can be imitated in this way by twist-welding and grinding. All investigators have agreed that the cutting edges were welded separately on to the core, and this was done in the case of Anstee's sword. Then nearly half the total weight was removed from the rough forging by grinding, and the total cross-sectional area of the original core reduced by 70 per cent. Anstee did not harden and temper his sword, as it did not contain sufficient carbon for this to be effective, and it may be noted that a number of swords examined by Salin from the Merovingian period had not been tempered, presumably for the same reason. The best pattern-welded blades, however, built up from carburized bars and with cutting edges of carburized iron, would almost certainly be quenched and tempered, as was one sixth-century sword of fine quality from grave 58 of the cemetery of Villey-St-Étienne.[1]

In the case of the sword made by Anstee, it was found that the

[1] Salin, iii, p. 72.

twisting process made it necessary to deepen the groove left on both surfaces of the core with a cold chisel and a wet sandstone wheel before polishing. The cutting edges were filed, and the sword was then ready for the finishing process. This final stage in the making of a sword was important for bringing up the pattern and for leaving a clear, smooth surface. The smith would use some kind of acid for this, and Liestøl (p. 88) suggests tannic acid, acetic acid (from vinegar), and urine as possibilities; others are fruit juice, sour beer, and vitriol.[1] Tannic acid would give a deep blue-black colour to steel, and would offer considerable resistance to rust,[2] so that it would be very suitable for treatment of a sword-blade. Probably special polishing agents were used as well (p. 107 below).

It is interesting to note that Anstee's first sword was completed in 75 hours' working time, 43 of this being taken up with the making of the blade and the rest with hilt, scabbard, and belt fittings. He was working alone, and possibly a smith with assistants and long experience might reduce this time, but on the other hand extra time would be needed if the iron were case-hardened. In any case the process is one of trial and error, and the possibility of the blade breaking before completion is great.

When Neumann examined the Nydam blades, he noticed that several swords differed from those in which the patterned strip formed the centre of the blade; they had a core of steely iron which was not pattern-welded, and the patterned strips were welded on either side of this. Klindt-Jensen (p. 205) found swords of this type in the collection of blades from Vimose, and suggested that these might be native work in imitation of those with the core built up in patterns. Another blade of this type, a Viking sword from Brandenburg, was described by Rohde,[3] and it seems that

[1] Smith, p. 200. Cf. Robinson, p. 58, on the finishing of damascened blades, and on the renewal of patterns on them. In a recipe which he quotes the polishing was done with fine emery paper and oil, the oil being removed by lime and a final treatment given with tobacco ash and water.

[2] Knowles and Whate, 'The Protection of Metals with Tannins', *Journal Oil and Colour Chemists' Association*, xli (1), 1958, pp. 10 f.

[3] *Z.f.h.W.* iv (N.F.), 1932–4, pp. 38 f. Examples from England are fragments from Rainham (Evison 1, p. 168) and the sword from the River Witham in Sheffield Museum.

both methods were practised throughout the whole perod. Liestøl thought that the smiths of the Viking Age tended to prefer blades with an iron core, but it is not easy to prove this, since patterns on this type of sword are not always revealed by X-ray photography. Janssens (p. 99) examined a blade with an iron core in the museum at Munich, and suggested that the method might have been a means of reusing old strips of pattern-welding from worn swords to make a new blade. He quotes an account of a Persian method of remaking a damascened sword which had worn thin with use:[1] the smith lengthened the old blade to twice its normal length and then welded it over a core of ordinary iron, so that this was covered by damascened steel on both sides and could not be distinguished from a new sword. Salin (iii, p. 65) assumes that such blades would be very inferior ones, but there seems no reason why a skilful smith should not produce a good-quality sword by such means.

It is only recently that the fine quality of workmanship put into the best pattern-welded swords has been appreciated. Maryon was the first to point it out: 'I do not know of finer smiths' work anywhere, at any time', is his comment on the sword from Ely Fields, while the conclusions of the French investigators on the cutting power, toughness, and flexibility of the blades which they examined are impressive.[2] They could cut like razors and were extremely hard and flexible. There is no doubt that they were also weapons of great beauty, when the surfaces now uneven and corroded were brilliantly smooth, and the variable colour of the background brought out by etching and polishing: the sword made by Anstee gives clear proof of this. There was considerable difference in quality among pattern-welded blades, and Salin's reports on various swords bear this out, for several had a low carbon content and had not been tempered. But even in such cases, the building up of patterns from narrow strips of iron by a twisting technique was more than a mere decorative device, for it meant that a blade could be built up from variable metal, and that small pieces of iron

---

[1] Massalski, 'Préparation de l'acier damassé en Perse', *Annuaire du Journal des Mines de Russie*, 1841.

[2] France-Lanord 1, pp. 19 f.; Salin, iii, pp. 65, 72.

could be utilized. In the finest swords produced by this method, the smith was able to introduce carbon into the centre of the blade, while any soft iron present was dispersed and strengthened by welding and no longer remained a source of weakness; the result was a weapon of extremely fine quality, uniform throughout its whole length. It is no longer difficult to understand the popularity of the pattern-welded blade in north-western Europe for so many centuries.

4. WHEN AND WHERE WERE THEY MADE?

As a result of the new interest in pattern-welded swords, many weapons in museums have been re-examined, and careful cleaning and X-ray photography have revealed that a surprisingly large number of Merovingian and Anglo-Saxon swords have patterns on their blades. On the Continent we have the sword from Pouan, probably of fifth-century date,[1] and a number of swords from Alamannic and Frankish cemeteries examined by France-Lanord and Salin. From Anglo-Saxon England there is the sword from the Sutton Hoo royal grave of the seventh century, and two others from rich graves in burial mounds at Taplow and Broomfield,[2] as well as one from a mound at Brushfield in Derbyshire, probably of seventh-century date.[3] A number of other examples have come from Anglo-Saxon cemeteries, and the list is rapidly increasing.[4]

There are not many examples of short swords made by the pattern-welded technique, but one of the Rainham fragments was thought to come from a short sword,[5] and there are other examples from Walthamstow and Reading.[6] Sonia Chadwick pointed out

---

[1] Salin and France-Lanord, p. 65.   [2] Bruce-Mitford, p. 68.

[3] The barrow was opened in 1820 (T. Bateman, *Vestiges of the Antiquities of Derbyshire*, London, 1848, p. 27). Mr. Bartlett of the City Museum, Sheffield, has kindly given me information about the sword.

[4] The list includes: two swords from Howletts, Kent, and three fragments from Rainham, Essex (Evison 1, pp. 167 f.); two from Holborough (Evison 2, pp. 100, 118–19); a sword from Finglesham and all surviving swords from Bifrons (information supplied by Sonia Chadwick); the sword from Ely Fields described by Maryon (p. 24 above); one from Waterbeach, in the British Museum (*V.C.H. Cambridgeshire*, i, pl. 16); and one in the museum at Rochester, on which the patterns are visible.   [5] Evison 1, p. 169.

[6] I owe this information to Mr. L. Biek.

that what appears to be an iron weaving sword in a rich woman's grave at Finglesham has a pattern-welded core, built up of four composite rods in a standard pattern.[1] Other iron weaving swords, from both England and the Continent, come from exceptionally rich graves, and it is possible that these short 'swords' might have been symbols of authority rather than implements of practical use. In the case of the Finglesham weaving sword, it may have been made from an old pattern-welded blade, but may on the other hand have been made for its owner on the model of her husband's sword.

Examples of pattern-welded spearheads, with a patterned core built up in the same way as in a sword, are also known.[2] These must be distinguished from spearheads where a decorative panel of work resembling pattern-welding has been inserted.[3]

So far no examples of pattern-welded blades from Scandinavia have appeared which are as early in date as the earliest Anglo-Saxon and continental finds. One of the two swords from the Swedish ship-burial Valsgärde 6 seems to be the earliest example from Sweden; this burial is thought to be mid-eighth century, and the weapons may be a little earlier in date. Greta Arwidsson (1, pp. 47 f.) when discussing this gave two other examples of pattern-welded swords of approximately the same period, one from Skane and one from Denmark.

Many swords of the Viking period have long been recognized as pattern-welded ones, since they have been recovered from rivers or marshes with the blades in good condition and the patterns clearly visible. Lorange showed some in his book of 1899, and Liestøl worked on two examples from Norway. The sword from the River Witham (Fig. 66), now in Sheffield Museum, is pattern-welded, and this is thought to be of late eighth- or ninth-century date.[4] Other examples from this period are the sword from

---

[1] I am most grateful to the author for allowing me to read her account of the Finglesham cemetery before it appeared in *M.A.* ii.

[2] I owe this information to Mr. L. Biek.

[3] A. E. P. Collins, 'Some Viking-Period Weapons from the Thames', *Berks. Archaeological Soc.* li, 1949, p. 17. Cf. report in *Man*, l, 1950, p. 1241 (misleading); also Coghlan, pp. 150, 162.

[4] Described in the Annual Reports for Sheffield City Museum, 1954-5, 1955-6.

Westminster (Fig. 76) found in 1948 and two swords recovered from the Thames.[1]

By the ninth century the art of pattern-welding was on the decline. This was probably because better ores were obtainable as conditions became more settled, and possibly also because the design of the furnaces had improved.[2] But existing pattern-welded swords continued to be used late in the Viking Age, and their renown permeated the literature, as we shall see. Nor was the process forgotten, since letters produced by a similar technique were frequently inlaid in the form of inscriptions in the blade, and decorative panels of pattern-welding are sometimes found on a short sword or knife, as well as on spearheads. A good example is the fine sax from Little Bealings (Fig. 16) in the British Museum,[3] and another of similar type examined by Liestøl (pp. 87 f.).

We know that the art of pattern-welding was practised in western Europe before Anglo-Saxon times. At Nydam as many as 90 swords out of a total of 106 had patterned blades, so that the technique was evidently well known by the fourth century A.D. The bog-finds at Vimose, which are perhaps a century earlier, included 14 pattern-welded blades out of a total of 67 two-edged swords.[4] This gives us a long period over which patterned swords were made, and a recent discovery, not yet published, enables us to extend this still further.

In 1953 fragments of two sword-blades from South Shields Museum,[5] found under the ramparts of the third-century Roman fort at South Shields, were examined at the British Museum and discovered to be pattern-welded blades, with a pattern of the two-strand herringbone type. Since these swords were lost when the rampart of the fort was being built, between A.D. 197 and 205, we

---

[1] One from the Thames at Westminster (*P.S.A.* xvi, 1897, p. 390), and one from the Thames at Windsor (Kendrick, p. 393).

[2] *H. of T.*, p. 62.

[3] Kendrick, p. 393. Small knives with such decorative panels can be seen in the Ashmolean Museum and at Cambridge (two examples from Barrington and Wicken Fen). See France-Lanord 2, p. 418, and Coghlan, pp. 150, 162.

[4] Klindt-Jensen, p. 204.

[5] I am most grateful to Professor I. A. Richmond for permission to see these fragments and for the information given here.

know that they must have been in use in the second century. One of the fragments[1] is of especial interest, for it bears finely executed and elaborate figures in gilt inlay on both faces: one is an eagle standard between manipular standards, and the other Mars in panoply holding shield and spear (Fig. 15a). These figures are of provincial workmanship and may have been made in Gaul; it is suggestive that the sword fragments were found associated with a belt with enamelled mountings which must have come from a workshop in Gallia Belgica. Richmond believes that these fragments formed part of officers' swords; when more work has been done on them they should add greatly to our knowledge of pattern-welded blades during the Roman period, while examination of Roman swords in other museums may yield interesting results.

The inlaid figure of Mars upon the blade does not stand completely alone. In a cremation grave from Øvre Stabu, Norway, a pattern-welded sword was discovered with a barbaric figure of a Roman Victory inlaid in bronze below the tang, and the letters s, f below (see Fig. 15b). The figure was placed so as to be the right way up when viewed from the hilt. From the resemblance of the sword to those from Vimose, Shetelig[2] dated this (and the spear with a runic inscription found with it) to about A.D. 200.

The process of pattern-welding then was known at least from the second to the ninth century A.D., a far longer period than was formerly realized. Neumann, who was interested in Roman processes of manufacturing iron and steel, appeared to be unaware that the technique continued after the fall of the Empire. Baldwin Brown was puzzled by the gap in time between the Nydam swords and the patterned blades of the Viking Age. But now we know that they were made continuously throughout the period which intervened, and were treasured as rich possessions by Anglo-Saxon kings and warriors and by their Frankish and Alamannic contemporaries across the Channel. Our former ignorance was due to the fact that in most cases Anglo-Saxon swords were rusted

[1] Shown by Plenderleith, *Conservation of Antiquities*, 1956, pl. 46, p. 321.

[2] H. Shetelig, 'Arkeologiske Tidsbestemmelser av ældre norske Rune-indskrifter', in M. Olsen, *Norges Indskrifter med de ældre Runer*, Christiania, 1914–24, iii, p. 6, fig. 2.

in their scabbards, and the patterns could only be revealed by X-ray.

Pattern-welded swords may not have been made in many workshops, and as yet there is no evidence that they were ever produced in England or Scandinavia, though there seems no convincing reason why they should not have been. Many of these swords are fitted with hilts of characteristic Anglo-Saxon or Scandinavian workmanship, and Liestøl believes that some of the Viking swords were made in Scandinavia. There seems to have been an increase in the number of patterned blades about the sixth century, and France-Lanord suggested the possibility that at this time more workshops began to produce them. It may be, however, that the process remained a secret in the hands of a few smiths only.

Lorange thought the most likely centre for the manufacture of the Nydam blades was the Rhineland. Other possible regions famed for the working of metals are Noricum and the Pyrenees, and France-Lanord and Salin (iii, pp. 110 f.) favour Noricum, thinking that skilled smiths from this region may have brought the technique westwards to Ratisbon and the Rhine. The general opinion now is that it was Celtic smiths who first practised pattern-welding, and Forbes (p. 464) suggests that the Romans copied it from them and perhaps developed it to some extent. An argument against Noricum, however, is that the smiths there could obtain good steel for swords, and presumably would have no need to resort to elaborate welding processes to build up their blades; similarly Roman smiths were able to rely on good steel from the East as well as that from their own mines for the making of weapons.

A possible origin of the pattern-welding technique may be seen in the Celtic practice of forging weapons of laminated or 'piled' wrought iron. This seems to have been known as early as the eighth century B.C. and perhaps even earlier, from the evidence of certain Iron Age blades. Coghlan[1] discusses this process, which was a method of carburizing the iron and so improving the quality

---

[1] Coghlan 2, pp. 130 f.; cf. *Antiquity*, March 1956, p. 27, for a description of a blade from the Bern Historical Museum examined by Dr. René Wyss.

of the weapons made from it. Thin plates of iron were separately carburized, piled one above the other, and then forge-welded together, so that there was a fairly even distribution of carbon throughout the whole mass. Only certain La Tène smiths seem to have adopted this method, and it must have meant a considerable technical advance; it may be noted that some of these layered blades show superficial marks indicating welding, and have been thought to be damascened.[1] The process of layering was still used in later times, for Salin (iii, p. 52) has examples of scramasaxes of the sixth or seventh centuries A.D. which have been built up by this method; in the best of these, the layers making up the body of the blade alternate in quality between low-carbon steel and pure iron, and he points out that these one-edged swords would make excellent weapons. Thus the pattern-welding method was not the only means of building up a good sword-blade in Merovingian times, but it is to be noted that in the case of the scramasaxes the smiths appear to have procured iron ore which was remarkably free from impurities, according to Salin's analysis.

If experiments in building up sword-blades from layers of wrought iron had gone on for so long in western Europe, it would seem reasonable to suppose that the method of twist-welding could develop naturally out of such experiments, and that there is no need to assume that the process of pattern-welding began as an attempt to imitate the damascened swords of the East.[2] The building up of a patterned structure by a forging technique is something which has been known and practised with local variations at different periods in many parts of the world. Examples of it are the *kris* of Malay, 'damascened' gun-barrels, which were made in Sweden in the eighteenth century and in Belgium still more recently, and the Japanese sword, which was a weapon of superb quality built up by a most elaborate technique from many layers of steel.[3]

---

[1] Déchelette, *Manuel*, ii (3), p. 1117; cf. Salin, iii, p. 78.
[2] As Lindenschmidt and others have suggested; see Salin, iii, p. 97.
[3] France-Lanord 2, p. 416; Smith, pp. 201 f.; and for the Japanese sword, Coghlan, pp. 166 f.; A. Dobrée, *J.R.A.I.* lxii (xii), 1905, pp. 1 f.; and M. Chikashige, *Alchemy and Other Chemical Achievements of the Ancient Orient*, Tokyo, 1936, pp. 87 f.

It is scarcely surprising, then, to find such a method of producing sword-blades flourishing in western Europe, where for
many centuries it was to result in the making of fine weapons,
prized by kings and leaders among the Teutonic peoples.

5. THE TEUTONIC SWORD

The complicated question of the origin of the pattern-welded
blade is bound up with that of the Teutonic sword. This has been
discussed at length by Behmer in his survey of the swords of the
Migration period. Short swords of the type used in the Roman
army were popular among the Germans and were apparently
copied by native smiths, but they disappear about halfway through
the Roman period in northern Europe. The swords from Vimose
and Nydam with pattern-welded blades were long swords, and it is
not easy to see how such weapons could have developed out of the
short *gladius* used by the Roman legionaries, with a blade made
for thrusting and not for cutting. The origin of the long cutting
sword of the Germans might be looked for in the weapon used by
the Roman cavalry, in the long sword of the Gauls, or possibly in
the sword of the Sarmatians and Alani in south Russia, a long
cutting weapon which reached the Goths fairly early.[1] But the line
of development is not clear, and the earliest surviving examples of
the Teutonic sword in north-western Europe have hilts of a very
primitive type, bearing no resemblance to more elaborate Roman
or Celtic examples.

The series of swords from the Danish bog-finds (p. 6 above)
throws some light on changing fashions in sword forms. Brøndsted
(iii, pp. 201 f.) distinguishes three main groups of finds. The
swords from Thorsbjerg and Vimose belong to the first group,
which he dates to the period between A.D. 100 and 300. This group
contains three types of swords: first a short sax or single-edged
sword-knife, usually with curved hilt (Fig. 1*a*); secondly a short
two-edged sword resembling the Roman *gladius* in type, with round

---

[1] With regard to swords of this class, the difficulty is that practically no information is available about swords of Hungary, central Russia, and the Steppe
regions, as Salin points out (iii, pp. 91 f.).

pommel, indented grip, and semicircular guard (Fig. 1*b*); and thirdly a long two-edged sword, sometimes but by no means always with the same type of hilt as the *gladius*. One sword from Vimose has a ring-formed pommel of Scythian type and another a hilt with a guard ending in a spiral at each side (Fig. 1*c*). The two-edged swords, both long and short, frequently have smiths' marks of various kinds, and some have pattern-welded blades. The sax, however, has no mark, possibly because this type of weapon was of native manufacture.

The next group of finds can probably be dated from the third to the end of the fifth century A.D., and the rich collection of swords from Nydam forms part of this. There are very few single-edged blades or short two-edged swords of the *gladius* type to be found from this period. The *gladius* type of hilt is found on a few of the long swords, but a hilt with a small pommel and a grip shaped like an hour-glass is more common (Fig. 1*d*). Most of the blades in this group are pattern-welded and these frequently bear smiths' marks on blade or tang.

It would appear from these finds that the long sword with a pattern-welded blade gradually increased in popularity as the weapon of Teutonic warriors fighting in Denmark between the second and sixth centuries A.D., and that workshops were supplying this new type of sword from about A.D. 100 onwards, and seeking a market mainly outside the Roman Empire for their wares. When the first deposits of arms were laid down at Thorsbjerg and Vimose, the northern peoples were using either swords of the Roman type or large knives probably of native manufacture. But about two centuries later practically all the swords were of the new type with pattern-welded blades.

The position may be comparable to that of glass-making at the close of the Roman period in the Rhineland. Expert craftsmen still went on producing glass there when the Empire came to an end, but since their old customers and the well-established trade with Rome and her colonies had gone, they continued work on a smaller scale, and produced new types of luxury glass such as would appeal to their new customers, the Teutonic peoples who were

settling in the north-west. While trade might suffer from the un-
settled conditions which prevailed in the Migration period, there
would be more demand than ever for good swords. It is not easy
to determine the nationality of the craftsmen who were producing
them at the time when the Nydam swords were in use and through
the centuries afterwards; the names on blades from Vimose and
Nydam, when recognizable, suggest romanized Celtic smiths (p. 43
below), while inscribed names on later swords are Teutonic in
form; no doubt a workshop of first-class reputation would in any
case attract craftsmen of many different nationalities. The geo-
graphical situation must be important, since smiths had to obtain
their own ore and charcoal locally, but there are many regions
where this would be possible. Now that widespread interest has
been aroused in pattern-welded swords, we shall probably gather
sufficient evidence in time to give us a definite answer to the question of where the finest blades were produced, and this is a question
which will be further discussed in a later section.

In size and shape the blade of the Teutonic sword varied comparatively little during the long period of its use. Behmer distinguishes between *broad*, *narrow*, and *long* types of sword in use
during the Migration period. Most surviving swords are of the
narrow type, varying in width from 4·5 to 5·5 cm. Behmer's
type III, which is broader (6 to 6·5 cm.), is probably Alamannic
in origin, and there are two other types of blade, found in central
Europe and also used by the Alamanni, which are relatively broad.
The normal length of a sword of the Migration period he gives as
between 85 and 95 cm., apart from one class of longer blades
(type IV) found mainly in south Russia. Salin similarly gives the
average length of a Merovingian sword as 85 cm. without the
tang.[1]

Measurements of blades from Anglo-Saxon cemeteries agree
with these estimates. Swords from the cemetery at Sarre vary from
34 to 37 inches (86·4 to 94 cm.), and there is plenty of minor
variation, since no two swords from this cemetery are precisely the
same length. One sword from Acklam (in the museum at Hull)

[1] E. Salin, *Le Fer à l'époque mérovingienne*, Paris, 1943, p. 117.

measures as much as 39·5 inches (100 cm.). With this may be compared a Viking sword from Dublin, said to be more than 99·5 cm. long.[1] Salin quotes similar examples of a few unusually long swords from Merovingian France.

Gessler (p. 102) took the measurements of thirty-two swords of Carolingian times, mostly from the Rhine area; he found that the average length was 94 cm. including the tang (84 cm. for the blade alone), and the width below the hilt 5·5 cm. During the Viking Age there was no great difference in the length of the blade, but an interesting development took place in the shape. Arbman (2, pp. 223 f.) and Gessler (p. 100) note that Carolingian swords tended to become heavier about A.D. 800, as was shown by the weapons from the cemetery at Landern, Westphalia. But by about A.D. 900 there was a change in the type of blade, and swords of this time are found to be better balanced, with the centre of gravity no longer halfway down the blade but nearer the hilt, so that they must have been more efficient weapons both for thrusting and cutting. Jankuhn thought the makers of *Ulfberht* blades may have been largely responsible for this change, since many of their inscribed swords were of the new type.

Blades of the ninth and tenth centuries also have edges slightly tapering from shoulder to point instead of running parallel for most of their length, and from about the eighth century onward there is a strongly marked groove or *fuller* down the blade. Such a groove is popularly known as the 'blood-channel', although this term is not found in early literature; its function is to give deeper backing to the edges without extra weight or decrease in flexibility.[2] It is not altogether a new feature, since it is present on some of the Nydam blades, and is clearly visible on the sword depicted on the panel on the Sutton Hoo helmet. Anstee's experience in making a pattern-welded blade showed that the practice of twist-welding necessitated the hollowing out of a groove down the centre of the blade before etching and polishing, and it is evident that this was a feature of the blades described by Cassiodorus in the fifth century (p. 106 below). Two swords from Abingdon, Berkshire (which

---

[1] *V.A.* iii, p. 16 (Wk. 34 A–B, 1881: 362).　　　　[2] Cowen, p. 171.

were not pattern-welded), had each a wide, shallow groove on one face and a pair of narrower grooves on the other; and these were thought to come from the neighbourhood of Namur, from the style of one of the scabbard chapes.[1] Such shallow grooves are usual also on one-edged swords. At the close of the Viking period the form of the blade changed as new defensive armour came into use, and swords of the twelfth century became longer and more slender, with a narrower groove down the centre.

The use of the Anglo-Saxon term *seax* (ON *sax*) is complicated by the fact that there is no complete agreement as to its meaning. The term *scramasax* was employed by Gregory of Tours for the daggers of the Franks, and this term is sometimes adopted by archaeologists for the long one-edged sword.[2] Beck distinguishes between *sax* (short sword), *langsax* (one-edged long sword), and *scramasax* (dagger), a useful distinction if it could be generally maintained. The terms used for a short sword in West Gothic and Burgundian Laws were *scrama* and *semispatha* respectively.

One type of short sword was two-edged with a blade of about 27 inches in length. There were two swords of this type in the cemetery at Sarre,[3] and another fine example is the sword from Lough Gur (in the British Museum) which has a blade 27 inches long and a grip only 2·2 inches between the rings at either end (Fig. 27). This sword has a fine hilt with gold ornament and a blade with impressive smiths' marks,[4] and may have been made for a high-born boy. Short swords of this type might be pattern-welded. Salin mentions shorter weapons, averaging about 40 cm. in length, but only as rarities. The earliest example of the scramasax in a Frankish grave was that which accompanied the long sword in the tomb of Childeric (A.D. 482).

Another class of weapon which can be included under the general heading *sax* is the long, one-edged sword, rare in Anglo-Saxon England. The sword in the British Museum which was

[1] Leeds and Harden, pp. 59 f. See p. 90 below.
[2] See Wheeler 1, p. 176; Beck, i, p. 710.
[3] *A.C.* vi, p. 169; vii, p. 308.
[4] Bruce-Mitford, *Congrès International des Sciences Préhist., Actes de la IIIᵉ session*, Zurich, 1950 (pub. 1953), p. 321.

found at Little Bealings has a blade 32·8 inches long, and there are three one-edged swords from the Thames, now in the London Museum,[1] and three from Kilmainham, now in the museum at Dublin.[2] The long sword with one sharpened edge was popular in Norway in the eighth century;[3] like the swords from the Thames, it usually had two or three grooves along the back of the blade. The blade is curved on a number of Scandinavian one-edged swords. Of one-edged blades reported on by Salin from sixth- and seventh-century cemeteries none were pattern-welded, but the quality of the iron was in some cases very good.

Brief mention may here be made of the short dagger or dirk (*scramasax* or *handseax*). There are a number of very varied examples of this in the English museums, and some have Anglo-Saxon or runic inscriptions (p. 43 below). A knife from Sittingbourne (in the British Museum) has panels of mosaic inlay and champlevé work resembling that on some of the more elaborate sword-hilts, and bears an inscription in Anglo-Saxon (Fig. 17 and p. 80 below). Kendrick (p. 398) pointed out that there must have been a considerable number of such knives made in England in the tenth century, and it seems probable that they were being produced in the north of England some time earlier. Schubert (p. 65) suggests that the Sittingbourne knife was probably made in Northumbria, and mentions the Thames scramasax with the runic alphabet (Fig. 18) and another inlaid knife from Hurbeck Farm near Lanchester as other examples of fine native workmanship. He refers to two letters written in the eighth century in the monasteries of Wearmouth and Jarrow;[4] these allude to presents of small knives (*cultelli*) sent to the Rhineland, and a priest who sends four such knives refers to them as 'made in the fashion of our country' (*cultellos nostra consuetudine factos*). As Schubert points out, it is most unlikely that knives would be sent to the Rhineland, a region with

---

[1] Wheeler 1, pl. xiii.

[2] Coffey and Armstrong, pp. 110–11.

[3] For a full account of these Norwegian swords, see S. Grieg, *Merovingisk og Norsk eneeggede Sverd fra VII og VIII Aarh.*

[4] P. Jaffé, *Monumenta Moguntina*, Berolini, 1866, Epistola 77, p. 215; 134, p. 300.

a high reputation for tools and weapons, unless they were of out-standing quality.

Such daggers were frequently worn as additions to the sword, usually in a sheath on the belt. In the fifth century a sax might also accompany a sword, as not only Childeric's grave but also those at Pouan and Lavoye held both weapons (p. 64 below). A one-edged sword or a short sword might be occasionally preferred to a long two-edged weapon, as was the case with the Icelandic hero Grettir the Strong; his saga tells how he took a fine sax from a burial mound,[1] and when allowed to keep it for his services to the family, he preferred it to his own family sword. This weapon was probably a short, two-edged sword, with a full-sized hilt (*meðalkafli*).[2] Salin (p. 53) rightly emphasizes the usefulness of short and one-edged swords, but the evidence of the cemeteries shows that they never replaced the long two-edged weapon in general popularity in north-western Europe.

6. INSCRIBED BLADES

The earliest sword inscriptions are found on blades from the Danish bog-finds, and they form a varied and interesting collection. There are none from Thorsbjerg, since the blades there were almost wholly lost. Two swords from Vimose bear stamps on the tang, one reading CAXB and the other TASVIT (Fig. 2a, b).[3] Some blades also have marks which must have been stamped by the makers: a star or scorpion is found below the hilt on one sword (Fig. 2c), and twice on the tang of another, while a third has a circle on both faces of the tang (Fig. 2d). The largest collection comes from Nydam.[4] Here there are four examples of what appear to be names (Fig. 3): RICUS (with a 'herring-bone' stamp) on the tang; RICCIM; COCILLUS; and what appears to be UMORCD (with a stamp in the form of a half-moon with horns). In addition there

---

[1] *Grettis Saga*, xviii.

[2] A. R. Taylor, 'Two Notes on *Beowulf*', *Leeds Studies in English*, vii–viii, 1952, p. 13, notes this use of the term *meðalkafli*, but it is hardly surprising. The term *mundriði*, which he seems to expect here, is presumably used of the handles of the small dagger-knives.

[3] Engelhardt 1, pp. 14 f. [4] Engelhardt 2, pp. 22 f.

are various marks: a double X on the tang (Fig. 4*a*), and a mark in the form of a circle with a cross and a smaller circle in each segment (Fig. 4*b*), which is found on several swords with an unusually long tang. One sword has gold symbols inlaid on the blade below the hilt (Fig. 4*c*), which Engelhardt suggested might be runes; it seems probable that this was an owner's rather than a maker's mark.

It will be seen that this collection of swords contains a large variety of inscribed letters and symbols, and that most of these are on the tang where they could not be seen when the hilt was in place. Of the names on the blades, it may be noted that Cocillus is known to have been a Celtic name;[1] it occurs in a number of inscriptions on the Continent and also in one from Wilderspool near Warrington, the site of the great ironworks of Roman Britain.

After this early period, inscribed swords of any kind are rare until the ninth century, when recognizable names are found. Schmid notes an interesting example of a blade from Nördlingen cemetery[2] (the only inscribed one out of a large number found in this area). The cemetery was of seventh-century date, but he thinks that the inscription O2 may go back to Roman times. There are rare examples of motifs on pattern-welded blades.[3] Not until the ninth century, however, did it become usual to inscribe names on the blades, as well as symbols such as circles, lines, crosses, and single letters. Contrary to popular belief, runes are not commonly placed on sword-blades, and all the known examples are on hilt or scabbard. This supports the assumption that blades were made on the Continent in districts where runes had gone out of use, while hilts and scabbards were frequently made by Anglo-Saxon and Scandinavian craftsmen.

There are, however, examples of runic inscriptions on the blades of knives. A scramasax from the Thames[4] bears the twenty-eight

---

[1] A. Holder, *Altceltischer Sprachschatz*, Leipzig, 1896, under *Cocillus*. I owe this reference to Mrs. N. O'Sullivan.

[2] W. M. Schmid, 'Frühgeschichtliche Schwertinschrift', *Z.f.h.W.* ix, 1921, pp. 72 f.

[3] Salin, iii, pl. vi; Arbman 2, p. 256. Cf. Jankuhn, p. 216.

[4] In the British Museum; *B.M. Guide*, p. 96.

characters of the runic alphabet or *futhorc* in order, together with eight further runes which may spell the owner's name (Fig. 18). Two smaller knives, probably of seventh-century date, from Alamannic cemeteries at Steindorf and Hailfingen,[1] bear runic inscriptions. Arntz believes that the runes in each case include a shortened dedicatory formula for 'I dedicate the sax.' The question of how far such knives were intended for ritual use, and whether the runes carved on them were in the nature of a magic spell, is a difficult one to answer with confidence. In his book *Malruner og Troldruner*, Bæksted has firmly opposed the view that the runes on the Thames knife, for example, were used with any such purpose. On the other hand, there is a significant body of evidence in the form of runic inscriptions on spearheads, which suggests that runes were placed on weapons to bring strength, luck, and victory to their owners, and these will be referred to later.

An unusual example of runes in connexion with a sword may also be mentioned here. A runic inscription was cut on a small model of a sword in wood, 24 cm. in length, found in a *terp* near the village of Arum in West Frisia[2] (Fig. 22). It could be a model of a short sword of the Roman type, or of a longer weapon; since the edge of the blade has suffered from burial for many centuries it is impossible to be sure. The sword is of yew-wood, and like another inscription cut in yew from Britsum[3] probably belongs to the late sixth or early seventh century. The runes cut on the blade run as follows:

$$\text{M M F : B F M F}$$
$$\text{e d æ : b o d a}$$

There is some doubt as to whether the last rune is to be taken as F, 'æ', or F, 'a', but Arntz thinks he can distinguish an upward stroke. Von Friesen[4] and others have taken the inscription to be a

---

[1] E. Moltke and G. Neckel, 'Ein alamannischer Sax mit Runen?', *Germ.* xviii, 1934, pp. 36 f.; and H. Zeiss and H. Arntz, 'Ein bajuwarischer Sax mit Runen von Steindorf', ibid. xx, 1936, pp. 127 f. Also Arntz and Zeiss, pp. 240 f., 350 f.   [2] Arntz and Zeiss, pp. 106 f., pl. vi.

[3] Ibid., pp. 154 f. For inscriptions on yew, see Elliott, 'Runes, Yews and Magic', *Speculum*, xxxii, 1957, p. 256. The Britsum piece—another Frisian inscription—begins with an injunction always to carry the yew.

[4] *Nordisk Kultur*, vi, p. 49.

personal name, but it may, as Arntz is inclined to believe, have the meaning *renuntius*, 'return-messenger'. The point of the blade shows signs of burning, and it has been suggested that the sword was a summons to war.[1] Other wooden swords were found at Vimose and Thorsbjerg,[2] but no runes were recorded on them.

Sword inscriptions which have sometimes been mistaken for runes are those on blades of the ninth and tenth centuries which are made up of Roman letters, sometimes accompanied by smiths' marks. A sword recovered from the Thames near the Temple and now in the British Museum has been cleaned to show the inscription *Ingelrii* on the blade below the hilt[3] (Fig. 30). Another of the tenth century recovered from the River Witham about a hundred years ago was recently examined at the British Museum and found to bear the name *Leutlrit* (perhaps for Leutfrit) (Fig. 23), while on the reverse is a large s.[4] An account of this sword by Maryon describes how such inscriptions were produced: a number of small iron rods were hammered into the white-hot blade and the whole then reheated and the inlay hammered until secure.[5]

There are other swords bearing inscriptions on their blades which are visible but cannot be made out. A sword from the Thames in the Tullie House Museum, Carlisle, probably about A.D. 1000 in date, has at least four letters on the blade[6] (Fig. 24). Another from the Thames near Shifford (Fig. 25) is in Reading Museum; this is in good condition and appears to be of tenth- or eleventh-century date, and bears an illegible inscription, as does another sword from the Thames at Battersea (Fig. 26).[7] These inscriptions are all of the same type, with fairly large letters inlaid in

---

[1] Saxo Grammaticus (v. 153, p. 188, Elton) states that 'an arrow of wood, looking like iron, used to be passed on everywhere from man to man as a messenger' for an urgent summons to war. Arntz compares this with the Scandinavian custom of sending round a piece of burnt wood for a war summons.

[2] Englehardt, *Thorsbjerg Mosefund*, i, p. 38, pl. ix, 3; *Vimosefundet*, p. 15, fig. 7.   [3] Oakeshott 2, p. 69.   [4] Maryon 2, p. 175.

[5] T. Petersen ('Gravfundene pa Flemma i Tingvoll', *Aarsskrift for Nordmär Historielag*, 1925, pp. 31 f.) discusses some *Ingelrii* inscriptions and quotes from a tenth-century Latin account of how letters were inlaid on knives.

[6] Cowen, pp. 181 f.

[7] *P.S.A.* (2) iv, 1868, p. 143. See App. B.

the central panel of the blade. A sword from Canwick Common, which Grove (p. 256) mentions along with the other inscribed blades of this period, has quite a different type of inscription: ANTANANTANANAN in small neat silver letters; and this is almost certainly considerably later in date.

Probably, as Cowen (p. 181) points out, many of these inscriptions would not be comprehensible even if the letters could be identified with certainty. He suggests that sword-makers in the tenth century often imitated genuine inscriptions by 'letters and senseless marks' because of the employment of illiterate craftsmen. This, however, is unlikely to have happened in workshops of good repute, providing luxury articles for distinguished customers, and it is probable that letters and marks often formed a trade code, conveying much to the tenth-century connoisseur of good swords. There is certainly no reason to assume that all inscriptions were in the form of personal names. The use of recognizable personal names like *Ulfberht* and *Ingelrii* seems to have been an innovation, probably instituted by the makers of the *Ulfberht* blades. An example of an attempt at a Latin inscription on a blade probably of eleventh-century date in private possession at Munich is given by Schmid.[1] This has a pattern on one side and on the other an inscription which he reads as:

†B̄H̄⊥IOMEŁECI

He suggests that the last part is an attempt at ME FECIT, following a personal name. This inscribed blade has been mended by the addition of an inferior piece, suggesting that a local smith repaired it.

The largest and most interesting group of inscribed swords in the Viking Age is formed of those bearing the name *Ulfberht* (Fig. 32). A number of these come from Norway and East Prussia, and a few from Finland and Russia. Jankuhn has published some valuable work on these swords, with a distribution map of the places where they have been found[2] (Fig. 28). He came to the

---

[1] W. M. Schmid, 'Beiträge zur Geschichte der Schwertmarkierung', *Z.f.h.W.* viii, 1918–20, p. 244.

[2] H. Jankuhn, 'Ein Ulfberht-Schwert aus der Elbe bei Hamburg', *Festschrift f. Gustav Schwantes*, Neumünster, 1951, pp. 212 f. Cf. *Archaeologia Geographia*, i, 1950, pp. 1 f.

conclusion that they were distributed from a centre in the Middle Rhine district, over a period extending from the late ninth to the early eleventh centuries, mainly through the port of Hedeby. They are rare in Sweden and very few seem to have reached the British Isles. One example from Ballinderry Crannog in Ireland is on the blade of a sword which also bears the name HILTIPREHT on the hilt (Plate IV*a* and p. 81 below). Oddly enough, neither of the two published accounts of the sword mentioned this blade inscription, interest having focused on the hilt.[1] A second Irish sword from Kilmainham, Dublin, bears an inscription now illegible, and this was photographed during the preservation process and read as ULFBERHT.[2]

Another example from the British Isles is claimed in *Viking Antiquities* (iv, p. 61), where a sword found in the bed of the Old Nene in 1895, described as 'from Raven's Willow, Peterborough', and now in Wisbech Museum (Fig. 31), is said to bear the inscriptions VLFBERHT II and INIEFIR II on its blade. My own rubbings of these inscriptions, however, have inclined me to substitute INGEL-RII for INIEFIR II; though BERH can be made out on the other side, it does not seem very likely that this inscription, now very hard to decipher, is a genuine *Ulfberht* one.[3]

The swords inscribed *Ulfberht* were made of fine-quality steel, and were not pattern-welded. Petersen (pp. 208 f.) tested one of the Norwegian examples and found it to have a carbon content of 0·75 per cent., while one from Hamburg was found to be as high as 1·2 per cent. The blades are efficiently shaped and well balanced, and they are good examples of the tendency towards lighter, better-balanced swords for both cutting and thrusting, noticeable about A.D. 900.[4]

The name which occurs most frequently after *Ulfberht* is that of *Ingelrii*, appearing with several slight variations in spelling such

[1] A. Mahr, 'Ein Wikingerschwert mit deutschem Namen aus Irland', *Mannus*, vi (Ergänzungsband), 1928, pp. 240 f., and *V.A.* iii, p. 77.

[2] *V.A.* iii, p. 62.

[3] My thanks are due to the Curator of Wisbech Museum for allowing me to examine the sword and for assistance in making rubbings of the inscription.

[4] Jankuhn, pp. 225 f.

as *Ingelrd* and *Ingelrilt*. This group of swords seems to have been produced a little later than the earliest *Ulfberht* blades, and they continued to be made over a longer period, since one inscription *Ingelrilt* is found on a twelfth-century sword. Oakeshott (2, pp. 69 f.) noted thirteen examples of this inscription in 1951, and I would support his suggestion of the Wisbech sword as a possible fourteenth. The distribution of these blades differs from that of the *Ulfberht* ones, since they are found in both England and Sweden (Fig. 29), but they seem likely to be of Frankish origin. Two variations of the inscription are INGRLRIIMEFECIT, on a sword from Sigridsholm, Sweden,[1] and INGELRIH FECIT on one from Flemma, Norway.[2]

It seems likely that both Ulfberht and Ingelrii were individual smiths, whose names were either handed down in the family or came to be used as trade names in the workshops where these special swords continued to be made and inscribed over several generations. It is now clear that the names cannot represent the owners of the swords, and that Ulfberht cannot be a place-name.[3]

A few isolated examples of inscriptions have been noticed. There is so far no parallel to *Leutlrit* mentioned above (p. 45); a blade in Dresden has the words HOMO DEI,[4] and in Leyden Museum there is a blade inscribed ATALBALD IE.[5] Petersen (p. 151) gives a Viking sword of tenth-century date with the inscription REX, which might possibly refer to the owner and not to the maker. Finally there are two inscriptions BENNO ME FECIT and NISO ME FET in Stade Museum, the first with INOMINE DNI on the reverse; Jankuhn (p. 277) dates these to the eleventh century. Such inscriptions, together with the latinized form of the *Ingelrii* inscription mentioned above, point forward to the more elaborate Latin ones of the medieval period.

An unusual example of a stamp upon a sword-blade, differing from the various examples discussed by Jankuhn and Schmid, is

---

[1] Arbman, *Z.f.h.W.* v (N.F.), 1935, p. 145.
[2] T. Petersen, *Aarsskrift for Nordmär Historielag*, 1925, p. 31.
[3] A place near Solingen was suggested by Kelleter in *Geschichte der Familie J. A. Henckels*, pp. 21 f.
[4] Schmid, *Z.f.h.W.* viii, 1918–20, p. 244.   [5] Jankuhn, p. 227.

found on a weapon recovered from the Thames and now in the British Museum. On the blade are two small circular stamps, one below the other, a short way below the hilt (Fig. 19). The stamps are identical and have been covered with gold foil, and it would seem that the die employed was similar to one used for stamping coins.[1] The design can be identified with one found on *sceattas* of the early eighth century, and nos. 173 and 111 in the British Museum *Catalogue of Anglo-Saxon Coins* are very close to it[2] (Fig. 20a, b). These bear a figure described as 'dragon-like figure, head turned right'; no. 173 is dated about A.D. 700, and no. 111, which has a different figure on the reverse, a little later. These stamps are unlikely to be maker's marks, and it seems probable that the sword was reheated and stamped when it came into the possession of some influential person who had the right to impress the symbol of his own coinage upon it; it is perhaps significant that the design chosen is one of native type and not based on a Roman prototype. It has been suggested that a reference to a sword 'on which the hand is marked' in a tenth-century Anglo-Saxon will (p. 121 below) may refer to the symbol of the Hand of God used on certain coins of the tenth and eleventh centuries[3] (Fig. 20c), and the sword in question may have been stamped in the same way as this one with a die resembling that used for coins.

There is another interesting example of a stamp on a sword, apparently added by the Anglo-Saxon owner, on a weapon dredged up from the River Lark and now in Cambridge Museum. This has three figures of boars either stamped or punched into the blade, two on one side and one on the other[4] (Fig. 21). As far as I know, there is no other example of a naturalistic animal stamp of this kind upon a sword blade of this period. The creature depicted is

---

[1] My thanks are due to the authorities of the British Museum for the opportunity to examine this sword and to compare the stamps with Anglo-Saxon coins in their collection.

[2] *Catalogue of English Coins in the British Museum*, Anglo-Saxon series, 1887, vol. i, pl. iii (1, 4); iv (3, 5); cf. p. 13.

[3] The device of the Hand is found on coins of tenth-century kings of Northumbria, and also on those of Æthelred II. See *B.M. Catalogue*, op. cit., pl. xxviii (1084), and other examples there given.

[4] T. Lethbridge, 'A Sword from the River Lark', *C.A.S.* xxxii, 1931, p. 64.

a small, plump boar, whose ears, eye, and tail are clearly visible in profile, and the closest parallel seems to be the stamp of a duck on one of the pots from the Lackford cremation cemetery.[1] This sword is not pattern-welded; its hilt is missing, except for a narrow bronze guard, and it is dated by Lethbridge to the seventh century.

These two Anglo-Saxon stamped blades are of special interest, since the stamps do not appear to have been added merely as a decoration. It seems likely that they are there either to denote ownership or that they are special symbols of some kind. The boar we know to have been placed on helmets as a protective symbol; not only have we the statement in *Beowulf* to that effect, but there is also a helmet from an Anglo-Saxon grave at Benty Grange with a boar figure on the crest, to be compared with other boars depicted on helmets from Sweden.[2] The other sword has a stamp showing an animal, though it is hard to identify it, and here the clue seems to be the close resemblance to coinage, which presumably bore the symbol of a local ruler. Certain pommels on Kentish swords also bear marks which suggest symbols, either for luck or protection or marks of ownership (p. 66 below).

Patterns on blades of the Viking Age are usually of a very simple kind, accompanying smiths' marks. A sword from the River Bann in Ireland (Fig. 70), which has no inscription, but an inlaid silver pattern on one side, is exceptional if, as is claimed, it is a Viking sword. The hilt, with oval pommel and wide, straight, slender guard, is not, however, characteristic of the Viking Age, and suggests a twelfth-century date. The pattern also, which appears to be a 'palm-tree' motif, may be compared with that on a twelfth-century sword from Zurich, described by Wegeli. Although the Swiss sword has far more elaborate ornament, it may be noted that the hilt is almost identical with the River Bann sword.[3]

---

[1] *C.A.S.* Quarto Publications, 6, fig. 31, pp. 12, 21.

[2] See Cramp, p. 59, and Hatto, pp. 12-15. The Benty Grange helmet is described with photographs by Bruce-Mitford in the *Annual Report of the City Museum of Sheffield*, 1955-6, p. 13.

[3] Included by Bøe among Viking swords in Dublin, *V.A.* iii, p. 83. Fig. 56 shows the pattern on the blade, but not the hilt. For the Swiss sword, see Wegeli,

7. THE CONSTRUCTION OF THE HILT

If the blade on the whole varied little, this is not true of the hilt; it is the variation in shape and decoration of the hilts of swords which survive from Anglo-Saxon and Viking times which provides the chief evidence for dating. The hilt offered fine opportunities for elaboration and enrichment, and those used by the Anglo-Saxons and Vikings were often beautiful and complex pieces of craftsmanship. This does not, however, mean that the hilt was a mere ornamental appendage to the blade. It was essential that it should be well constructed, since should it become loose, slip off the tang, or shift under the weight of a heavy blow, it would lose the fight and perhaps bring death for its owner; and the continual shock and vibration of sword fighting must have been a gruelling test.

There were a number of necessary functions for the hilt to perform. It had to cover the tang, and particularly the pointed end, lest this should wound the warrior who held the sword; consequently it was topped with a cap or knob, forming the pommel. This pommel had to be well and securely fastened to keep the whole in place, and various methods were tried to ensure this; sometimes a bar was fixed below the pommel to strengthen it. Secondly, the hilt had to offer a comfortable grip for the hand, so that the sword could be effectively controlled; and to ensure this the tang was covered either with some kind of binding or with an outer shell of wood, metal, or horn, which might be indented or divided into ridges to afford a surer grasp for the fingers. Thirdly, the hilt had to offer protection to the hand, to prevent it slipping down the blade or being reached by the sword of an opponent; so that a guard of horn, wood, or metal had to be fitted over the shoulder of the blade. In a later period, when swords were used increasingly for thrusting as well as cutting strokes, a rounded guard was provided like a small shield (as on the fencing foil); this protected the hand from the point of the opponent's sword, while the

'Inschriften auf mittelalterlichen Schwertklingen', Z.f.h.W. iii, 1902–5, p. 221, fig. 12. This resemblance has been pointed out to me by R. E. Oakeshott, with whom I hope to publish a detailed note on the Bann sword.

cross-guard gave protection from a cutting stroke. Swords of the Anglo-Saxon and Viking periods, however, seem to have been fitted with the guard in the form of a cross-bar only.

There seems little doubt that the hilts were often made separately from the blades. As far as we know at present, the blades for the most part came into England and Scandinavia from abroad, but the hilts were often made at home. Rich hilts may have been the work of royal and famous smiths and jewellers, like one mentioned in the will of Prince Æthelstan in the eleventh century (p. 120 below). The fact that some hilts have makers' names inscribed on the guards (p. 81 below) led Morawe (p. 298) to suggest that groups of hilt-makers existed in the ninth and tenth centuries to whom blades could be sent to be fitted with hilts before they were sold. Passages in the literature suggest that it was a comparatively easy matter to fit a new hilt to a blade, and this is borne out by what we know of the construction. A possibility to be borne in mind when dating swords is mentioned by Jankuhn (p. 215), when he suggests that the fitting of new hilts upon old blades was probably a general practice.

Since much of the hilt was made of perishable material, in many cases the covering of the grip and also the pommel and guard have not survived on Anglo-Saxon swords, and it is not easy to establish an accurate typology of the weapons of the pagan Anglo-Saxon period. From the Viking Age more material has survived, and Norwegian sword-hilts have been divided by J. Petersen into twenty-six main classes in *De Norske Vikingesverd*;[1] although modifications are necessary in considering swords outside Norway, this remains the most valuable classification of hilts of this period.

8. THE POMMEL

The main feature on which we rely for the dating of swords is the pommel, for this varied considerably in accordance with changing fashions. In the earliest Teutonic swords from the Danish bogs the pommel was often of a primitive kind and consisted merely of

[1] A simplified classification based on this for hilts found in the British Isles is given by Wheeler in *London and the Vikings* (pp. 31 f.).

a flat, diamond-shaped washer of metal through which the tang passed, the end of the tang being hammered into a knob to hold the washer in position. It is reasonable to suppose that this, like the grip, was covered by some perishable material. During the early Anglo-Saxon period this simple pommel was elaborated in various ways. Metal pommels which survive are sometimes boat-shaped (Fig. 33a), or of the popular 'cocked hat' type (Fig. 33b), or in the form of two animal heads flanking a central projection (Fig. 33c). The use of animal heads developed early, for they are found on the hilt of King Childeric's fifth-century sword (one head now lost), with garnets for the eyes and clearly marked nostrils (Fig. 9a). Arbman (1, p. 128) suggests that Roman pommels with animal heads may have been the origin of this fashion; he instances two striking examples of swords with naturalistic heads of eagles forming the pommels, on a fifth- (or possibly fourth-) century carving of the Tetrarchs at St. Mark's in Venice. The Teutonic treatment, however, is very different, and in the whole history of the Teutonic sword there is no instance of the whole pommel forming a bird or animal head in this way.

The importance of a securely fixed pommel is obvious; the sword with the boar-stamps from the River Lark (p. 49 above) had lost its pommel, and Lethbridge suggested that it had come loose because the pommel-bar was not secure, so that the sword flew out of its owner's hand into the river. The normal method of fixing the pommel was to fit the pommel-bar over the tang, the top of the tang being clinched over it to hold it securely. The cap hid the top of the tang and was fixed to the pommel-bar by two rivets. Sometimes a second bar was added below, and four rivets used instead of two; these all passed down into the lower bar, as on the Sutton Hoo hilt (Plate IIIa) and many others from England and Scandinavia in the sixth and seventh centuries. The use of the double bar continued for a considerable time, and the reason may have been that since the space between the bars was filled with wood, the hilt would offer good resistance to shock, the metal fittings providing toughness while the filling gave elasticity. A double guard with the filling between the bars of the same perishable material might also be used; on the Sutton Hoo hilt the spaces between the gold bars on pommel and guard have now been filled with perspex.

Many Viking Age swords were fitted only with a small straight bar as a pommel (Fig. 34), a simple but effective shape. Another favourite form was the triangular one (Fig. 77), which could have developed from the 'cocked hat' pommel. This was popular in Norway and is found in Ireland and in other Viking settlements round Great Britain, but is rare in England; there are as many as ten swords with pommels of this type—some elaborately ornamented—in the museum at Dublin, most of them from the Kilmainham cemetery. Two are one-edged swords; and it may be noted that this type of pommel was often fitted to one-edged blades.

From the ninth century onwards a very popular form of pommel was the lobed or lobiate one. It was divided into three or five lobes, the central one usually higher than the others; they were separated by lines and sometimes by deep indentations, which might be marked out by strands of silver or gilt wire. Laking,[1] quoting 'an eminent authority', suggested that this form originated from the practice of tying an amulet on to the pommel, but although there is literary evidence for relics or amulets in the hilt (p. 182 below) there is no indication that they ever formed 'parcels' of this kind, which would be clumsy appendages to a sword. It seems more probable that the lobed pommel is a natural development from the animal-head type; a sword in the British Museum (traditionally from the Earl of Pembroke's tomb, but probably from the Thames)[2] has three lobes in the centre and one on either side, the two outermost carefully modelled in the shape of horses' heads (Fig. 37); another from the Seine, also in the British Museum, has a stylized head on each side, and in the centre a panel of gold filigree work in the style of an earlier period (Fig. 38). Another possible line of development suggested by Wheeler (2, p. 34) is from the cocked-hat pommel with a rivet on either side. A pommel from Askeaton,

---

[1] Laking, i, p. 18.
[2] *Arch.* l, 1887, pp. 531 f., fig. 11–12; *V.C.H. London*, i, pp. 156 f., fig. 11.

Co. Limerick, might be noted in support of this, for it has two slightly upturned ends which suggest rivets (Fig. 82).

Reginald Smith[1] instanced a pommel from Fetter Lane (Plate III, b, c) as an early example of the lobed type, and this like the Seine pommel has in its central division a pattern in a spiral design which seems to be an imitation of filigree ornament. Here the lobes are set on a straight bar, and he compares with this pommel another in the form of a partly hollow bronze casting divided into five lobes with deep indentations between them, now in Norwich Museum (Fig. 40). The central design seems to be ninth-century Anglo-Saxon work, based on the palmette. In general this type of pommel with three or five lobes above a straight bar is rare in the British Isles. Good examples are the swords with inscribed guards from Kilmainham and Ballinderry[2] (Fig. 85 and Plate IVa).

Two other types of lobed pommels are easier to draw than to describe. They are fitted to hilts with curved guards, and the base of the pommel is curved also, so that the lobes are enclosed in a curve with the ends turning upwards while those of the guard turn downwards. The curve may be acute or gentle. Wheeler calls the acutely curved hilt the Wallingford type, after the well-known hilt in the Ashmolean Museum (Fig. 67) which was thought until recently to have been found at Wallingford, but is now known to have come from Abingdon.[3] Other good examples of this type are the sword from the Thames at Westminster[4] (Fig. 68) and the sword in Sheffield Museum taken from the River Witham[5] (Fig. 66). A hilt from Wensley churchyard[6] is of this type, with five lobes inside the curve instead of three (Fig. 71). Wheeler suggested

---

[1] P.S.A. xxiii, 1910, p. 302. Cf. B.M. Guide, p. 93, and V.C.H. London, i, p. 154, figs. 8, 9, on coloured plate. Cf. pommel from Rossabø, Norway, Brøgger, p. 19.

[2] Coffey and Armstrong, p. 113; for other references, see p. 81 below. A third sword from Galway in the museum at Dublin appears to have a pommel of the same type, but is in bad condition.

[3] First described Evans, Arch. l, 1887, p. 534. Records now in the possession of the Ashmolean Museum establish Bog Mill, Abingdon, as the place of the find (Oxoniensia, xvii–xviii, 1952–3, pp. 261 f.).

[4] P.S.A. xvi, 1897, p. 390; V.C.H. London, i, p. 156, fig. 9.

[5] See p. 8 above, and p. 60 below.

[6] P.S.A. xxviii, 1916, p. 228.

that this class of hilt originated in England, since the fine Abingdon hilt appears from the decoration to be Anglo-Saxon work; it may be noted that some hilts of this type found in Norway have ornament which is not Scandinavian in style but in the Trewhiddle manner, resembling that on Anglo-Saxon metal objects of the second half of the ninth century[1] (p. 69 below).

The second type of pommel, with the lobes within a less acute curve and the guard curved slightly to correspond, is found mainly south and east of the Baltic and may be a Danish fashion, which evolved a little later than the other. A number of examples come from England, notably three inscribed swords from the Thames near the Temple (Fig. 30), the River Witham (Fig. 23), and the Thames at Shifford (Fig. 25 and p. 45 above), the last with five lobes.

Another group of pommels shown by Wheeler forms a link between the lobed ones and those of 'tea-cosy' form mentioned below. In these the centre of the pommel is still divided into three, but there are no true lobes and the pommel is dome-shaped, fitting on to a slightly curved bar. In a sword from the River Lea at Edmonton[2] (Fig. 69) this type of pommel is inlaid with a chequer design in bronze, and a sword from the Kilmainham collection had a similar design carried out in silver[3] (Fig. 79). A less elaborate example is the inscribed sword from the River Nene (Fig. 31 and p. 47 above). This group of pommels belongs to the tenth century.

R. E. Oakeshott (1, p. 51) has shown that two types of pommel, which he names respectively 'brazil-nut' and 'tea-cosy', must have been used at least as early as the first half of the tenth century and been contemporary with the lobed forms. These pommels have no bar and are fastened directly over the tang and usually left without decoration. The tea-cosy shape has some resemblance to the lobed pommels, but is without divisions; a good example from England is the hilt of an inscribed sword taken from the Thames at Battersea (Fig. 26 and p. 45 above), which is interesting on account of a

---

[1] A. W. Clapham, *English Romanesque Architecture before the Conquest*, Oxford, 1930, pp. 129 f.   [2] *P.S.A.* xxvii, 1914–15, p. 217.
[3] Coffey and Armstrong, p. 112; *V.A.* iii, p. 19.

simple pattern of foliage spirals which is probably Frankish work. Pommels of this type are usually found in Western coastal regions and are associated with areas settled by the Danes; some of the earliest are found in the Seine and may have been lost during the fighting for Paris in the ninth century. The brazil-nut form (Fig. 35) is similar to the tea-cosy but seems to have been more popular, probably because it was more comfortable to hold. It first appears in tenth-century Norwegian graves and is distributed through central and eastern Europe. Many examples of both types of pommel are shown in manuscript illustrations and carvings of this period (Fig. 114). By the mid-eleventh century the 'disc' and 'wheel' pommels were coming into favour and replacing other types, together with a new form of 'cocked hat' pommel, rather heavy and massive and easily distinguishable from the earlier ones.

It is not always easy to see how a pommel is secured to the tang. In a description of a hilt with an inscribed guard, Morawe (pp. 292 f.) suggested that the pommel-knob, which was missing, had been fastened to the pommel-bar by two rivets, passing through holes slanting inwards to allow the points of the rivets to go through the bar into the wooden covering of the grip; he thought the oblique position of the rivets would prevent the bar from slipping, and resin or some other cementing substance could be used to make the whole secure. In another article in the same volume of *Mannus*,[1] however, Kossinna rejected the idea of slanting rivets as most unlikely, and in any case an impossible form for fastening the pommel in many types of hilt. When the grip has been covered by metal or bound with gold or silver thread or leather a pommel could not be riveted on to the grip, nor could those which have a metal ring fixed over the grip below the pommel-bar. He shows that occasionally a semicircle of iron was riveted on to the pommel-bar through a hole at each end, and the loop of iron then acted as a support for a hollow pommel-knob placed over it (Fig. 39). Kossinna found seven examples of

---

[1] *Mannus*, xxi, 1929; F. Morawe, 'Hiltipreht', pp. 292 f.; G. Kossinna, 'Die Griffe der Wikingschwerter', pp. 300 f.

this type of hilt, which must have been frequent in the Viking Age.[1]

In the case of two swords from the Anglo-Saxon cemetery at Petersfinger, Wiltshire, with rather fine little bronze pommels (Fig. 36a, b), one of these became detached during the excavation, and no trace of a transverse pin securing it could be found, although one was present on the other hilt. Atkinson (pp. 57 f.) suggested that the pommel had been filled with lead or solder in which the tang-point was embedded, but this seems a precarious method of fastening. On further examination, however, it appeared that the tang had been covered by a wooden grip in three pieces and a bar of wood fastened under the pommel by two iron rivets, so this no doubt made it secure. When the hollow pommels in brazil-nut and tea-cosy shapes were introduced, they were fastened directly on the tang, presumably by heating and then allowing to shrink into position so that they were firmly fixed.

9. THE GRIP

The grip of the sword might be covered in a variety of ways. A well-known hilt from Cumberland (Fig. 63) in the British Museum[2] had grip and guard of horn, and the grip is indented to fit the fingers. This fact, together with the broad boat-shaped pommel, suggests an earlier date than the decoration, in plates of gold filigree work, which is at least as late as the seventh century in style.

The two swords from Petersfinger mentioned above had a wooden covering for the tang, made in three pieces: in the central portion, which served as a grip, the grain of the wood ran parallel to the tang; this fitted on to a transverse bar above, below the bronze pommel, and on to a second bar which served for the guard below. The three sections could have been pegged or mortised together.[3]

The rich gold-adorned swords from various parts of Europe which are thought to date from the mid-fifth to the early sixth

---

[1] Other examples may be seen in Petersen, pp. 92, 175.
[2] *B.M. Guide*, pl. vii.   [3] Atkinson, p. 58.

centuries had their grips enclosed in precious metal. The hilt of King Childeric's sword (Fig. 9a) was of this type,[1] and other fine examples are from Pouan[2] (Fig. 10) and Klein-Hüningen[3] (Fig. 11); they have survived to show grips covered with gold plating. The gold might be confined to one side only, to show in the scabbard, while the back was of silver, as on a sword of this type from Lavoye[4] (Fig. 12). Another characteristic of these grips was that they were divided into three or sometimes four divisions. Metal grips also became fashionable in the sixth century in Scandinavia, and some fine examples may be seen in Behmer.[5]

Some grips are fitted with a metal ring at either end, which would have served to hold the covering in place as well as for ornament. These are seen on Anglo-Saxon swords of the sixth century, as on two hilts from Gilton (Fig. 50) and Faversham (Fig. 49a); and a hilt from Crundale Down (Fig. 64), in the British Museum, has two gold rings ornamented with interlacing. The Sutton Hoo hilt (Plate IIIa) has two slender rings with a delicate raised pattern in gold, and also curved mounts in filigree work on one side of the grip only. Mounts of a similar type but without rings are fitted on a hilt from Nocera Umbra (Fig. 60a), and a second sword from the same cemetery has two deep metal plates in the same position[6] (Fig. 60b). Such mounts seem to have been rare in England, but one parallel to those on the Sutton Hoo hilt is found on the hilt from Cumberland mentioned above.

It is possible that such curved metal mounts may be all that has survived of a metal grip. In grave 1 at Vendel[7] there was a

---

[1] This sword is described in detail by Böhner, 'Das Langschwert des Frankenkönigs Childerich', *B.J.* cxlviii, 1948, pp. 218 f., and Arbman, 'Les Épées du tombeau de Childerich', *Bulletin de la Société Royale des Lettres de Lund*, 1947–8, pp. 7 f. These give full references to previous work.

[2] Salin and France-Lanord, 'Sur le trésor barbare de Pouan', *Gallia*, xiv, 1956, pp. 65 f.

[3] Laur-Belart, 'Eine alamannische Goldgriffspatha aus Klein-Hüningen bei Basel', *IPEK*, xii, 1938, pp. 126 f.

[4] G. Chenet, 'La Tombe 319 et la buire chrétienne du cimetière mérovingien de Lavoye (Meuse)', *Préhistoire*, iv, pp. 34 f.

[5] Behmer, pls. xxix, xlvi, &c.

[6] Ibid., pl. xli, 6 and 7. These are in Rome.

[7] Stolpe and Arne, p. 11; Behmer, pl. xlvii.

sword with a richly ornamented grip, with three raised ridges, clearly derived from the rich gold-ornamented hilts of the Continent in the fifth century (Fig. 59). There are deep mounts of metal at either end, elaborately ornamented with animal forms with garnet eyes, while there is silver and niello work on the pommel bar and guard. Another metal grip survives from Gotland.[1] Unfortunately few rich Anglo-Saxon hilts of the early Viking Age survive to tell us how the grip was covered. The upper half of a metal covering can be seen on a hilt from Fetter Lane (Plate III*b*) in the British Museum (p. 68 below). This has a raised ring which must have come about half-way down the grip, and the hilt from the River Witham at Sheffield (Fig. 66) has a silver decorated ring which must also have been fastened over the middle of the grip, as there are already rings at either end. Probably this hilt and other rich hilts like the one from Abingdon decorated in the Trewhiddle style had a metal covering when complete.

Surviving hilts from the Viking Age show that there were other metal-covered grips with no break in the pattern. An elaborate example survives at Dublin,[2] a grip of bronze (Fig. 78) inlaid with chevrons of white metal terminating in small circles, marked in the centre with a silver ring set in niello or some similar material. At either end of the grip are round knobs in the form of cast animals' heads with protruding snouts. Another hilt with a metal grip from Søndersø, Denmark, is in the National Museum, Copenhagen;[3] this has an effective diamond pattern on grip, guard, and pommel (Fig. 83). It may be compared with a hilt from Ophus, Norway,[4] with a design of crosses in bronze on a silver ground (Fig. 80). A different method of covering a narrow grip was to use silver wire, finished at either end with a plaited wire ring, as on the so-called Earl of Pembroke's sword (p. 54 above). Another Viking hilt of eleventh-century date from Sydow, shown by Kossinna,[5] illus-

---

[1] Behmer, pl. xlix.

[2] Coffey and Armstrong, p. 112, no. 2361; *V.A.* iii, p. 22, and fig. 6. Bøe points out that the number given by Coffey and Armstrong is incorrect.

[3] O. Klindt-Jensen, *The Vikings in England*, Copenhagen, 1948, p. 11.

[4] Kossinna, p. 300; Petersen, p. 72, fig. 59.

[5] Kossinna, p. 302.

trates a more elaborate use of metal thread, for here it is used to make a step pattern up the grip (Fig. 81); he gives another instance from Hungary of a grip built up in a pattern of circles with gold and silver thread.

A number of Viking hilts retain the ring at either end of the grip. Petersen (p. 124) shows a hilt with rings of iron; rings of plaited wire have been mentioned above, and on the short sword from Lough Gur (Fig. 27) there are plain gold rings. Sometimes, on a metal-covered grip, the ring takes the form of a circle of tiny heads, whether human or animal is hard to say. A good example of this is the ring which has now been restored to the elaborate hilt from Kilmainham[1] (Plate IVb). Kossinna shows other rings of this kind on the hilt from Ophus, mentioned above, on another from Hungary, and on a third from Norway, on which the heads have become a ring of points, like a little crown. The animals' heads on the grip from Dublin mentioned above may be an early form of this ring.

The grips of Anglo-Saxon and Viking swords often seem surprisingly small. One sword found at Reading (now lost) is said to have had a grip too small for a grown man's hand,[2] and it may be noted that other swords in this museum, including the one from Shifford, have small grips. On the Lough Gur sword the grip is only 2·2 inches long. It was noted by Hillier (p. 35) that of the swords found at Chessel Down hardly one of the ten was large enough for an average man's hand. Some of these swords may have been made for boys or slenderly built men, but another possible explanation was given by R. E. Oakeshott,[3] who suggested that grip and pommel might be grasped together, and confirmed this by illustrations from early manuscripts (Fig. 114); the brazil-nut pommel in particular fitted easily into the hand in this way. Another possibility for swords without true guards was suggested by Werner. He noted that swords from the Steppe region, fitted

---

[1] Not shown in Coffey and Armstrong's drawing (pl. iv, 3). It was among uncatalogued finds from Island-bridge, and shown in place close to the upper cross-bar, in a drawing made in 1846 (V.A. iii, p. 22).

[2] P.S.A. iii, 1867, p. 461; V.C.H. Berks. i, p. 243.

[3] Oakeshott 1, p. 55.

with small guards, were held in the hand so that the index finger passed over the guard and the others went round the grip; there is again confirmation for this in illustrations.[1] It is possible also that if the hilt had to be renewed and the tang was worn, the pommel might be fixed farther down, and the grip shortened for the sake of retaining a good weapon.

10. THE GUARD

Swords from the early Anglo-Saxon period are usually found without guards, presumably because these were of perishable material and were not intended to give much protection to the hand. The guard of the Cumberland hilt survived because it was made of horn, like another example in the British Museum from Lakenheath Fen. The richly decorated fifth-century swords with gold hilts have very narrow guards, scarcely wider than the blade, but these are elaborately ornamented with gold and precious stones. It is possible, as Arbman suggested was the case with the hilt of Childeric's sword (2, p. 103), that the jewelled guard was set between two thin layers of bone or ivory. Wider guards were certainly in use fairly early. An elaborate hilt in Oslo Museum from Snartemo (Fig. 14), dated as early as A.D. 500,[2] has a guard composed of two layers of metal with decoration to match the double layer below the pommel cap, and there is another sword with a well-defined guard from the same cemetery. Two hilts from Nocera Umbra[3] have a double pommel-bar and a double guard secured by rivets in the same way (Fig. 60), and the double guard is also found on hilts from Vendel I, of mid-seventh-century date,[4] where the spaces between the bars are filled with decorative work in silver and niello (Fig. 59), and again on the Sutton Hoo sword (Plate IIIa), where part of the guard—in gold—has survived, but the filling is lost. Swords with clearly marked guards may be seen on the top panel of the Franks Casket[5] (Fig. 107), but these appear to be single cross-bars only.

[1] J. Werner 2, pp. 38 f.   [2] Behmer, pl. xxix, and Cramp, pl. xi, B.
[3] Behmer, pl. xli, and pp. 166 f.
[4] Behmer, pls. xlvi, xlvii; cf. Stolpe and Arne, pp. 11 f.
[5] B.M. Guide, pl. viii (centre); Baldwin Brown, vi (1), pl. viii.

Where the guard survives on swords of the early Anglo-Saxon period it is straight. Later two distinct types of hilt developed (p. 55 above), one with a straight bar beneath the pommel and a straight crossbar (as seen on the Franks Casket)[1] and the other with a curved pommel-bar with the ends turned upwards and a curved guard with the ends turned downwards. Both these types of hilt were used by the Vikings of the tenth and eleventh centuries, but they were probably of different origins.[2] Hilts with brazil-nut and tea-cosy pommels usually have straight guards, but this is not invariable, since the Battersea sword has a tea-cosy pommel and a curved guard with inlay decoration (Fig. 26). Wheeler (2, p. 35) puts the swords with curved guards within the period 875–950, and gives a map of their distribution, while the gently curved guards are a little later in date and were popular in Danish territory. It is possible that the curved hilt originated in Anglo-Saxon England, for the Abingdon hilt (Fig. 67) is a very fine example of the curved guard which appears to be of Anglo-Saxon workmanship, and this type of sword is frequently shown in Anglo-Saxon illuminated manuscripts of the eleventh century. An extreme form of a guard with a drooping curve is seen in London Museum (Fig. 73), where there is an isolated guard of bronze, ornamented in a pattern in the Ringerike style of ornamentation, which is thought to have come from Sweden or been influenced by East Scandinavian traditions.[3] A similar curve is seen on the carving of a sword in Ebberston Church near Scarborough[4] (Fig. 115); Grove dates this as late eleventh or early twelfth century, and it may be even later. Hoffmeyer (pp. 35 f.) has pointed out the close resemblance between the hilt of this sword and that of the Norwegian sword with a runic inscription from Korsøygarden (Fig. 89), but the dating of the latter also presents difficulties and it too may be late (p. 80 below).

Straight guards are rare in England in the late Viking Age.

[1] For example, a sword in the London Museum, found in the Thames near Waterloo Bridge; Laking, i, p. 18, fig. 23; Wheeler 2, p. 36, fig. 16, 4.

[2] Reginald Smith, 'East Anglian and Fetter Lane Pommels', *P.S.A.* xxiii, 1910, pp. 307 f.

[3] Wheeler 1, p. 182.   [4] Grove, p. 256.

Wheeler[1] shows a drawing of one from the River Lea at Enfield (Fig. 75), said now to be in Rome, which may have been the sword found in a ship-burial discovered in 1900 and never properly recorded. The guard of this sword appears to be identical with the sword found in the Palace at Westminster[2] (Fig. 76). Another sword with a straight guard came from the River Lea at Edmonton (Fig. 69 and p. 56 above), and there are several examples in Dublin.[3]

II. THE DECORATION OF THE HILT

The decoration of hilts might be described at great length, for much elaborate and varied work has survived; but there would be little profit in repeating the material collected by Behmer, Petersen, Montelius, and Lorange, and only a brief account will be given here, emphasizing points of interest relating to descriptions of swords given in the literature.

The series of impressive gold-ornamented hilts from various parts of Europe dating from the mid-fifth to the early sixth century has been mentioned earlier (p. 58 above). Among them is the splendid hilt of King Childeric's sword (Fig. 9a), recovered from his tomb in 1653 and unfortunately treated with so little consideration afterwards. This sword is of outstanding importance, since we know it to have been a king's weapon, and we know also the date at which it was placed in the tomb on the death of the king in 481. It was accompanied by a gold-hilted scramasax, and both weapons were in jewelled scabbards; it has been suggested that they were weapons made for the king's coronation.[4] Another fine sword and scramasax came from a rich grave at Pouan[5] (Fig. 10), and a third pair of weapons from Lavoye[6] (Fig. 12). Böhner and Laur-Belart show a number of gold-hilted swords decorated with jewels belonging to this group, and these, found in many cases in gold

[1] Wheeler 1, p. 184; 2, p. 34; Laking, i, p. 16, fig. 20.
[2] A resemblance pointed out to me by R. E. Oakeshott.
[3] Coffey and Armstrong, pp. 112 f.
[4] H. Rupp, 'Der Herkunft der Zelleneinlage . . .', *Rheinische Forschungen zur Vorgeschichte*, ii, Bonn, 1937, p. 57.
[5] Salin and France-Lanord, pp. 65 f.
[6] Chenet, pp. 34 f.

scabbards which match the hilts in magnificence, must have been the treasures of kings and leaders. They form a clearly defined group, recognizable by their plated grips, divided by ridges, and by the cloisonné work on pommel, guard, and mouthpiece of scabbard. This effective style of decoration is often in the form of square cells set with garnets, and divided from one another by thin zigzag or by wavy lines of gold, as on the guard of Childeric's hilt. Alternatively these cells may be set round a flower-shaped cell, as on the mount of his scramasax, or they may be heart-shaped, as on the wonderful guard of a sword from Altlussheim (Fig. 13), the complete hilt of which has unfortunately not survived.[1] In the earliest group, to which Childeric's sword belongs, there is usually one dominant colour for the fillings, with a central cell in a contrasting colour.

This bright and effective type of decoration was very widespread in Europe in the fifth century. It was practised in the region round the Black Sea, and also in Hungary, Italy, Spain, and North Africa. Consequently there has been much argument as to how it reached the Franks, and this is summarized by Böhner and Arbman in their detailed papers on Childeric's sword.[2] Many scholars have urged that these jewelled swords came into Childeric's kingdom from eastern Europe, from either Gothic or Alamannic territory. Böhner and Arbman, however, both believe that Childeric's sword was made at home, and that it marks the adoption of new fashions in sword ornament at his court. They are not in agreement, however, as to the source of this new influence. Böhner thinks that craftsmen from the Black Sea region may have come into France, and that another line of influence may have been from Visigothic jewellers in Spain; Arbman, however, emphasizes the importance of Roman influence on the Franks, and thinks that craftsmen skilled in cloisonné are just as likely to have come over the Alps from northern Italy. The sword from Lavoye may be one of the earliest of this type, for its decoration is relatively simple. Childeric's sword and the one from Pouan are two of the finest examples, and it is possible that the Pouan sword also was a king's

[1] Garscha, p. 192.   [2] Böhner, pp. 218 f.; Arbman, pp. 124 f.

weapon, the sword of Theodoric the Visigoth who was killed in 451; it is thought to be Gothic in origin and slightly earlier in date than Childeric's sword.[1] The hilt from Altlussheim is more Eastern in type, resembling a number of rich hilts from eastern Europe. A group of less elaborate hilts in the same tradition (Böhner's type III) come mostly from Alamannic territory, and are probably later in date, imitated by Alamannic craftsmen from Frankish models.

The second half of the sixth century is the period in which swords with rings or ring-knobs on the hilt were in use in Kent and in parts of the Continent. The question of the rings and their significance will be discussed later (p. 75 below), and it may merely be noted here that the decoration on early hilts of this type was mostly in the form of linear designs on bronze or silvered hilts. Fine examples are a ring-hilt from Gilton (Fig. 50) and two from Bifrons[2] (Figs. 51, 52). The designs are simple but delicately and skilfully executed, and close examination of the loose rings on these and other Kentish hilts reveals them to be elaborately shaped and decorated, with encircling bands of ornament, like valuable finger-rings. A pommel fitted with a ring-knob from Sarre was silvered[3] (Fig. 53) and an elaborate bronze pommel from Orsoy, also fitted with a ring-knob, was gilded with niello ornament[4] (Fig. 58). Another pommel from Sarre was silvered, with a single red garnet set in a round cell on one side, the rest of the space being occupied by a linear design which suggests an imitation of cellwork[5] (Fig. 44). A similar design can be seen on a pommel with a ring (Fig. 49) from Faversham.

One interesting feature of the pommels of this period from Kentish graves is that in some cases there seems to be special significance in the designs chosen. A ringed pommel from grave 39

[1] Salin and France-Lanord, p. 75.
[2] *Arch.* xxx, 1844, p. 132, and *A.C.* x, 1876, p. 312. For detailed descriptions of these and other ringed hilts, see H. R. Davidson, 'The Ring on the Sword', *Journal of the Arms and Armour Society*, ii, 1958, pp. 211 f.
[3] Described in the account of the excavation (*A.C.* vi, 1866, p. 172) as 'purple vitreous enamel inlaid with silver'. This, however, appears to be misleading.
[4] From a late sixth-century Frankish grave (Böhner 2, p. 167).
[5] Jessup, p. 140.

at Bifrons has a swastika on one side (Fig. 51), and on the other, zigzag and wavy lines; these lines are repeated on both sides of a second ringed pommel from the same cemetery[1] (Fig. 52). Plaques from the sword-belt survived in grave 39, and on these both the swastika and zigzag lines are repeated (Fig. 55). We know that the swastika had either religious or magical significance for the Anglo-Saxons, and it may have been connected with the worship of the god Thunor (though definite proof of its significance is hard to find).[2] The zigzag lines may also have some special meaning: they suggest a lightning symbol, and there are other devices on pommels of this period which seem to be symbolic rather than purely ornamental. One of these is on a pommel from Grove Ferry, Wickham (Fig. 43); it is inlaid with silver wires in a pattern which Payne once suggested might be a runic monogram.[3] Another is a device on a pommel from Lower Shorne (in Maidstone Museum), which resembles a standard topped with horns (Fig. 45). The pommel marked with runes from Gilton (Plate II*a* and p. 78 below) may also be borne in mind in this connexion. Such designs or symbols placed on the pommel might be marks of ownership or protective signs to bring luck in battle; they certainly give the impression that they are more than mere ornament, and in the case of the runes there is no doubt of this.

Anglo-Saxon sword-hilts of the sixth and seventh centuries continue a traditional style of decoration which relies on delicacy of workmanship to gain its effects. The horn hilt from Cumberland (Fig. 63 and p. 58 above) has small plates of spiral decoration in gold filigree work[4] and a little cellwork with garnet filling; there is no attempt to cover the whole surface. A curved plate runs round the grip on one side only (as on the Sutton Hoo hilt), perhaps in order to ensure that the sword was replaced the correct way in the scabbard. A fine example of delicate gold work is the hilt from

---

[1] *A.C.* xiii, 1880, p. 553, grave 62.   [2] J. de Vries, ii, p. 127.

[3] *P.S.A.* xv, 1895, p. 178. The pommel has recently been described as Frankish work: *A.J.* xxxviii, 1958, p. 244, fig. 3, and pl. xxvi, *g, h.*

[4] For an interesting parallel from the Viking Age, see a guard found near Wicklow which has a plate of spiral decoration set in the centre (*V.A.* iii, p. 83, fig. 55). Now in the National Museum, Dublin.

Crundale Down (Fig. 64), also in the British Museum, and probably late seventh century in date.[1] This is boldly and skilfully decorated in an interlacing pattern in Salin's style II, while the grip is encircled by two slender gold rings with a raised pattern of interlacing.

From the seventh century onwards sword-hilts in northern Europe become increasingly elaborate, with much decoration in gold and silver and jewelled settings. The Sutton Hoo hilt (Plate III*a*) is an exquisite example of gold and cloisonné work, retaining the delicacy of the Cumberland and Crundale Down examples, while it is as splendid in its jewelled ornament as the earlier Frankish hilts. The garnets are curved to fit the cells into which they are set, and fitted to the convex and concave surfaces with great skill. The pommel of this sword has much in common with Swedish pommels decorated with gold and cloisonné, although certain resemblances in workmanship to other pieces of Sutton Hoo jewellery suggest that it was fitted and perhaps made in England.[2] But few really elaborate hilts of this period have survived; one is a hilt from Coombe, Kent (Fig. 65), now in Saffron Walden Museum in a poor state of preservation. This hilt can hardly be earlier than the late seventh century,[3] so that the report that it was found with burnt bones and objects of the Roman period appears to be misleading. Examples from Norway and Sweden given by Behmer[4] show that Scandinavian hilts at this period were becoming increasingly large and elaborate with much gold decoration, many of them set with large hollow ring-knobs on one side of the pommel.

During the Viking Age there was less use of gold and cellwork on sword-hilts, and silver, bronze, and niello work became more popular. The unusual hilt from Fetter Lane (Plate III*b* and p. 60 above) has been dated about A.D. 800, although its pommel is in a

---

[1] *B.M. Guide*, p. 11.   [2] Bruce-Mitford, pp. 53, 67 f.
[3] Baldwin Brown, iii, p. 222. This hilt may have had a ring fixed on the pommel: Jessup, p. 140; Montelius, p. 18.
[4] Behmer, pls. xlvii, xlviii; cf. the hilt from Valsgärde 8, with wooden grip decorated with bronze, an earlier example of a ringed hilt, of the seventh century, Arwidsson 2, pp. 61 f., Abb. 82.

form resembling those of an earlier period, being fastened on to a bar with two rounded rivets. The effective ornamentation in animal and foliage designs is characteristic of what we know of Anglo-Saxon decoration on metalwork in the late eighth and ninth centuries. Another famous hilt from this period is the Abingdon hilt in the Ashmolean Museum (Fig. 67 and p. 55 above). It is decorated with silver mounts inlaid with niello work in a style reminiscent of late ninth-century ornament in Anglo-Saxon manuscripts. Designs based on animal ornament and the acanthus leaf are arranged in panels over the curved guard and pommel-bar and the high pommel. This is the style to which Kendrick[1] has given the name of 'West Saxon baroque', and which is found on metalwork from the Trewhiddle Hoard. In the first published account of the sword[2] it was suggested that the four creatures depicted on the pommel-bar represent the symbols of the Four Evangelists, and Leeds[3] has strongly supported this idea. It is true that one of the figures is that of a man (rare at this period, but found on the Fuller Brooch and the Alfred Jewel) while another figure bears some resemblance to an eagle, but the so-called 'calf' and 'lion' (the last a serpent-like creature) do not seem to justify this interpretation. It is more likely that such vague animal forms are the direct descendants of fantastic creatures of heraldic type found in Anglo-Saxon carvings and manuscripts of a slightly earlier period.

The Trewhiddle style was evidently a popular one for hilts. The fine sword in Sheffield Museum, found in the River Witham at Lincoln (Fig. 66 and p. 60 above), has a hilt richly decorated with silver bands inlaid with niello and animal figures in panels, recalling those on the Abingdon hilt, but unlikely to have any symbolic meaning. Another incomplete pommel decorated in this style, from Ingleton, Yorkshire (Fig. 46), is in the British Museum,[4] and here the band of decoration round the curved base has survived, and is in gold and niello work. Three other hilts in this

[1] T. D. Kendrick, *Anglo-Saxon Art*, London, 1938, p. 184.
[2] *Arch.* l, 1887, p. 534.
[3] E. T. Leeds, 'The Wallingford Sword', *Antiquary*, xlvi, pp. 348 f.
[4] *British Museum Quarterly*, xv, 1941–50, p. 74; I am indebted to Mr. Bruce-Mitford for bringing this pommel to my notice.

style with nielloed silver mounts are from Høven, Dolven, and Grønneberg in Norway (Figs. 41, 42),[1] the last two very similar to the Witham hilt, while the Hoven example, as Bruce-Mitford has pointed out,[2] has contorted birds and animals in curved frames, offering a most interesting parallel to those on the Fuller Brooch. There seems no doubt that these three pommels were all made in Anglo-Saxon England. A bar from a hilt in this style is in the Tullie House Museum, Carlisle[3] (Fig. 47), while a lost sword from Reading with a decorated pommel and guard said to show 'figures of men and animals imperfectly executed'[4] was somewhat similar in type. In a quite different style is a silver pommel from the hilt of either a sword or knife found at Windsor (Fig. 48), now in the Ashmolean Museum. This has a gold panel of interlacing, executed with great artistry, let into one face, and is a fine example of Anglo-Saxon metalwork.

An idea of the variety of decoration used on the finest swords of the later Viking period is given by the collection of hilts in the museum at Dublin, found at the extensive Viking cemetery at Kilmainham. One of these, from which the pommel is missing, was in bronze inlaid with chevrons of white metal in an elaborate pattern (Fig. 78 and p. 60 above); another, with a pointed pommel, was ornamented on this and the pommel-bar and guard by narrow silver strips beaten into the iron (Fig. 77); a third had pommel and guard inlaid in a chequer pattern in silver (Fig. 79), while a fourth, with an unusually heavy hilt, was decorated with gold and small circles in silver[5] (Plate IVb). The sword which survived burning in the Hesket cremation (Fig. 72 and p. 11 above) was covered with a thin silver plating decorated in an elaborate interlacing pattern recalling those on the Manx crosses.[6] A hilt from Wensley churchyard (Fig. 71) was decorated with niello work on silver.[7] There are other hilts with panels of gold-coloured copper alloy, hammered

[1] Brogger, pp. 15 f. Cf. Arbman 2, p. 130 (taf. 42, 1), for a pommel in the Nat. Mus., Copenhagen.

[2] R. L. S. Bruce-Mitford, 'Late Saxon Disc-Brooches', *Dark Age Britain* (ed. Harden), London, 1956, pp. 181 f.

[3] Cowen, p. 180.   [4] *P.S.A.* iii, 1867, p. 461.

[5] *V.A.* iii, p. 22, fig. 6; p. 16, fig. 2; p. 20, fig. 4; p. 22, fig. 5.

[6] Cowen, p. 175.   [7] *P.S.A.* xxviii, 1915–16, p. 228.

into channels chiselled in the iron: for instance, the hilts from the Thames near Shifford (Fig. 25 and p. 56 above) and at West-minster (Fig. 68 and p. 55 above), another from the River Witham (Fig. 23 and p. 56 above), and another from Wareham in Dorset[1] (Fig. 74).

The swords which survive in our museums must be a very small remnant of those made in Anglo-Saxon and Viking times, so that it is clear that there were many skilled and gifted craftsmen at work on the sword-hilts of kings and leaders. The gold hilts of the Migration period, the Kentish ring-hilts, the hilt from Sutton Hoo and the rich Swedish ones which it resembles, the elaborately decorated Vendel hilts, those in gold, silver, and niello from the Viking Age with their bold, bright decoration—these are sufficient to establish the high standard of workmanship and originality to which these unknown craftsmen attained, and to show that the standard remained very high throughout the whole period. Increase in knowledge and improved technique in conservation help us to appreciate the quality of craftsmanship more than formerly, and we have come now to realize the importance of what might be called local traditions in metalwork of this kind. The blades of these swords vary comparatively little, and may have come from a few centres only. But we now have several groups of hilts, each showing definite and individual characteristics. Those decorated in the Trewhiddle style, for instance, are found in England and Norway, but are typically Anglo-Saxon in choice of motif and ornamental treatment, and probably came from one workshop. Similar claims may be made for other groups of hilts, associated with various regions in north-western Europe. In time we may be able to speak with some assurance about the district and the workshop where each particular group was produced, and even to recognize the royal courts to which these workshops belonged.

12. THE RING ON THE HILT

Apart from the decoration of the hilt there are certain occasional features which appear to have special significance. One of the most

[1] *A.J.* viii, 1928, p. 361.

interesting is the ring which is found attached to certain hilts from Anglo-Saxon graves in Kentish cemeteries. Two hilts from Faversham (Fig. 49a, b),[1] two others from Bifrons (Figs. 51, 52),[2] and one from Gilton (Fig. 50)[3] have each a fixed ring fastened to one side of the pommel-bar and a loose ring linked with this. A sixth example, also from Kent, has not yet been published.[4] These loose rings vary in size, and are all elaborately made, with bands of ornament which usually matches decoration elsewhere on the hilt. No example of a loose ring fastened to the pommel in this way has been yet found outside Kent, although an elaborate hilt from Snartemo (Fig. 14), probably early sixth century in date, has a loose ring hanging from the guard.[5]

Leeds suggested that there might have been a ring on the pommel of a sword (Fig. 36a) from grave XXI of the Petersfinger cemetery;[6] this is an interesting pommel of bronze decorated with silver and gilt, the rivet on one side covered by a beak-like projection which reminded Leeds of allusions to eagles and ravens feasting on the slain in Anglo-Saxon heroic poetry.[7] It recalls also the pommel of Childeric's sword (Fig. 9a and p. 53 above). The small notch on the other side might possibly have had a ring on it, and the date, estimated as mid-sixth century, corresponds to that of the Kentish ring-hilts. Another possible example of a ringed hilt is that from Combe, Kent (Fig. 65), in Saffron Walden Museum.[8]

In grave 88 of the Anglo-Saxon cemetery at Sarre, which contained many swords, there was a pommel of silvered bronze, now in Maidstone Museum (Fig. 53 and p. 66 above). This has

[1] In the British Museum. The first is shown by C. Roach Smith, *Coll. Antiq.* vi, 1868, p. 139, and Behmer, pl. xxxvii, 6a; the second by Baldwin Brown, iii, pl. xxvii, 4, and Behmer, pl. xxxviii, 2.

[2] In Maidstone Museum. One is shown by Faussett, *A.C.* x, 1876, p. 312; the other is the 'sword with the bronze hilt' mentioned *A.C.* xiii, 1880, p. 553 (grave 62), and shown by Behmer, pl. xxxviii, 1.

[3] *Arch.* xxx, 1844, p. 132.

[4] I have permission from Miss Vera Evison to mention this; it was found in the Anglo-Saxon cemetery at Dover.

[5] Behmer, p. 117 and pl. xxix; Cramp, p. 65 and pl. xi, b.

[6] Leeds and Shortt, p. 53.

[7] Cf. the Old Norse sword-names *Trani*, 'Crane', *Qrn*, 'Eagle', given in the list in the *Thulur*.

[8] See Montelius, p. 18, and Jessup, p. 140.

a metal fitting on one side which clearly represents one ring held inside another, the upper 'ring' ornamented like the loose rings on the other hilts. Such fittings may be called 'ring-knobs', and they are found also in sixth-century Frankish graves. One from Kastel,[1] Mainz (Fig. 56b) has a fitting composed of one complete ring and a second incomplete ring rising from it and joined on to the pommel, and a second fitting of this type is in the museum at St-Germain and was found at Chaouilly[2] (Fig. 56a). There is another from Orsoy (Fig. 58), with ring and mount in heavy gilded bronze.[3] The Sarre pommel differs from these in that the two 'rings' are made in one piece.

These hilts are all dated to the second half of the sixth century. Throughout the seventh century the ring-knob was very popular in Sweden. An early example is the hilt from Valsgärde 8 (Fig. 62), with a knob made in two pieces, in gilded bronze, on a bronze pommel fitted to a wooden hilt.[4] A fine hilt from Vendel I (Fig. 59) had a ring-knob, the top part of which is now missing,[5] and one from Väsby (Fig. 61), with cloisonné work and garnets, had a ring-knob of gold.[6] Swedish knobs are usually larger than the one from Sarre, with plain rings, swollen in shape, sometimes separated from the ring-mount by a line of gold or silver beading. Other examples are the two fine hilts (Fig. 60a and b) from Nocera Umbra, Italy,[7] a hilt with a silver knob from the Alamannic cemetery at Schretzheim[8] (Fig. 57), two hilts from Norway,[9] and several from Frankish cemeteries.[10] Montelius shows some gold ring-knobs which have been found detached from hilts, and a ring-knob (Fig. 54a) was found in the grave at Sutton Hoo which at first was thought to have belonged to a sword, but which was afterwards seen to have a fitting of a different type; it is similar to one fixed to a drinking-horn in the Swedish boat-grave Valsgärde 7

[1] Lindenschmidt, v, p. 165. [2] Behmer, pl. xxxix, 1. See Evison (1967), p. 91, n. 1.
[3] Böhner 2, p. 164. [4] Arwidsson 2, pp. 61 f., Abb. 82, p. 128.
[5] Stolpe and Arne, p. 11 and pl. 1; Behmer, pl. xlvii.
[6] Bruce-Mitford, pls. xii, xiii. [7] Behmer, pl. xli, 6, 7.
[8] P. Zenetti, pp. 275 f. [9] Montelius, pp. 18, 30.
[10] J. Werner, 'Die Schwerter von Imola, Herbrechtingen und Endrebacke', A.A. xxi, 1950, p. 57.

(Fig. 54*b*), and may have come either from a horn or possibly from the shield.[1] Pictures of warriors with swords fitted with ring-knobs may be seen on helmet plates from grave XIV at Vendel and from Öland (Fig. 106).[2]

The relationships of the various types of ringed hilt have been much discussed,[3] but the problem of the origin and purpose of the ring has not been wholly solved. Behmer and Arwidsson believe that the ringed hilt originated in Europe, the earliest type being represented by the hilts from Haroué and Mainz Kastel; while Arwidsson suggests that the forerunners of metal ring-knobs may be seen in the beads and balls of amber, glass, and other materials which are found with Alamannic and Frankish swords from the fifth century onwards (see p. 83 below). These attachments may well have had some special significance, but since there is no attempt to make them resemble rings, the connexion seems a doubtful one. The meerschaum balls in particular are very different from the fine and delicate rings on the Kentish hilts. Böhner argues for a Scandinavian origin, on account of the extreme popularity of the ring-knob in Sweden, and the fact that its development can be traced there without a break. But since the Kentish ring-hilts are as early as the earliest Frankish examples, and earlier than any known examples from Scandinavia, there seems some reason for supporting Baldwin Brown's suggestion[4] that the type originated in Kent. We now know of six early examples from Kent, as well as one ring-knob. Out of these, one of the Faversham hilts (Fig. 49*a*) has a mount of a different type from the rest, for it is simpler, and gives the impression that it has been fixed on to a completed pommel and not made as part of the hilt like the other rings on the Kentish swords. Behmer thinks that this hilt may be as early as the mid-sixth century, which would make it earlier than any Frankish ring-hilt. It seems reasonable to suppose, moreover, that the loose ring, moving freely on

---

[1] Bruce-Mitford, p. 58.
[2] Stolpe and Arne, pl. xli, and Montelius, p. 151.
[3] By Montelius (pp. 1 f.), Behmer (pp. 135 f.), and more recently by Böhner (2, pp. 167 f.) and Arwidsson (2, pp. 64 f.).
[4] Baldwin Brown, iii, p. 221.

the hilt, would be an earlier stage in the development of the ring-sword than the fixed ring of the earliest Frankish examples; the moving ring might well prove inconvenient when a sword was used in battle. The fixed ring, whose development can be traced continuously from the hilts of the Mainz Kastel type to the great hollow ring-knobs of the late seventh century, seems more likely to be a second stage of development.

Two suggestions for a utilitarian purpose for the ring on the hilt are, first, that it was intended for the attachment of a cord or thong,[1] and secondly that it was used for the attachment of a charm or amulet.[2] We know from literary evidence that a thong was often attached to a hilt (p. 184 below), but if this were the purpose of the ring it seems strange that there are so few surviving examples of an open ring, since the ring-knob, especially in its later form, would not be a convenient substitute. The ring on the guard of the Snartemo sword may well have been meant to fasten it securely into the scabbard,[3] and is much better placed for such a purpose. A charm fastened to the ring is also unlikely, since it would disturb the balance of the sword, and again the later forms of the ring-knob would be unsuitable for any such intention. Nor could the knob have been meant to act as a counterweight to the blade, since it was usually hollow and always on one side only. The general conclusion, then, which has been reached by archaeologists is that the ring had some symbolic or ritual significance.

Allusions to ringed swords in the literature are few and rather vague, but they confirm the suggestion that such swords were of special value (p. 180 below). Böhner, following an earlier theory of Lindenschmidt (v, p. 165), thinks that the ring might have been set on the hilt to commemorate the gift of a sword from one warrior to another, making them, as it were, 'sword-brothers', with the double ring to symbolize their alliance. This is an attractive idea, but one for which no trace of confirmation can be found in the literature. We know, however, that the gift of a sword from

---

[1] Behmer, pp. 135 f., and Böhner, pp. 167 f., discuss this and other theories.
[2] This was Akerman's suggestion (p. 50), based on knowledge of a Kentish sword with a loose ring only.
[3] As suggested by Cramp, p. 65.

the king or leader to a warrior entering his service was considered to form a bond of mutual obligation and loyalty between them. Moreover, as some of Böhner's quotations show very clearly, the ring has always been a symbol of a pledge between two parties, and frequently used for the swearing of a binding oath. Of particular interest is the custom in medieval Germany of letting a bride and bridegroom set their hands upon the hilt of a sword when they took an oath of fidelity to one another, and again the custom of presenting the wedding-ring to the bride upon the hilt of a sword; for both these there is literary evidence of fairly early date.[1] The fact that a ring might be set upon a drinking-horn is not inconsistent with such a usage, since we know from Old Norse literature that the oath made in the hall when receiving the horn at a feast was judged to be binding on the man who uttered it.[2]

Taking all this into consideration, it is possible to go further than Böhner does, and to emphasize the fact that the hilt of the sword had special significance as a symbol of kingly power. It is stated in early Norwegian law[3] that the hilt of the king's sword had to be presented to the man who entered his service, and that as the follower swore the oath of allegiance to his new lord he had to touch the hilt of the royal sword as it lay across the king's knee:

At the time when the king appoints hirðmen, no table shall stand before the king. The king shall have his sword on his knee, the sword which he had for his crowning, and he shall turn it so that the chape goes under his right arm, and the hilt is placed forward on his right knee. Then he shall move the buckle of the belt over the hilt, and grasp the hilt, so that his right arm is over everything. Then he who is to become

---

[1] In the eleventh-century Latin poem Ruodlieb (ed. Serler, lines 63 f.) and a prose story of Catherine de Gebeswiler, not later than the fourteenth century. They are discussed by Meyer, 'Die Eheschliessung im Ruodlieb und das Eheschwert', Zeitschrift der Savigny Stiftung f. Rechtsgeschichte (Germ. Abt.), lii, 1932, pp. 276 f., a reference which I owe to Professor Hatto.

[2] For the bragarfull or 'promise cup', see Grönbech, ii, p. 153. There is an example in Óláfs Saga Tryggvasonar, xxxv (Heimskringla), where a cup is drunk in memory of the dead king by his heir, King Svein, and he utters a vow to invade England. Cf. Beowulf's speech on receiving the cup, Beow. 628–38.

[3] Hirðskraa, Norges Gamle Love, Keyser and Munch, 1848, ii, p. 422. A man received as a gestr (member of the royal bodyguard of lower rank than a hirðman) is also directed to touch the sword, putting his right hand under the grip while he kisses the hand of the king (ibid. ii. 43, p. 439).

a *hirðman* shall fall on both knees before the king on the floor . . . and
shall put his right hand under the hilt, while he keeps his left arm down
in front of him in the most comfortable position, and then he shall kiss
the king's hand.

This account has come down to us in its thirteenth-century
form, but there seems good reason to believe that it reveals a custom which went back to Viking times and possibly earlier still.[1]
The name of 'ring-giver' for a king, familiar in heroic poetry,
might help to account for such a custom; it is normally taken to
mean the king as treasure-giver, dealing out rings to his followers,
and the fact that he was so regarded would make the ring a particularly apt symbol to hold out to his liegemen when they approached
his sword. Regarded both as a pledge on which an oath could be
sworn and as a token of the link of generosity between the lord
and his followers, the ring was a rich symbol, and the popularity
of the ringed hilt in north-western Europe becomes understandable when we consider it in this light.

Such an explanation of the ringed hilt implies that the swords
on which the ring was placed were owned by kings and leaders,
the men who gave out swords to their followers, and in return
could call upon them to follow to the death, if need be. In view of
the richness of the swords bearing the rings, and the large number
of petty kings and princes among the Teutonic peoples of the
sixth and seventh centuries, this does not seem an unreasonable
assumption; indeed both Zenetti and Garscha[2] have already suggested that the ringed hilt was a symbol of leadership, though not
for the reason given here.

13. INSCRIBED HILTS

A number of hilt inscriptions are known, either in Roman letters
or in runes, and these are of considerable interest in view of
references to inscribed hilts in the literature. Runes are not common, although it is possible that many examples have disappeared

---

[1] It is known to be a revision of a twelfth-century one. See L. M. Larson,
'The Household of the Norwegian Kings', *American Historical Review*, xiii,
1908, p. 60.

[2] Zenetti, p. 281; F. Garscha, *Volk und Vorzeit*, i, 1939, p. 4.

together with the perishable portions of hilts. The earliest known is on a silver mount (Fig. 5), probably from a hilt, found in the peat bog of Thorsbjerg;[1] on one side are two engravings of an elaborate swastika, and on the other side two of the rune ᛟ ('o' in early runic inscriptions and 'œ' in Anglo-Saxon times). Other runic inscriptions from the Danish bog-finds are on scabbard-mounts and will be discussed later.

An Anglo-Saxon sword-pommel from the cemetery at Gilton, Kent (Plate IIa), has a long inscription in runes on one side, which is still legible, and five runes faintly discernible on the other. It was read by Haigh in 1872 as follows:

ᚡᚲᛗᛁᚣᛉᛁᚷᛁᛗᚻᚠᚱᛗᚻᛁᚣᚠᛁᛉᛁ

but neither his interpretation nor that of Stephens is reliable.[2]

In a paper on the Sandwich runic inscription published in 1938[3] Bruce Dickins referred to this inscription, and suggested that the central part should be read: *Sigimund ah*, 'Sigimund possesses', and that its purpose was to record the owner's name on the pommel. The marks on either side of this he believed should be disregarded, since they are lightly and casually formed and those on the extreme right roughly resemble those on the extreme left, suggesting the possibility that they are only scratches added to fill up the space on either side. In 1957, however, the pommel was examined by R. W. V. Elliott, and he came to the conclusion that there are reasonable grounds for going further than this. He has given an interpretation of the inscription which makes good sense,[4]

---

[1] Krause, p. 600 (Abb. 98).

[2] My thanks are due to Miss Tankard, Keeper of the Dept. of Archaeology at Liverpool, for an opportunity to examine the pommel and to check Haigh's reading. His interpretation is: *icu ik sigi muarnun ik wisa / Dagmund*: 'I increase victory by great deeds, I prince Dagmund' (*A.C.* viii, 1872, pp. 259 f.). This does not inspire confidence, nor does Stephens's interpretation, which concludes: *merge mik wisæ, Dægmund*: 'merrily brandish me, Dægmund' (Stephens, iii, p. 165). That of Bugge is no better; he concludes: *Me ær nim ic wisi*, 'Grasp me early; I point the way' (ibid., p. 164).

[3] B. Dickins, 'The Sandwich Runic Inscription RÆHÆBUL', *Beiträge zu Runenkunde und nordische Sprachwissenschaft* (ed. Schlottig), Leipzig, 1938, p. 83.

[4] 'Two Neglected English Runic Inscriptions: Gilton and Overchurch', in *Mélanges de linguistique et de philologie in memoriam Fernand Mossé*. Mr. Elliott most kindly allowed me to read this paper before publication, and I should like to express my gratitude here.

and which utilizes all the symbols with the exception of two very slight strokes at either end of the pommel. He reads it as:

EIC SIGIMER NEMDE
Sigimer named the sword.

To obtain this reading he takes the symbol ᚺ which occurs three times as a formal, deliberate variant of the regular 'e' rune, M. The symbol 's' appears to be in the archaic form ᛉ, for which there is a parallel on a sixth-century coin. The symbol ᚤ is taken to be an upturned ᚲ, 'c', accounted for by 'a combination of the writer's own uncertainty and the early date of the inscription'. *Eic* is a recorded variant of OE *ecg*, 'sword',[1] and is here an accusative singular without ending, an occasional dialect feature. *Sigimer* is found as an Old English name (*mer* a Kentish variant of WS *mær*).

The suggestion that the runic symbols on the other side, which are now too worn to be deciphered, completed the inscription by recording the name of the sword, is an attractive one. Elliott thinks that the fact that the pommel is more worn on one side might be due to superstitious touching or rubbing of this part; it might, however, be accounted for by the fact that the sword was always replaced the same way in the scabbard, and therefore was subjected to wear where it rubbed against the body on one side. Lightly carved runes such as these would certainly suffer.

The type of pommel suggests a late sixth-century date, and other swords from Gilton, including one with a ringed hilt (p. 72 above), are thought to be of this period. On linguistic and runological grounds Elliott inclines towards a seventh-century date, so there is no great measure of disagreement here.

A Viking sword of considerably later date bearing an inscription in runes on the hilt is the sword from Korsøygarden (Fig. 89), now in Oslo Museum.[2] This was found in 1880 during work on the

[1] Cf. *seic* for OE *secg*, 'sedge', in the Leiden Glossary. Recorded variants of *Ecg* in personal names are *ec, eg, eche, ecce, aig*, and *eic* in *Eicmund* on a ninth-century Kentish coin.

[2] I am grateful to Mr. Oakeshott for bringing this late inscription to my notice, and for passing on to me a report on the dating of the sword from the museum in Oslo. The find was first published by O. Rygh, *Aarsberetn*, 1880, pp. 183 f., and an account of the inscription is given in Olsen, *Norges Innskrifter med de yngre Runer*, Oslo, 1941, 1. 28, pp. 66 f. See also Hoffmeyer, pp. 35 f.

railway, in a stone cist which also held a shield-boss, but no traces of human remains were recorded. The runes are inscribed on a band of metal encircling the grip, below the pommel, and on the corresponding band at the other end is simple linear ornament. The inscription runs:

: ᛆᚢᛘᚢᛐᛆᚱ : ᚴᛂᚦᛂᛘᛁᚴ : ᛆᛋ ᛚᛁᚴᛆᚱᛆᛘᛁᚴ
:a u m u t æ r : g e þ e m i k : a a͡s l i k æ r a m i k

and this is interpreted:

> Auðmundr gerði mik. Ásleikr á mik.
> Auðmundr made me. Ásleikr owns me.

The form of the hilt suggests an eleventh-century date, and Petersen gives a date of about A.D. 1050. But the runes suggest a later date than this, and Moltke and Rygh date the inscription as late as the first half of the twelfth century. The runes may, of course, have been placed on the sword after it had been in use some time, but the reference to the maker of the sword makes this on the whole unlikely.

This double reference to owner and maker is paralleled on a knife from Sittingbourne of much earlier date (Fig. 17), which has an inscription in Anglo-Saxon, not in runes, on its blade:[1]

> Biorhtelm me worte; S(i)geberiht me ah.
> Biorhtelm made me; Sigeberiht owns me.

A further point of interest concerning the Norwegian hilt is the position of the runes, which are inscribed round the metal ring to which the name of *véttrim* was given (p. 179 below). We are told in one of the *Edda* poems that this was one of the places where runes should be carved, but this late hilt is the only known surviving example of such a practice.

A curved pommel bar from Exeter (Fig. 84), now in the British Museum, probably of tenth-century date,[2] bears an inscription: EOFRI MEFE, which has been read as *Leofric me fecit*, Leofric made me.

[1] J. Evans, 'Notes on an Anglo-Saxon Knife', *Arch.* xliv, 1873, pp. 331 f., and *B.M. Guide*, p. 95.
[2] Ibid. and *V.C.H. Devonshire*, i, p. 373.

Leofric may have been a local craftsman who made the bronze hilt, but he may also have been the patron who ordered it to be made for his sword. The letters are placed on the upper side of the bar, and so would be visible when the sword was worn. The form of the inscription may be compared with two in Latin on *Ingelrii* blades (p. 48 above).

There are five other hilts with inscriptions on the upper side of the guard and probably of tenth-century date, but these are not in Latin but in the form of Teutonic names. Two were found in Ireland: a hilt from Kilmainham (Fig. 85) bears the inscription *Hartolfr* on the guard,[1] while one from Ballinderry Crannog, West Meath, which has an *Ulfberht* inscription on the blade (Plate IVa and p. 47 above) has the name *Hiltipreht* on the guard.[2] In 1928 A. Mahr published a description of the Ballinderry sword,[3] which had then just been acquired by the Irish National Museum, and mentioned two other hilts with inscribed guards, both bearing the inscription *Hliter*. One of these (Fig. 86) came from a grave in Malhus, Trondhjem, in Norway,[4] while the second (Fig. 87) he stated to be in France, although it was in fact at that time in the Wallace Collection in London.[5] Mahr commented on the fact that these inscriptions were not in runes, and accounted for it by these being Frankish swords, the names denoting in all probability the smith or the workshop rather than the weapon's owner; the fashion could be a variant of the tenth-century custom of inscribing a maker's name on the blade. The following year (1929) Morawe added a fifth example to the list of inscribed hilts, when he described a Viking sword (Fig. 88) in the Armoury at Berlin. This bore the word *Hiltipreht* on the guard,[6] which is identical with

[1] *P.R.I.A.* xii (xxviii), 1910, p. 113; *V.A.* iii, p. 20; Coffey and Armstrong, p. 113.　　　　　　　　　　　　　　　[2] *V.A.* iii, p.77, fig. 49.

[3] *Mannus*, Ergänzungsband vi, 1928, pp. 240 f.

[4] Petersen, Abb. 89.

[5] Catalogue of the Wallace Collection, *European Arms and Armour*, Supplement iii, 1945, p. 567. I am indebted to Sir James Mann for information about this sword, and for allowing me to examine it. It probably came from the Nieuwerkerke Collection in 1870, and Mahr was misled by references to the hilt being in France which are found in Petersen, Lorange, and Viollet-le-Duc (*Dict. du mobilier français*, v, p. 365).

[6] F. Morawe, 'Hiltipreht', *Mannus*, xxi, 1929, pp. 292 f.

the one on the hilt from Ballinderry. This sword in Berlin had a pattern-welded blade and appeared to be of ninth- or tenth-century date, while guard and pommel-bar were inlaid with silver, as on the Irish hilt; the pommel, however, was missing. Morawe thought it most unlikely that the smiths who made the blades had their names put on the hilts, but suggested as an alternative that the blades were manufactured separately and then dispatched to merchant craftsmen who fitted them with hilts before disposing of them to their customers.

There are some isolated examples of sword inscriptions on the outside of the guard. Jankuhn (p. 214) mentions a sword from Buxtehude with the inscription *Benedict* and another from Amrum no longer legible.

The majority of inscriptions surviving on sword-hilts have been made for the purpose of recording the owner's name, and the new interpretation of the Gilton pommel suggests the possibility that runes may sometimes have been used to record the names of both owner and sword. In the tenth century we have the group of what appear to be the names of the craftsmen who made the hilts, and since such a named hilt could be fastened on to a blade which already bore a different smith's name upon it, Morawe's suggestion of a workshop to which blades were sent to be finished seems a likely one. Inscriptions of a more individual kind, like the runic ones and the Latin words on the Exeter hilt, are more likely to have been specially executed for a patron by a craftsman in his service. The Gilton inscription in particular is of interest because of its uncertain touch, which while it renders it difficult to interpret also suggests that it is the work of an amateur who was not accustomed to inscribing runes upon a sword-hilt.

14. SWORD ATTACHMENTS

There is archaeological evidence for various attachments worn with swords, although it is hard to be certain whether they were fixed to hilt or scabbard. Akerman (p. 50), who thought the rings on the Kentish hilts were intended for the attachment of charms, commented on large crystal beads found beside swords in a number of graves. Unfortunately, records of early excavations seldom tell us the precise position of such beads. A sword from grave 31 of the Anglo-Saxon cemetery at Brighthampton (Fig. 100) had a large amber bead on one side of the hilt, not far from the pommel. A second sword from grave 44 had two glass beads, said to lie not far from the hilt and both on the same side.[1] At North Luffenham, Rutland, a sword was found with a large glass bead near the hilt, beside the left arm of the sword's owner, and Reginald Smith suggested this might be a 'sword-knot'.[2] Two others were found at Petersfinger,[3] in each case under the sword and about a third of the way down, and there are other examples from Fairford[4] and Little Wilbraham.[5]

Veeck (p. 78) noted the presence of such beads beside swords in Alamannic cemeteries. He gives instances of one large bead of amber, one of crystal, and one of blue glass. Lindenschmidt had thought the presence of a bead meant that a woman had been buried with the man who owned the sword, but Veeck realized that this could not be the correct explanation, but that the beads were connected with the swords themselves in some way; on the strength of a sword from south Russia with a round pommel (in the Berlin Museum), he suggested that they were pommels which had become detached from the hilt. But Reginald Smith's idea of a 'sword-knot' is confirmed by the discovery of the fine sword from Klein-Hüningen near Basle, dated by Laur-Belart to the second half of the sixth century (Fig. 11 and p. 59 above). The attachment in this case was a ball of amber with a knob of silver-gilt in the centre, which had been fastened to the end of a leather strap. While this establishes the position of the attachment, however, it does not fully explain its purpose. Similar balls at Bülach were fastened to leather straps, and it seemed as if the other end of the strap was fastened round the top of the scabbard below the

[1] *Arch.* xxxviii, 1860, pp. 87, 88, 96.
[2] *Arch. Soc. Leicester,* xxvi, pp. 251 f., and *V.C.H. Rutland,* i, p. 100.
[3] Leeds and Shortt, pp. 16, 17, 44.
[4] W. M. Wylie, *Fairford Graves,* Oxford, 1852, p. 20.
[5] R. C. Neville, *Saxon Obsequies,* London, 1852, p. 10.

mouthpiece.[1] Werner thought that they may have been worn as special tokens like the rings on hilts of a later period, while Arwidsson went further and suggested that they represented an earlier form of the metal rings and ring-knobs fitted on sword-hilts of the sixth century. But the form of these balls bears little resemblance to rings; there is no example of a metal ring lying beside a sword in this way, while Werner noted that a ring-hilt from Chaouilley had a ball of this kind beside it.[2] Böhner emphasized the fact that balls of meerschaum were found beside Frankish swords of the fifth and sixth centuries, and since this was a fragile substance unlikely to be chosen for any practical purpose, he thought that the beads and balls had some magical significance. Such a ball of meerschaum (Fig. 90), measuring 2·5 cm. across and 2·1 cm. in height, was found just below the hilt of a fine sword discovered in a grave under the church of St. Martin, near Cologne.[3] It illustrates the care with which such sword attachments were made, for the ball has a gold plate set in the top, decorated with cloisonné work.

In *Beiträge zur Archäologie des Attila-Reiches*,[4] Werner has discussed the significance of such balls, following up the suggestions made in his account of the Bülach cemetery. He puts evidence from eastern Europe beside that of the West, and shows that these sword attachments appear to have been a fashion among the Persians and Alani and to have come westward with the Huns about the fifth century A.D. He gives a long list of examples from Frankish and Alamannic graves, and shows how the fashion spread through northern France and Belgium to Anglo-Saxon England, to last in western Europe until the mid-seventh century. It may be noted, incidentally, that there are no elaborate examples of such fittings recorded up to now from Anglo-Saxon graves. Werner gives illustrations of attachments of many different types found with swords, and he makes it clear that the long metal shanks on the back of

---

[1] In graves 7 and 1; Werner, p. 57.   [2] Werner (see below), p. 32.

I am grateful to Dr. Herrnbrodt of the Rheinisches Landesmuseum for information about this before publication. An account of the discovery appeared in the *Illustrated London News* of 26 May 1956, pp. 601 f.

[4] J. Werner, *Beiträge zur Archäologie des Attila-Reiches*, Abh. d. Bayer. Akad. d. Wissenschaften, N.F. xxxviiia (3), 1955, pp. 31 f.

some of these would make it impossible to fasten them like buttons on to the front of a scabbard. They are presumably intended for suspension from a leather thong or cord. The fragile nature of these fittings and the fact that they are also found with Eastern swords worn differently from the Germanic ones seems to rule out the possibility that they were meant for the attachment of the scabbard to the belt. Consequently Werner concludes that they were worn as amulets, and he argues that the materials used—glass, rock-crystal, amber, meerschaum—are likely choices for such a purpose. The glass balls found in women's graves in Kent and in Frankish cemeteries are probably amulets of a similar type.

It is unfortunate that up to now we have no literary allusions to such amulets nor any picture of a warrior with such a fitting upon his scabbard to help us. There are, however, allusions to 'life-stones' in the Icelandic sagas, and although these are much later than the seventh century in date, it is not impossible that some memories of such a custom remained. The stones seem to have been rare, and the sword possessing one about which we hear most was Skofnung, which was said to have been taken from a grave of the Migration period (p. 181 below). The chief purpose of such amulets, according to the sagas, was to heal wounds given by the sword.

In the seventh century, sword attachments which replace the balls are little metal pyramids, sometimes richly ornamented, which are found in many Anglo-Saxon and continental graves. Werner[1] gives a list of continental finds, but includes only two examples from England, and many more are now known. In the British Museum are three of these pyramids which came from the cemetery at Faversham (Fig. 91); although no records survive as to how they were found, it is probable that all three came from one grave, and it is interesting to note that they are of three different sizes.[2] These pyramids are of hollow bronze, with a bar at the base to which a cord or narrow strap could be fastened. Two

---

[1] Werner, p. 59, note 23.
[2] This has been pointed out to me by Mr. Bruce-Mitford, to whom also I owe information about the pyramids from the Thames and Linlithgow.

other examples in bronze were found in a grave on Salisbury race-course,[1] and another from Tuddenham, Suffolk, is in the museum at Cambridge, while there are other examples from Long-bridge, Warwickshire,[2] and from Uncleby, Yorkshire. The Uncleby pyramid was found in a mound containing a large number of Anglo-Saxon secondary burials, and was said to have come from the grave of a woman, together with ear-rings and a girdle-hanger.[3] No full account of this excavation, however, has ever been published, and even if the record is reliable, which is doubtful in view of various inconsistencies in the existing evidence, there is no inherent reason why a woman should not wear such a pyramid at her waist, either as an ornament or for sentimental reasons.

More richly ornamented pyramids, with coloured glass or garnet decoration, have also been found. One came from the Thames and is in the British Museum; the filling from the cell in the top has now disappeared. Another from Sarre[4] has a garnet in the top, and ivory and coloured glass set in gilt foil on the sides (Fig. 92); this was found beside a sword. Another, set with garnets and with gold filigree work (Fig. 93), came from the rich grave at Broomfield, unfortunately never properly excavated;[5] on the plan in the British Museum it is shown a little to one side of the hilt. Another example with gold filigree and garnet filling from Dalmey Church, Linlith-gow, is in the National Museum at Edinburgh. The finest examples yet found, however, are the pair of pyramids in the ship-grave at Sutton Hoo (Plate IIIa), which lay one on each side of the sword and a short distance from it. These are described as being of 'miraculous workmanship',[6] and are formed of gold, the upper edges cut in solid garnet and ornamented with gold cellwork and mosaic glass to form a square of chequer pattern on the top. Ornamented pyramids have been found in Europe, but the only parallel yet known to the pair from Sutton Hoo is a pyramid from

---

[1] R. C. Hoare, *Ancient Wiltshire*, 1821 (Roman Æra), ii, pp. 26 f.
[2] *J.B.A.A.* xxxii, 1876, p. 108.
[3] *P.S.A.* xxiv, 1912, p. 152, fig. 4 on plate.
[4] *A.C.* vii, 1868, p. 310.
[5] A good account, with references, is given in *V.C.H. Essex*, i, pp. 320 f.
[6] *Sutton Hoo*, p. 59.

a cremation grave in Old Uppsala, which may possibly have been made in England.[1]

Some kind of fastening presumably ran from either scabbard or hilt and ended in beads or metal pyramids. Its purpose could have been either to keep the sword secure within the scabbard or to fasten the scabbard to the belt. Anglo-Saxon illuminated manuscripts of about A.D. 1000 show narrow straps fastened near the mouthpiece of the scabbard which seem to be intended for some such purpose, and a sword with two such straps, for example, may be seen in B.M. Tib. C. VI, fol. 10 (Fig. 108), while an illustration in the Lothair Gospels, of earlier date, shows a sword slightly raised in the scabbard, and two red straps encircling it ending in gold strap-ends[2] (Fig. 111). A sword in the Utrecht Psalter (probably ninth century in date)[3] has two slender cords too narrow to be a belt, fastened to two buttons on the scabbard (Fig. 112). But so far no illustration has been found to explain the exact function of the pyramids in use in the seventh century, and there is considerable variety possible in methods of securing a sword within the scabbard.[4]

In his report on the Bülach cemetery, Werner classes the metal pyramids with other forms of fastening attached to the scabbard and intended to slip on to narrow straps which join it to the belt. According to his theory, however, they would be found farther down the scabbard than appears to be the case in graves which have been carefully excavated, and they would be placed one below the other on the same side. The Sutton Hoo scabbard is provided with buttons to fit on to the belt, so that presumably there at least the pyramids had some other function. The Faversham set, of diminishing size, might fit in better with Werner's suggestion. But only careful excavation of swords and detailed study of

[1] Bruce-Mitford, p. 52.

[2] I am indebted to Miss Barbara Raw for this reference. The original is in the Bibliothèque Nationale (Bib. Nat. latin MS. 266, Lothair Gospels IX, Tours).

[3] In the Univ. Library, Utrecht. For its dating, see Wormald, *English Drawings of the Tenth and Eleventh Centuries*, London, 1952, p. 21.

[4] A possible alternative to pyramids in the form of 'two thin iron objects . . . like inverted boats' was noted 'just below the haft' of a sword found at Alfriston (*Sussex A.C.* lvi, 1914, p. 35).

contemporary illustrations are likely to help us to a solution of the problem. The use of the metal pyramids appears to have come to an end after the seventh century, and we do not yet know why they were no longer needed.

15. THE SCABBARD

The scabbard was usually buried in the grave with the sword which it enclosed, but since it was generally of wood it seldom survived, and in most cases only the metal fittings are left. However, Behmer has collected a good deal of information about the scabbards of the early period, and traces occasionally left when the wood is not wholly decayed have given us some information about the form.

A good example is the scabbard of the sixth-century sword from Klein-Hüningen[1] (Fig. 11), which was covered with fine leather, parts of which survived, and was lined with leather inside. At the foot was a space of about 3·8 cm. below the sword-point, and here traces of wool were found, as though the space was stuffed with wool or the point rested in a pocket of woollen material. Other examples of scabbards with traces of woollen lining have been found in Anglo-Saxon graves at Holborough, Finglesham,[2] and Harrold, Bedfordshire.[3] At Holborough and Finglesham sheepskin was probably used, and this is paralleled by a scabbard found in a Frankish grave at Orsoy, which had an inner lining of sheepskin with the fleece on the inside, coming into direct contact with the blade. Detailed examination of this showed that the direction of the hair was towards the mouthpiece, to facilitate the easy removal of the blade from the scabbard.[4] It seems possible that the lanolin present in sheeps' wool would help to protect the blade from rust.

The favourite covering for the scabbard in western Europe seems to have been leather. This might be decoratively applied over

---

[1] Laur-Belart, p. 130.   [2] A.C. lxx, 1956, p. 100.
[3] M.A. ii, 1958, p. 28.
[4] Böhner 2, p. 165. It is difficult to see how in this case the blade could be easily replaced in the scabbard. It is possible, however, that there was a thin inner lining (of linen or leather).

carved wood, as on the Klein-Hüningen scabbard, so that the
pattern could still be seen when the leather covering was fitted over
it. The same feature was noted in the case of the swords from
Valsgärde 6, 7, and 8.[1] A scabbard from the cemetery at Petersfinger was fairly well preserved, and was found to have been of
wood covered with leather, with strips of bronze to hold the
covering in place, while inside it was lined with strips of leather
and also fitted with thin laths of wood slightly narrower than the
blade, probably to serve as guides so that the point of the sword
did not catch in the leather lining. Some kind of strap may have
passed through the back, but the traces were not clear.[2]

The Sutton Hoo scabbard was too badly decayed to be restored,
but it showed traces of leather lining inside a wooden framework,
bound in places with cloth.[3] The scabbard of the Broomfield
sword also appeared to have been bound with cloth below the
mouthpiece, and the same was noted of the scabbard from the
Swedish ship-grave Valsgärde 8, though in this case it may have
been a repair.[4] Some scabbards were probably covered outside
with linen over the leather, as in later medieval times, for the
Lavoye scabbard, dated late sixth century, had a leather covering
under a second cover of stout linen.[5] Veeck (p. 79) mentions a
scabbard from Zöbingen, part of which survived, as being of wood
bound with birchbast, which must have given it a shining white
appearance when new. Birchbast was used on a number of scabbards in Alamannic cemeteries, e.g. at Herbrechtingen[6] and Oberflacht.[7]

Behmer gives some examples of wooden scabbards covered with
metal, but these seem to be confined to the South Russian region,
where they were used by the Goths. The scabbard from Altlussheim (Fig. 13) had sides of thin wood, believed to be poplar,
held together by metal bands down the edges and covered with

---

[1] Arwidsson 2, p. 63. It may be noted that this scabbard also was thought to
have had a hairy lining (ibid., p. 62).   [2] Atkinson, p. 59.
[3] *Sutton Hoo*, p. 58.   [4] Arwidsson 2, pp. 62–63.   [5] Chenet, p. 48.
[6] J. Werner, 'Die Schwerter von Imola, Herbrechtingen und Endrebacke',
A.A. xxi, 1950, p. 48.
[7] Veeck, *Der Alamannenfriedhof von Oberflacht*, 1924, p. 24.

gold leaf;[1] this held a richly decorated sword with a gold hilt which showed Eastern influence in the decoration (p. 66 above). An odd feature of this scabbard, to which I know no parallel, was part of a hilt, according to Werner a narrow straight guard,[2] made of lapis lazuli, fastened to the silver chape.

Some of the metal fittings which survive from scabbards are of very elaborate workmanship. The chief of these were the chape, riveted over the tip of the scabbard to hold down the outer covering, and the mouthpiece at the top, through which the sword passed. Sometimes additional mounts were added at the side, or belt fittings in the centre for the strap to pass through. The scabbard of Childeric's scramasax (Fig. 9b) gives a good idea of the ornamental possibilities; although the fittings are now incomplete, they can be reconstructed from earlier drawings.[3] Two right-angled metal fittings appear to have run along one side of the scabbard mouth, down one side of the scabbard, and along the straight base, fastened by rivets to the leather. They were richly ornamented with garnets and cloisonné work, with tiny stones like pearls set along the edge, and in the centre of the long side a flower-shaped cell enclosing a large garnet. There are other examples of jewelled mouthpieces from Scandinavia, and also of elaborate gold plates covered with animal ornament.[4]

A scabbard from the Anglo-Saxon cemetery at Abingdon (Fig. 97) is interesting because of close links in decorative motifs on mouthpiece and chape with those from scabbards taken from late fifth-century graves at Samson and Éprave in the neighbourhood of Namur.[5] The chape is in the form of a bearded head between two birds, and a clearer form of this was found in 1957 on a chape from Krefeld-Gellep[6] (Fig. 98). The ornament on the mouthpiece is in an ovolo design, and parallels to this are found on several

[1] Garscha, pp. 192 f.
[2] Garscha takes it to be a pommel. But see Werner, *Beiträge* (op. cit. p. 84), p. 39.   [3] Arbman 2, pp. 107 f.   [4] Behmer, pls. xxxvi, xli.
[5] Leeds and Harden, pp. 59–60 and pl. ix.
[6] A. Sleeger, 'Ein frühfränkisches Kriegergrab von Krefeld-Gellep', *Germ.* xxi, 1937, pp. 183 f. There is probably some connexion here with the head between two birds with large beaks on the Reinstrup brooch (Bruce-Mitford, p. 55, fig. 10).

scabbard mounts and buckles in early Frankish cemeteries. Werner[1] points out that these scabbards with silver inlay are evidently in a separate artistic tradition from the gold-ornamented swords and scabbards of the fifth century. They must have been contemporary with them, and it is possible that this tradition may go back to late Roman times; if, as seems probable, they were made in the neighbourhood of Namur, then the workshop there may have been producing swords continuously from the late Roman period to the Middle Ages. He suggests also that the pattern on the mouthpiece of the scabbard from grave 21 at Petersfinger comes from the same source.

An unusual example of a rich mouthpiece from the seventh century is that on a scabbard which was taken from the River Seine at Villeneuve-la-Garenne[2] (Fig. 99), and which held a pattern-welded sword. The mouthpiece is of copper, elaborately decorated with various motifs and bird and animal figures inlaid in gold, while there is a gold edging running round the edge of the scabbard. The scabbard which belonged to the Anglo-Saxon sword from Brighthampton must also have been a fine one, for it has a chape of bronze, inlaid with animal figures in gilt (Fig. 100).[3]

Further opportunity for decoration was afforded by the strap-holders. The most usual form was two bars of metal, held by rivets on the upper part of the scabbard parallel to one another so that the strap could pass underneath them. Examples can be seen on Childeric's scabbard (Fig. 9) and on the one from Klein-Hüningen (Fig. 11); in the first case they are slender and gracefully shaped, and in the second they are shorter and almost cylindrical, and decorated with silver inlay. Possible variations on straight bars are cross-shaped, hammer-shaped, and square strap-holders (Fig. 96). On the Lavoye scabbard (Fig. 12) the holders were one above the other on the same side,[4] and Werner (Fig. 95) shows how a narrow strap could pass through one of these, then round the

---

[1] J. Werner, 'Zu fränkischen Schwertern des 5. Jahrhunderts', *Germ.* xxxi, 1953, pp. 39 f., and 'Fränkische Schwerter des 5. Jahrhunderts aus Samson und Petersfinger', ibid. xxxiv, 1956, p. 156. [2] Salin, iii, p. 260.

[3] *Arch.* xxxviii, 1860, p. 92, pl. 2. In the Ashmolean Museum, Oxford.

[4] Chenet, p. 49; Werner, p. 57.

scabbard and over the wearer's shoulder, to return to finish at the second strap-holder.

On the Lavoye scabbard (Fig. 12) the end of the strap was fastened down by a silver star decorated with a garnet set in gold. On those from Bülach, however, metal plates which could slide along the strap were used, and these could release the scabbard when necessary, while its weight held them in place when it was worn. On one scabbard the plates had a hollow, pyramid-shaped knob at one end, resembling the metal pyramids discussed earlier (Fig. 94).[1] Werner thought that a rounded strap passed up and under the pyramid to join the scabbard to the belt, which would work if the sword were worn on a belt round the waist instead of on a strap over the shoulder. He suggested that this might explain the pyramids from seventh-century graves, the date of the Bülach grave being late sixth or early seventh century.

The scabbard from Sutton Hoo (Plate IIIa) had two circular bosses differing from the examples of strap-holders given in Behmer. They appear to have been used as buttons, standing out from the scabbard so that a leather strap with holes could be buttoned over them. Another scabbard with two buttons can be seen on one of the Vendel helmet plates (Fig. 106).[2] The Sutton Hoo buttons are particularly interesting because they are ornamented with garnets and cellwork in the form of a cross (Fig. 101), corresponding, as Bruce-Mitford pointed out,[3] to certain cruciform designs on Anglo-Saxon jewelled pendants. The Brighthampton scabbard (Fig. 100) was also ornamented with a cross, in this case a silver mount in the form of a cross *patée*,[4] which must presumably be a Christian symbol. Another example on a scabbard from Bülach also consists of a silver cross of this form, accompanied by two other silver mounts in the shape of an arrow, and this scabbard is dated by Werner (p. 51) to the second half of the sixth century. The scabbard from Villeneuve-la-Garenne (Fig. 99), thought to be seventh-century in date, may also be noticed here. It has two

---

[1] Werner, op. cit. For other examples see H. Zeiss, *Germ.* xvii, 1933, pp. 208 f.
[2] Stolpe and Arne, xli, 4, from grave XIV.
[3] *Sutton Hoo*, pp. 32 f.   [4] *Arch.* xxxviii, 1860, p. 96.

equal-armed crosses on one side of the rich mouthpiece, which appear to be Christian symbols, while they are matched on the opposite side of the central panel by one undoubted swastika and what appears to be a second swastika of unusual form.[1]

The idea of a Christian symbol of a cross set on a scabbard for the protection of the sword within is borne out by the reference to such crosses on the sword of Charlemagne (p. 113 below). His sword was also said to be protected by linen and wax, which agrees with the archaeological evidence for the careful protection against rust given to the precious blade within the scabbard. The crosses which have survived on the scabbards of the sixth and seventh centuries were in all probability intended, like those on the scabbard of Charlemagne, to protect the sword, hallowing and blessing it and guarding it in battle even as the boars on the helmets were said to guard the warriors who wore them from injury.[2] On the Anglo-Saxon helmet from Benty Grange the boar-figure on the crest is accompanied by a Christian cross,[3] so that it would seem that here the old emblem has been retained but the new Christian one added beside it; similarly on the Villeneuve scabbard, the swastika —which is also found on the hilt (Fig. 51a) and sword-belt (Fig. 55) of a sixth-century sword from Bifrons—is set opposite the cross.

The question of how the scabbard was worn can be answered to some extent by the evidence of archaeology and art. The natural position for a long sword worn by a right-handed man is on the left side, and this is the side on which swords are worn in the pictures of warriors on the Bayeux tapestry of the eleventh century (Fig. 113). These men wear their scabbards from a belt at the waist, fixed by straps so that the hilt is in a convenient position for the right hand and the chape of the scabbard not too near the ground. This position allowed a man to walk or ride without inconvenience, and is not very different from the arrangement of the modern sword-belt. When in some Anglo-Saxon graves the sword in its scabbard is placed diagonally across the body, the idea may have

---

[1] Salin, iii, p. 261 and pl. xxi.

[2] *Beowulf* 303-6. See Cramp, pp. 59 f.

[3] Bruce-Mitford, *Annual Report of the City Museum of Sheffield*, 1955-6, p. 13 and plate.

been to imitate the position in which the scabbard was worn, and to place the sword-hilt ready for the hand (see p. 12 above). Sometimes the sword was certainly worn higher than the waist, as may be seen from a drawing of Goliath (Fig. 109) in an Anglo-Saxon manuscript of about A.D. 1000[1] in the British Museum; his belt passes across the chest and under the right arm, where it is secured by another strap passing over the shoulder. This picture shows Goliath as a left-handed man, holding shield in right hand and spear in left. Another Goliath (Fig. 110) in a manuscript of the same period[2] has the strap to which the scabbard is fixed worn over his right shoulder. The Romans seem sometimes to have worn the long *spatha*, the cavalry-man's weapon, high on the shoulder. Such a fashion was occasionally adopted also by the Teutonic peoples, for swords are sometimes found in this position in Anglo-Saxon and continental graves, and in the fifth century Sidonius refers to Teutonic chiefs wearing their swords high (p. 104 below), while Falk (p. 35) gives instances from the Icelandic Sagas. In some of the saga references, however, the context shows that one sword was worn from a strap on the shoulder because a second was worn on the belt. In *Bjarnar Saga Hitsdœlakappa*, xviii, for example, a man uses the sword on his belt in a fight, and is saved from a wound in the arm and chest by the fact that another sword is worn high on the shoulder; his opponent has a sword on his belt and a shield slung on his shoulder. An earlier Scandinavian example of a strap over the right shoulder can be seen on a helmet from grave XIV at Vendel[3] (Fig. 106).

According to the Emperor Leo VI, who wrote an account of the arms of the Franks in *Tactica*,[4] they wore their swords in general suspended by a strap, but some preferred to hang them from their belts. At Bülach, Werner[5] found that scabbards from the earlier

[1] Tib. C. VI, fol. 9.

[2] B.M. Harley 603, fol. 8.

[3] Stolpe and Arne, pl. xli, 3.

[4] Migne, *Patrologia graeca*, cvii, pp. 964–8. Lot (*L'Art militaire et les armées au moyen âge*, i, p. 85) points out that this chapter is reproduced from the *Strategicon*, but the remark about the belt is one of Leo's additions, either from a better text than we possess or based on his own observations.

[5] Werner, pp. 53 f.

graves (nos. 124 and 17) were worn from a strap over the right shoulder; they hung by side-fastenings and the weight of the swords kept them in place. Scabbards from later graves, however, were found with the remains of wide decorated belts worn round the waists of the warriors (e.g. no. 106), and he suggested that in the seventh century the belt was replacing the shoulder-strap in popularity. For those fighting on horseback, it would perhaps be more convenient to wear the sword high, and this is a question to be discussed later. It seems certain that throughout the Anglo-Saxon and Viking periods both methods of wearing a sword were practised, and that the strap on the shoulder, on account of its obvious convenience, was never wholly abandoned, but the belt round the waist was probably more popular in the later part of the period, as may be seen from the Bayeux Tapestry.

Examination of scabbards from the bog-finds led Engelhardt and Brøndsted[1] to conclude that they had been worn on the right side. Diodorus and Strabo[2] stated that the Gauls wore their long swords on the right side; Procopius contradicts this, but there may be confusion here between sword and dagger, worn one on either side. The sword from Klein-Hüningen, dated about A.D. 500, was said by Laur-Belart to have been worn on the left, but it may be noted that it was placed on the right side of the warrior in the grave.[3] Evidence from the Anglo-Saxon cemeteries does not help much here, as although in many cases the sword was laid on the left side of the warrior,[4] there are many instances of its being placed on the right.[5] Nor does it appear that it was the general

---

[1] Brøndsted, iii, p. 203.

[2] Diodorus, v. 30; Strabo, iv. 4. [3] Laur-Belart, pp. 129, 133.

[4] For example, Horton Kirby (*D.D.A.S.* viii, 1938, nos. 75, 86, 87); Bifrons (*A.C.* x. 24, p. 312; xiii. 62, 72, pp. 552 f.); Howletts (*P.S.A.* xxx, 1918, p. 105); Sittingbourne (*Coll. Antiq.* i, p. 99); Sarre (*A.C.* vi, nos. 8, 11, 15, 18, 68, 86). Outside Kent: North Luffenham, Rutland (*Arch. Soc.* xxvi, 1902, pp. 246 f.); Alfriston, Sussex (*S.A.C.* lvi, 1914, p. 41); Linton Heath, Cambs. (*Arch. J.* xi, 1854, p. 107); Chessel Down, I.O.W. (Hillier, p. 35); Petersfinger (Leeds and Shortt, pp. 7 f.); Lapwing Hill, Derbyshire (T. Bateman, *Ten Years Diggings*, p. 68); Kempston, Beds. (*Arch. Soc. Bedford*, 1864, p. 292).

[5] Gilton, Sibertswold, Barfriston (Faussett, pp. 7, 118, 124, 143); Folkestone (Notes of excavation, Ref. Library); Finglesham (*A.C.* xli, 1929, p. 115, G 2); Holborough (*A.C.* lxx, 1956, pp. 119, 140). Outside Kent: Sherrington, Wilts. (*Arch.* xv, 1806, p. 345); Astockton, Notts. (*V.C.H.* i, p. 197); Abingdon (Leeds

practice for the belt or strap to be worn in the grave. In the Burgundian cemetery at Bourogne, where some attention was paid
to this question, there were two graves where the long sword was
placed on the left side of the warrior with the sword-belt folded
over it, but in another grave the belt appeared to have been
buckled round the body.[1] At Kempston, where the exact position
of the sword was recorded, it was described as being on the left,
between arm and body, reaching 2 or 3 inches below the knee.
Here it seems probable that, if not worn by the dead, the sword-belt
was at least placed over him to give the sword the position it
would occupy when worn. Similarly at Petersfinger, the sword in
grave XX was high up under the left arm, with the pommel at
shoulder level and the left arm across the scabbard,[2] and one
sword at Holborough was on the right side, passing over the right
leg so that the point was level with the knee.

It was extremely rare for a sword to be buried without its
scabbard. One is recorded to have been found so with a skeleton
at St. Giles' Hill, Winchester,[3] but this is exceptional. Great care
was usually taken to preserve swords placed in the graves, and it
is even possible that an outer case was sometimes provided for both
the sword and the scabbard. At Abingdon traces of what may have
been a leather case were found,[4] and at Chessel Down, traces of
what Hillier thought had been a box covering the scabbard, marked
by a row of nails.[5] Such cases may have been made for a sword
which was not in constant use. From the careful way in which the
sword was in most cases laid in the grave, and from what we know
of the construction of the scabbard, it is certainly safe to assume
that much time and effort were normally devoted to the preservation
of this valuable weapon.

16. SCABBARD INSCRIPTIONS

Three runic inscriptions set on scabbard-mounts can be dated

and Harden, p. 40, no. 49). One grave at Sarre (no. 39) was an exception to the
general rule and had the sword on the right.
[1] Scheurer and Lablotier, p. 18.   [2] Leeds and Shortt, pp. 7 f.
[3] Reported in the *Hampshire Chronicle*, 7 April 1894.
[4] Leeds and Harden, p. 60.   [5] Hillier, p. 35.

back to an early period. These are from the Danish bog-finds, and
the earliest, from Thorsbjerg, is on the chape of a scabbard
(Fig. 6) which has been dated between the late third and early fourth
centuries. This has runes on both sides, reading as follows:[1]

ᛟᚹᛚᚦᚢᚦᛖᚹᚨᛉ ᚾᛁᚹᚨᛃᛗᚨᚱᛁᛉ
o w l þ u þ e w a R / n i w a j m a r i R

Each group can be interpreted separately, and it is not clear which
should come first. Krause[2] and von Friesen[3] took the inscription
to consist of a double name, probably of the sword's owner.
Krause took the first group of runes as a title or personal name,
Wulþuþewar,[4] and since *wulþu-* is a stem meaning 'glory', 'lordli-
ness' which is also found in the name of the Scandinavian god *Ullr*,
the meaning with *þewar* ('servant', 'follower') could be 'Servant of
Ullr'. Such a title might belong to either a priest or a worshipper
of the god. The second group he took as a descriptive word 'Not
of bad repute', related to Gothic *wajamers*, 'Of bad reputation',
with a negative prefix. The first runic symbol is smaller than the
others, and this Krause suggested might be taken separately, to
stand for *opala*, meaning something owned, as a mark of possession.
In the Anglo-Saxon runic alphabet this rune bears the name *eþel*,
standing for 'native land'. There appears to be some special significance in its use, for not only does Krause give several instances
where it appears alone, but it is also found in Anglo-Saxon manuscripts as a substitute for the word *eþel*,[5] so that it was evidently
familiar as an effective symbol many centuries after its appearance
in the early runic inscriptions. It was also a potent word in heroic
poetry, and it is twice used in *Beowulf* in connexion with the giving
of a sword which is a token of the receiving of certain rights.[6]

[1] Jacobsen and Moltke, p. 19; Atlas, nos. 27–28.   [2] Krause, pp. 600 f.
[3] O. von Friesen, 'Runorne', *Nordisk Kultur*, 1933, vi, p. 18; also in *Uppsala
Universitets Årsskrift*, iv, 1924, p. 105, where he disagrees with the interpretation
'Servant of Ullr'.
[4] The 'o' rune may sometimes be used for 'w' and the 'w' rune for 'u'. If the
'o' rune is taken separately, however, the 'u' must be inserted.
[5] Three times in *Beowulf*, once in *Waldere*, once in Alfred's *Orosius*. See R.
Derolez, *Runica Manuscripta*, Brugge, 1954, pp. 399 f.
[6] Those who fail Beowulf are told that for them the giving of the sword and
the joys of their native land (*eþelwyn*) shall be denied them for ever (*Beow.* 2885);

The interpretation of the Thorsbjerg inscription as a double name seems the most satisfactory one up to now. A name like 'Servant of Ullr' could be interpreted in various ways: it might refer not to the sword's owner (or to the man who cut the runes) but to the sword itself. But we know little of the cult of Ullr in early times in north-western Europe,[1] and the name might be a personal one and not that of a deity. Marstrander[2] suggests that the word was originally a divine title—'Lord'—and might here stand for some other god. He also reads the name as *Wulþuþewar*, and points out that this reading gives us two halves of the inscription which can be taken as two halves of a line of alliterative verse. He suggests that *ni waje* is to be taken as the negative form of the subjunctive of an earlier form of the verb *vægja*, to yield: 'May the famous one never yield'. He would, however, prefer to derive *waje* from Germ. *wæja*, 'to blow'. To make sense of such an interpretation, however, he has to put forward a doubtful argument based on folklore: the sword is used in magic ritual to prevent a storm, or to drive out the hostile spirit believed to live in the smith's bellows and to prevent him from doing good work. This is not convincing.

A second chape from Vimose (Fig. 7) also bears a runic inscription, and this according to archaeological dating would belong to the second half of the third century.[3] It runs as follows:

ᛗᚨᚱᛁᚺᚨ   ᛁᛒᛚᛒ   ᛗᚨᚲᛁᚨ
m a r i h a / i a l a // m a k i a

Here again there is no certain interpretation. *Ala* is usually taken to be a personal name, corresponding to ON *Alli*, which appears again on the runic stone from Glavendrup. *Makia* is taken as 'sword' (cf. Gothic *mekeis*, OE *mece*). Suggested interpretations are:

(a) 'Alli to Mærr, this sword' (recording a gift).

---

when Beowulf receives a family sword and a part of the kingdom, he is told that the rights of his native land (*eþelriht*) are to be his (*Beow.* 2198).

[1] For evidence from later times see De Vries, ii, pp. 153 f. Evidence for the cult of Ullr in Denmark is singularly lacking.

[2] Marstrander, 'De Nordiske Runeinnskrifter i eldre Alfabet', *Viking*, xvi, 1953, pp. 10 f.

[3] Jacobsen and Moltke, 205, p. 243; Atlas, nos. 485–6; Krause, pp. 603 f.

(*b*) 'Alli possesses the Famous One, a sword' (taking *mari* as an adjective (cf. ON *mærr*) and the sword-name *Mæring* as analogy).

(*c*) 'I, Alli, possess the sword, Famous One' (recording ownership).

Marstrander (p. 37) tried to improve on these suggestions by placing a 'd' rune between the words *mariha* and *iala*, where he thought traces of another rune could be made out. He then read: *mari hadi ala makia*, 'Take in thy hand, Alli, the sword Mari'. This could be a record of the receiving of a sword by a warrior as a ceremonial gift, perhaps on his attainment to manhood. This can certainly not be deduced without hesitation from the presence of the inscription as it stands, although it is a possibility to be considered. At least it would seem from the presence of the word *makia* that here we have an inscription which is more than a personal name, a fact which is of some importance.

From Vimose also comes a silver scabbard-mount (Fig. 8) ornamented in gold with runes lightly scratched on it. Four runes can be made out, and Marstrander (p. 60) reads them from right to left as follows:

ᛊ ᛜ ᚹ ᚨ

s ng͡i w a = awings

He takes this as an East Germanic nominative in '-s', and compares it with an inscription *marings* on a buckle from Szabadbattyán. But the scabbard inscription is too incomplete for any firm conclusions to be drawn from it.

An inscription from early Anglo-Saxon times on a scabbard-mount from the cemetery at Chessell Down, Isle of Wight,[1] is one of considerable interest. The runes were lightly cut on the back of the silver mouthpiece of the scabbard (Fig. 103), and were only discovered when the sword was cleaned at the British Museum.[2] They are now clearly visible, and can be read as follows:

ᚫ ᚳ ᚩ : ᛋ ᛟ ᚱ ᛁ

æ c o : s œ r i

[1] Hillier, p. 35.

[2] Stephens, iii, 1884, pp. 459–60.

Stephens[1] could do nothing convincing with this. Hempl[2] suggested that the fourth rune was the 'w' rune, ᚹ, left open at the
top, and read the inscription as *æco wœri*, 'for self-defence'. This is
an ingenious suggestion, as he takes *æco* as an earlier form of the
OE adjective *æce* (corresponding to OHG *eichi*) 'one's own', and
wœri as 'defence', based on OE *wer*, 'dam'. But it is highly specula-
tive, being based not only on an emendation of the runes but also
on two hypothetical forms not found in existing records. Nor is it
easy to see how this burial could be as late as A.D. 800, his suggested
dating of the runes.

A more satisfactory reading is that put forward by R. W. V.
Elliott.[3] He takes the symbols as they stand, and interprets them to
read 'Increase to pain'. This depends on taking *ǣco* as a Kentish
variant of WS *ēaca*, 'increase',[4] and *sœri* as dative-instrumental[5]
(Kentish form) of OE *sorg*, 'sorrow', 'pain'. He gives parallels to
these forms to support his interpretation, and on the basis of these
would date the inscription to the late seventh or early eighth
century. This interpretation takes the inscription as a descriptive
name of the sword itself, which might be translated 'Augmenter of
Pain'. It may be compared with descriptive names of this type in
Old Norse, for example, *Angrvaðill*, 'Rushing Harm', and *Fjǫrs-
váfnir*, 'Life's Sleep-bringer'.[6] The date of the Chessell Down
cemetery is usually taken on archaeological grounds to be earlier
than the late seventh century, while Behmer (p. 179) puts the
sword to which the scabbard belongs into his type VII class, but
hesitates to date the hilt later than the end of the sixth century;

[1] Stephens, iii, 1884, p. 460.

[2] G. Hempl, 'The Runic Inscription on the Isle of Wight Sword', *P.M.L.A.*
xviii, 1903, p. 95.

[3] *Runes. An Introduction*, Manchester University Press, 1959, pp. 79–80,
fig. 10. I am most grateful to Mr. Elliott for letting me have information about
this before publication.

[4] *Ǣc* is frequently found for WS *ēac* when Kentish forms appear in the ninth
century. It seems reasonable, therefore, to assume that this and other early
ninth-century forms have earlier roots in Kentish, and that an eighth-century
smoothing process has taken place, similar to that in certain Anglian dialects.
On this see A. Campbell, *Old English Grammar*, 1959, paras. 226, 312, 314.

[5] It could also be the genitive; the dative, however, is found in two other
runic inscriptions: *rodi* on the Ruthwell Cross and *cæstri* on the Franks Casket.
See Campbell, op. cit., para. 587. [6] Falk, pp. 47, 49.

there is no reason, however, why a scabbard inscription should not be of a later date than the hilt.

A scabbard inscription of the Viking Age was found on a metal mount (Fig. 104) taken from the earth of a Norman motte at Greenmount in Ireland, which may have formed part of an earlier tumulus.[1] The runes run as follows:

ᛏᛆᛑᛘᚾᛆᛚ '᛫ᛋᚾᛚ᛫᛬᛭ᛋᛑᚠᛆᚦ ᛆ '᛫ᛑᛁᚱᚦ ᛁᛏᛆ

T o m n a l / s e l s h o f o þ / a / s o e r þ / e t a

Macalister[2] interprets this as 'Domhnall Sealshead owns this sword', doubling the sixth rune 'l' and the 'þ' which occurs fourth from the end. The runes are on a strip of bronze which is presumed to have come from a sword scabbard, and Macalister dates the runes and the rather poor ornament on the other side to the early twelfth century.

A runic inscription which has been tentatively dated to the twelfth century was cut on a leather scabbard (Fig. 105) of which the remains are in the museum at Lund.[3] A long inscription has been cut on the leather with a knife, but unfortunately the damaged condition of the scabbard and the difficulty of making out surviving runes make interpretation impossible.

One good and obvious reason to inscribe runes on a sword scabbard (as on a hilt) is to record the ownership of the weapon. There are obvious advantages in choosing a scabbard for this purpose, as a sword would probably pass through many hands; it would not, however, be difficult to give it a new scabbard or to add an inscribed mount to the existing one. Unhappily, too few inscriptions survive for firm conclusions to be drawn, but there is a possibility that runes were sometimes used in this way to give the name of the sword itself. Marstrander suggested that this was the intention of the inscriber of the runes on the Thorsbjerg mount, and others have thought that the sword's name is included in the Vimose inscription. A possible example from Anglo-Saxon times is

[1] Stephens, iii, 1884, pp. 307 f.; *V.A.* iii, p. 85; vi, p. 181.

[2] R. A. S. Macalister, *P.R.I.A.* xxxiii, 1916, p. 495; see also Marstrander, *Norsk Tidsskrift for Sprogvidenskap,* iv, 1930, p. 385.

[3] Jacobsen and Moltke, p. 586; Atlas, nos. 1055–6.

the Chessell Down scabbard-mount, and the allusion on the Gilton pommel to the naming of the sword, according to Elliott's interpretation, may be borne in mind.

Any evidence which archaeology can offer concerning the naming of weapons is of great value, for while a large number of sword-names—nearly two hundred in all—have been preserved in literary sources, these are relatively late. The earliest are those given in Anglo-Saxon heroic poetry, written down about the tenth century, although composed considerably earlier than this. Most of the names, however, come from Old Norse sources, and many of them from manuscripts of the thirteenth century or later. It is thus hard to determine how far the naming of swords was a literary convention only, and how far it existed as a practice among Anglo-Saxons and Vikings of an earlier period. But a possible source for such a practice may be seen in the group of runic inscriptions from spearheads collected and discussed by Krause (pp. 441 f.) which date back to the Migration period. He gives one from Suszyczno, Kreis Kowel, probably of third-century date, which reads *tilarids*, and which he interprets as 'Assailant'. Another spearhead from Dahmsdorf has the inscription *renja*, which seems to have a similar meaning: 'One rushing to attack'. These two may be Gothic in origin. A third from Øvre Stabu, Norway, found in a grave dated by Shetelig to the second century (which makes it the earliest runic inscription so far found in Scandinavia), reads *raunijaR*, which Krause interprets as 'One that puts to the test' (cf. ON *reynir*). Another from Mos has the inscription *gaois*, which he interprets as 'The whirring one'.

Such inscriptions would make very suitable names for weapons, emphasizing their power to do harm, to test the opponent, and to make a shrill noise rushing through the air. If the interpretations quoted above are correct, they show imaginative personification of the weapon at an early date. It may be that the runes are intended as a spell, to strengthen and perpetuate the desirable qualities to which they refer; as to this, opinions differ. It seems fairly reasonable to assume that the use of runes on weapons continued without a break in north-western Europe into Viking times, although few examples have survived. The inscription on the scabbard from Chessell Down may indeed be an example of an imaginative weapon-name in the same tradition as the inscriptions on the early spears. It is to be noted that this inscription was on the back of the scabbard, and could easily have been missed had the mount not been carefully examined and cleaned; while an inscription of this type cut on the perishable parts of the scabbard would vanish without trace. Inscriptions which survive are cut lightly on the metal, never laboriously engraved or inlaid as if added by the craftsman who made the hilt or scabbard-mount. The importance of single runic symbols or monograms must also be borne in mind, in view of the sign on an Anglo-Saxon spearhead from Holborough, revealed by radiography.[1] This, unlike the inscriptions on hilts and scabbards, was inlaid in the iron spearhead. Possibly other symbols of this kind were placed on sword-pommels in the sixth century (p. 67 above). Fragmentary though our evidence is for the use of runes on swords, it is sufficient to offer a valuable commentary on what we learn of weapon runes from the literary evidence.

[1] Evison, *A.C.* lxx, 1956, pp. 97 f.

II

THE TELLING OF THE SWORD

Then the sword related whatsoever had been done by it,
for it was the custom of swords at this time when unsheathed to set forth the deeds that had been done by
them. And therefore swords are entitled to the tribute of
cleansing them after they have been unsheathed.

The Battle of Mag Tured

I. HISTORICAL RECORDS

THE earliest descriptions of the Teutonic sword in literature
come from outsiders, who looked with interest on the already
famed barbarian weapon. In the fifth century Sidonius, the
cultured man of the world who finally became Bishop of Clermont,
watched the Germanic chiefs who attended the marriage of the
Prince Sigismer to a Burgundian princess:[1]

Green mantles they had with crimson borders; baldrics supported
swords hung from their shoulders, and pressed on sides covered with
cloaks of skin secured by brooches. No small part of their adornment
consisted of their arms: in their hands they grasped barbed spears and
missile axes; their left sides were guarded by shields, which flashed
with tawny golden bosses and snowy silver borders.

This picture, seen through the eyes of one not likely to be over-
impressed by the splendours of uneducated barbarians, reads like
a foretaste of later descriptions in northern literature: the poet's
picture in *Hrafnsmál*[2] (11) of the warriors of Harald Fairhair, for
instance, in ninth-century Norway:

By their array and their gold rings, it may be seen that they are asso-
ciates of the king. They possess scarlet cloaks with splendid borders,

---

[1] *Letters of Sidonius*, iv. 20 (Dalton's translation, Oxford, 1915, p. 35).

[2] Attributed to Thorbjorn *Hornklofi*, one of the poets at Harald's court;
edited Kershaw, pp. 76 f. I have used the familiar translation 'Fairhair' for
Hárfagr here and elsewhere: 'fair' in this case does not mean 'blond', but 'hand-
some', but alternatives like 'comely-haired' strike an awkward note.

swords bound with silver, coats of ring mail, gilded baldrics and graven helmets and rings upon their arms; such things has Harald bestowed upon them.

Another echo comes in the heroic picture of the wooers of Gudrun in the Eddic poem *Guðrúnarkviða II*[1] (v. 21):

In they came like kings, a company of long-bearded men. They wore red cloaks, short mailcoats and towering helmets, and were girt with swords (*skálmar*).[2]

Such, then, is the setting of the swords; from the fifth century onwards we may picture them worn by Teutonic warriors, in rich scabbards, against a background of shining weapons and armour, gold ornaments, and bright colours. As to the appearance and quality of the finest blades, here again we have a witness from the close of the fifth century who has left us what proves to be an amazingly exact commentary on the evidence of archaeology. It is a passage to which reference has often been made, but I make no apology for quoting it in full, since the only easily accessible English translation by Hodgkin[3] is neither complete nor wholly accurate. The letter is one written by Cassiodorus, secretary to Theodoric the Great; it expresses the thanks of the king for a gift of several swords which had been sent to him by another Teutonic ruler, described in the best manuscript readings as *Rex Varnorum*, King of the Warni.[4] The letter runs as follows:[5]

Cum piceis timbribus et pueros gentili candore relucentes, spathas nobis etiam arma desecantes vestra fraternitas destinavit, ferro magis

---

[1] References to Edda poems are based on G. Neckel's edition of the *Poetic Edda*.

[2] *Skálm* is probably an archaic word for sword; Falk (p. 14) derives it from early weapons of wood, and suggests it was used for short, one-edged blades. It is often the weapon said to be carried by giants and supernatural creatures in Old Norse literature. In poetry, however, it is used as a term for 'sword', as here, apparently without special significance.

[3] T. Hodgkin, *Letters of Cassiodorus*, 1886, p. 264.

[4] Hodgkin (following Migne, *Patrologia Latina*, lxix, p. 645) assumes that the recipient of the letter is Thrasamund, King of the Vandals, and this assumption has been repeated by many others. The reading *Wandalorum* is, however, not a reliable one; I am grateful to Mr. J. M. Wallace-Hadrill for information on this point.

[5] *Epistulae Theod. Variae*, ed. Mommsen (*Monumenta Germaniae Historica*, Auct. Antiq. XII. v. 1, p. 143).

quam auri pretio ditiores. Splendet illic claritas expolita, ut intuentium facies fideli puritate restituant, quarum margines in acutum tali aequalitate descendunt, ut non limis compositae, sed igneis fornacibus credantur effusae. Harum media pulchris alveis excavata quibusdam videntur crispari posse vermiculis: ubi tanta varietatis umbra conludit, ut intextum magis credas variis coloribus lucidum metallum. Hoc vestra cotis diligenter emundat, hoc vester splendidissimus pulvis ita industriose detergit, ut speculum quoddam virorum faciat ferream lucem. Qui ideo patriae vestrae natura largiente concessus est, ut huius rei opinionem vobis faceret singularem; enses, qui pulchritudine sui putentur esse Vulcani, qui tanta elegantia fabrilia visus est excolere, ut quod eius manibus formabatur, non opus mortalium, sed crederetur esse divinum.

Together with musical instruments of pitch-black wood[1] and boys with the fair skin of their race, Your Fraternity has chosen for us swords capable even of cutting through armour, which I prize more for their iron than for the gold upon them. So resplendent is their polished clarity that they reflect with faithful distinctness the faces of those who look upon them. So evenly do their edges run down to a point that they might be thought not shaped by files but moulded by the furnace. The central part of their blades, cunningly hollowed out, appears to be grained with tiny snakes, and here such varied shadows play that you would believe the shining metal to be interwoven with many colours. This metal is ground down by your grindstone and vigorously burnished by your shining dust[2] until its steely light becomes a mirror for men; this dust is granted you by the natural bounty of your land, so that its possession may bestow singular renown upon you. Such swords by their beauty might be deemed the work of Vulcan, who is said to have perfected his craft with such art that what was formed by his hands was believed to have been wrought by power not mortal but divine.

It would seem that this is a strikingly careful and accurate description of pattern-welded blades. The central part of the blade is said to be 'cunningly hollowed out', and Anstee found in making a pattern-welded blade that it was necessary to form a fuller or

---

[1] *piceis timbribus* is obscure. Professor J. M. C. Toynbee, to whom I am greatly indebted for help with the translation of this letter, suggests 'musical instruments as black as pitch'. A deliberate rhetorical contrast to the white skins of the boys is of course intended. Unfortunately we have no clue to the nature of the instruments. Mr. Anstee has suggested to me some kind of harp or lyre of bog oak.

[2] 'Shining sand' would be a reasonable translation, but some kind of polishing agent seems implied.

hollow running down the centre, where the patterns are found.[1]
These hollows were probably roughed out first with a cold chisel
(*excavata*) and then ground on a rotating grindstone (*hoc vestra
cotis diligenter emundat*). 'Grained with little snakes' is a fair description of the curving patterns on such a blade,[2] and the shadows
mentioned are accounted for by the hollow in the blade and the
high degree of polish, while the varying composition and texture
of the steel, brought up by polishing, would give the effect of
changing colours. The filing of the edges is said to be so exact and
regular that it might be thought that the weapon had been moulded
in one piece in the furnace; perhaps Cassiodorus had in mind
weapons cast in bronze when making this comparison, since such
seems the implication of *effusae*, conveying the idea of pouring out
molten metal. Since seeing the blade made by John Anstee,
however, I have realized that the central panel suggests molten
metal poured out in a narrow stream, as the light catches the
polished surface; and this may have suggested the term to the
writer.

Reference is made to the cutting power of these blades, capable
even of cutting through armour, and to their great beauty; these
are points confirmed by work done on pattern-welded swords in
museum laboratories (p. 29 above). Also the reference to the work
of grindstone and file confirms what we know of the making of the
blade. Of special interest is the mention of the substance described
as *splendidissimus pulvis*, since it may furnish a clue to the region
where the swords were made. The letter implies that it was of
great value for the burnishing of the blades, and that it was obtained in the kingdom of the Warni. On account of the 'bounty of
their land' in providing this *pulvis*, they have won fame, it appears,
as producers of fine swords. Presumably we must look for some
special abrasive material likely to be used in the finishing process,
and of this more will be said below. Finally the reference to Vulcan
recalls at once the traditional Germanic attribution of fine weapons

[1] See Appendix A.
[2] Cf. definition of *vermiculated* in the *Oxford English Dictionary*: 'inlaid in
a pattern resembling the sinuous movement of serpents'. This would serve as
a good description of a pattern-welded blade with curving patterns.

to a supernatural smith, the Weland of Anglo-Saxon tradition. If such a figure were known to the Germans of Cassiodorus' time, it is possible that he was making this reference deliberately, to form a graceful compliment which would be likely to be appreciated by the recipient.

Could we be sure of the region inhabited by the Warni at this date, then we might reach some conclusion as to the origin of certain pattern-welded swords in the early sixth century. Unfortunately their movements are somewhat obscure, and the tribe seems to have split up into at least two sections at an early date. Procopius in one place states that they were separated from the Franks by the Rhine, but elsewhere he declares that they were not far from the Langobards, at that time east of the Elbe.[1] A little before 507 Cassiodorus sent another letter to the King of the Warni, appealing to him, together with the kings of the Heruli and the Thuringi, to join Theodoric in an alliance against Clovis, so that the latter would be prevented from attacking the Visigoths; this again would imply that they were in or around the Elbe basin. Schulz gives reasons for placing the Warni farther up the Elbe in the fifth and sixth centuries, in *Werinerfeld*, which is situated east of the river and south-west of Berlin.[2] Possibly they also inhabited land farther north, nearer the coast, since according to Procopius they were attacked from the sea on one occasion. But it would certainly seem that we have good reason to believe on the evidence of this letter that pattern-welded swords were being made at this time some way east of the Rhineland, and that they were rare and desirable weapons.

It is possible that the *pulvis* referred to might be kieselguhr, a form of diatomaceous silica which is used in mildly abrasive polishing compounds, and which would be suitable for burnishing sword-blades.[3] It appears that there were not many places where

---

[1] Procopius, iv. 20 and iii. 35. See H. M. Chadwick, *Origin of the English Nation*, Cambridge, 1924, pp. 102 f., and L. Schmidt, *Geschichte der deutschen Stämme*, 1934 (2nd edn.), pp. 127 f.

[2] W. Schulz, *Vor- und Frühgeschichte Mitteldeutschlands*, Halle, 1939, pp. 199 f. I am most grateful to Professor K. Richter (Amt f. Bodenforschung, Hanover) for this reference and for other information.

[3] A suggestion made to me by John Anstee.

kieselguhr could be found near the surface and easily obtained in early times, but it was certainly worked very early in one area near the Elbe, and according to Schulz this was part of the region inhabited by the Warni in the fifth century.[1] While this is no more than a suggestion it may give a clue to an area which in the time of Cassiodorus was renowned for its swords with patterned blades.

Unfortunately, detailed descriptions of swords are all too rare. In the eighth century Offa, King of Mercia, is known to have received a sword of 'Avar workmanship' from the Emperor Charles the Great,[2] but no details about it have survived. A sword which had belonged to Offa was still in the possession of the royal family of Wessex two hundred years later, for it is mentioned in the eleventh-century will of Prince Æthelstan, and is bequeathed to his brother Edmund;[3] Akerman (p. 50) suggested that this might be the Hunnish sword which Offa had owned, but there seems no way to determine this.

In the ninth century King Æthelwulf of Wessex sent his youngest son Alfred, then a child of four, on a visit to Rome to receive the blessing of Pope Leo IV. The Pope invested the little prince with the honorary dignity of a Roman consul, and the ceremony included the girding on of a sword; it is interesting to note that the compiler of the *Anglo-Saxon Chronicle* regarded this as a ceremony of ordination to kingship.[4] Two years later, in 855, Alfred paid a second visit to Rome with his father, and they carried with them rich gifts of Saxon workmanship which Æthelwulf presented to the new Pope, Benedict III. The gifts are recorded in the contemporary Life of Pope Benedict, 855–8, in the *Liber Pontificalis*,[5] where they are described as a crown, two basins, and two statuettes, all of pure gold; four hanging disks of gilded silver, supports for sanctuary lights; a silk dalmatic, with gold stripes,

---

[1] Professor Richter (*supra*) tells me that kieselguhr was worked on Lüneburg Heath, west of Berlin.

[2] Epistolae Karolini Aevi (ed. Dümmler, *Monumenta Germaniae Historica*, Berlin, 1895), ii. 100, p. 146.

[3] Whitelock, p. 58.

[4] *A.S. Chronicle*, 853. See Plummer's note on this passage, and W. H. Stevenson's notes on Asser's *Life of Alfred*, Oxford, 1904, pp. 183 f.

[5] *Liber Pontificalis*, ed. Duchesne, ii. 148.

and an alb of silk embroidered with gold; two rich curtains; and a splendid sword. This last item is recorded in the list as *spata cum auro purissimo ligata*, 'a sword bound with purest gold', and this would suggest a long, two-edged sword with a gold-ornamented hilt, perhaps with a grip covered with gold wire. It is interesting to find a description of a sword of Anglo-Saxon workmanship in so early a source, since it was in the ninth century that the rich hilts of gold, silver, and niello work, with panels of ornament in the Trewhiddle style, were made in Anglo-Saxon England (p. 69 above).

This gift of a rich sword to the Pope may throw light on another reference to a royal sword found in William of Malmesbury, who is believed to have taken his information from a tenth-century Latin poem about King Æthelstan, the grandson of Alfred the Great.[1] William tells us[2] that Alfred recognized Æthelstan as his heir when he was still a boy, and realizing that he would be great, invested his grandson 'unusually early' (*praemature*) as a warrior (*miles*), giving him

. . . a scarlet cloak, a jewelled belt, and a Saxon sword with a golden scabbard.

The exact significance of *Saxon* here is not easy to establish,[3] but in the light of the earlier account it seems likely that this, like the gifts taken to the Pope, was of native 'Saxon' workmanship, and was a sword with a rich hilt made by craftsmen of Wessex. There seems little doubt that in so honouring a small boy, at about the same age as Alfred when he visited Rome, the old king was remembering the ceremony of his youth.[4]

Another sword was mentioned by William of Malmesbury in connexion with King Æthelstan, and this he stated was still in the royal treasury at the time when he was writing (*c.* 1125). This was said to have been found miraculously within the scabbard of

---

[1] See L. H. Loomis, 'The Athelstan Gift Story', *P.M.L.A.* lxvii, 1952, p. 521.
[2] *De Gestis Regum Anglorum*, i. 133 (ed. W. Stubbs, Rolls Series, 1887–9), *E.H.D.* i, p. 279.
[3] There is the possibility of a mistranslation of OE *seax*, as has been suggested in the case of the phrase *ensis teutonicus* in Saxo (p. 170 below), but this seems on the whole unlikely.   [4] See Stevenson, op. cit., pp. 184–5.

King Æthelstan when he dropped his own weapon as he rushed out in the dark to lead his men against a surprise attack. William adds:[1]

> It can, as they say, be engraved on one side, but never inlaid with gold or silver.

This implies that the reornamenting of a sword in the armoury was a familiar practice.

The third sword associated with the same king is one said to be among the gifts sent to Æthelstan by the Frankish Duke Hugh when he requested the hand of the king's daughter:[2]

> ... the sword of Constantine the Great, on which the name of the original possessor could be read in letters of gold, and on whose hilt (*in capulo*) above thick plates of gold an iron nail might be seen fixed, one of the four which the Jewish faction prepared for the crucifixion of the body of Our Lord.

L. H. Loomis has given her reasons for accepting this as taken from a good and reliable source, not much later than Æthelstan's own time.[3] In another study of the holy relics associated with the king[4] she points out that there is some corroboration from independent sources for the existence of this sword together with a lance (also mentioned by William). A sword and a lance are included in an eleventh-century list of relics at Exeter Cathedral, and are mentioned together: 'De mulcrone et de lancea unde latus Domini fuit apertum'. This entry comes in the Leofric Missal, given by Leofric, first Bishop of Exeter, to the new cathedral in the eleventh century. A second and apparently independent list of gifts was inserted in the tenth-century copy of the Gospels, another gift from the bishop, and this too mentions the relics. It seems probable then that the sword which William mentioned was given by the king to Exeter to be preserved as a relic there.

This is the earliest reference to a holy relic fixed in the hilt, presumably in the pommel (p. 183 below). The reference to an

---

[1] *De Gestis Regum Anglorum*, i. 131, *E.H.D.* i, p. 278.

[2] Op. cit. i. 135, *E.H.D.* i, p. 282.

[3] L. H. Loomis, op. cit., 'The Athelstan Gift Story'.

[4] 'The Holy Relics of Charlemagne and King Athelstan', *Speculum*, xxv, 1950, pp. 437 f.

inscription in gold on either the blade or the hilt is in accordance with archaeological evidence, for such inscriptions were frequent in the ninth and tenth centuries, and a number of references in Latin writers of the Carolingian period, collected by Gessler, confirm this.[1] There is, however, some divergence between literary and archaeological evidence here. There seems to be no reference to a smith's name recorded on a sword at this period, while on surviving swords there is no example of a sword-blade marked with the owner's name, though the name of the owner in runes may be given on the Thames scramasax, and there is the name of both owner and maker on the Sittingbourne knife.[2] Possibly the name of Constantine was inscribed on the hilt, and if so there are several known archaeological parallels, among them the hilt from Exeter bearing the inscription *Leofric me fec* (p. 80 above), which it is tempting to associate with the first Bishop of Exeter already mentioned. Gessler quotes an instance from Ademar's History (ii. 41) of a sword which bore the inscription *Hainricus imperator cesar augustus*, and gives other references to swords and spears called after saints. Some of these rather vague allusions, however, may have been influenced by later medieval customs.

Gregory of Tours[3] mentions another gift of a sword to a king, one presented to the Frankish King Gunthram by the sons of Waddo who hoped to bribe him:

... They appeared before the royal presence, offering as a gift a great baldric enriched with gold and gems, together with a marvellous sword, the hilt of which was covered with gold and stones of Spain.

Dalton, commenting on this passage, suggests that the reference is to a sword of Visigothic workmanship, and Böhner (1, p. 234) quotes it as a possible allusion to a sword with a hilt of gold and cloisonné work like the sword of Childeric, since he believes Visigothic influence may have been important for this type of jewelled hilt (p. 65 above).

Some information about the sword and scabbard of Charles the Great is given in the *Lives* of the Emperor by Ekkehard and the

---

[1] Gessler, pp. 133 f.   [2] See pp. 43 and 80 above.
[3] Gregory of Tours, *Historia Francorum*, x. 21 (Dalton's translation).

unnamed Monk of St. Gall. Ekkehard (xxiii) tells us that Charles always wore a sword 'with hilt and belt of either gold or silver'. Occasionally, too, he wore a jewelled sword, but this was only at great festivals or when he received ambassadors from foreign nations. From the Monk of St. Gall we learn some interesting facts about his scabbard. He says of the sword:[1]

. . . quae spata primum vagina, secundo corio qualicumque, tertio linteamine candidissimo cera lucidissima corroborato ita cingebatur, ut per medium cruciculis eminentibus ad peremptionem gentilium duraretur.

This sword was enclosed first by a scabbard, secondly by leather of some kind, thirdly by pure white linen rendered stronger by clearest wax and strengthened towards the centre by little raised crosses for the destruction of the heathen.

Leather and cloth to protect the sword have already been indicated by the archaeological evidence from scabbards buried in graves. The waxing of the linen would be an obvious advantage; there is evidence that linen was used as an outer covering for the scabbard from Lavoye (p. 89 above). The 'raised crosses' are also known on scabbards from Anglo-Saxon graves; that from Sutton Hoo had raised buttons ornamented with a cross, and that from Brighthampton had a small raised cross in silver; another silver cross adorned a scabbard from a sixth-century grave at Bülach, and two crosses were found on the rich scabbard from the Seine, probably seventh century in date (p. 92 above). The description of the sword of Charles the Great confirms the suggestion that these were worn as deliberate Christian symbols for the protection of the sword within the scabbard.

The Monk of St. Gall also recounts how the Emperor Louis tested the swords sent by the 'King of the Northmen' to him as a mark of their submission.[2] Louis ordered the swords to be brought to him 'that he might make trial of them', and the ambassadors nervously proffered them, holding them by the point, since they had evidently been taken from their scabbards. Then the Emperor . . . took one by the hilt and tried to bend the tip of the blade right back

---

[1] *Monachi Sangallensis de Gestis Karoli Imperatoris* (ed. Pertz, Monumenta Germ. Hist., Scriptores ii), i. 36, p. 747.

[2] Ibid. ii. 28, p. 761; trans. Grant, *Early Lives of Charlemagne*, 1905, p. 152.

to the base; but the blade snapped between his hands which were stronger than the iron itself. Then one of the envoys drew his own sword from its sheath and offered it like a servant to the Emperor's service, saying 'I think you will find this sword as flexible and strong as your all-conquering right hand could desire.' Then the Emperor . . . bent it like a vine-twig from the extreme point back to the hilt, and then let it gradually straighten itself out again.

This passage implies that swords were made in Scandinavia at this time, but that these were not of very good quality. A similar method of testing the flexibility of a blade will be found elsewhere (p. 164 below).

From the ninth century onwards there are some most interesting references to swords used by the Vikings in the east of Europe. These seem to have been regarded with great interest by their Eastern neighbours, and a number of Arab writers refer to them, some with considerable knowledge of their quality and appearance. The best known of these writers is the Arab traveller Ibn Fadlan.[1] He comments on the value placed on the sword by the Rus, the Scandinavian settlers on the Volga whom he visited, and tells how every man presents a sword to his son at birth: further, that every man among them carries axe, knife, and sword, and is never seen without his weapons. He goes on to describe the swords as slender, with a furrow running down the centre of the blade,[2] and of Frankish[3] workmanship.[4]

Other descriptions of European swords used by these settlers

[1] The account of the Rus can be found translated into German by C. M. Frähn, *Ibn-Foszlan und anderer arabische Berichte*, 1825, p. 5. A more recent translation, however, based on additional manuscripts is that by A. Zeki Validi Togan, *Ibn Fadlan's Reisebericht (Abhandlungen für die Kunde des Morgenlandes*, Deutsche Morgenländische Gesellschaft, xxiv. 3, 1939), pp. 80 f., 82 f.

[2] Zeki Validi points out that Frahn's translation of *muṣattaba* as *wellenförmig* is misleading; he translates *mit Blutrinnen versehen*.

[3] *Farang* is, according to Validi, to be understood as 'Frankish', and not as 'European', as in Frahn and previous translators.

[4] An obscure passage follows, which some scholars have interpreted as referring to these swords, describing them as marked with trees and figures from point to hilt. It would be tempting to take this as a reference to the patterns on the blades of pattern-welded weapons, which were known among the Rus, as we shall see from the evidence of other Arab writers. Validi, however, rejects this on grammatical grounds, and takes the description to refer to tattooing on the arms of the men from the finger-nails to the neck (ibid., p. 83, note 1).

have been discussed by Zeki Validi in an article of some importance for our subject, since it gives information not easily accessible
to those who have no knowledge of Arabic.[1] He deals in particular
with the writings of two Arab scholars concerning swords, al-
Kindi, a historian living in Bagdad in the ninth century, and
al-Biruni, a philosopher and mathematician, who was living in
Ghasna (modern Afghanistan) in the eleventh century. Both were
extremely versatile thinkers and writers, taking a wide field of
knowledge for their province. They knew a good deal about
damascened swords, and they were aware that the Europeans also
had patterned blades, which were made in a different manner.

Al-Kindi describes two kinds of swords, which he calls Frankish
and *Slimanish*. The Frankish swords are evidently those with
pattern-welded blades, for he describes them as swords which
taper to a rounded point, and with a broad channel running down
the centre of the blade, which resembles a stream of water. The
patterns on these blades he compares to those of *Tabaristan* cloth,
or to rings of chain-mail. They are of whitish colour, and when
the treatment of the blade is completed, he says, the background
is red. Some of the blades are marked in the upper part with half-
moons or crosses of bronze or gold, and sometimes a nail of gold
or bronze is hammered into a hole in the blade. This account of
the patterns and marked blades corresponds to what we know of
swords of this period, though it is not usual, in the swords which
have survived, to find blades bearing smiths' marks which are also
pattern-welded. Al-Kindi seems also to know a good deal about
the construction of the European swords. He tells us that both the
Frankish and *Slimanish* swords are of soft iron and steel, forged
together, the patterns being formed by this mixing of metals. The
Slimanish swords have smaller decoration, and the blades are
brighter. The points are less rounded, and the blades taper less
than the Frankish ones, while the hilts are not so richly decorated,
and the swords are not marked with crosses.

[1] A. Zeki Validi, 'Die Schwerter der Germanen, nach arabischen Berichten
des 9–11. Jahrhunderts', *Zeitschrift der Deutschen Morgenländischen Gesellschaft*,
xc (N.F. xv), 1936, pp. 19 f.

Al-Biruni has also a good deal of information about the actual making of swords, in which he takes great interest. He praises the wonderful blades made by the Indian smiths, with their rich damascened patterns. Then he tells us that the Rus also make swords; since they find that oriental steel cannot withstand the cold of their winters, they have found another way to produce patterns, by making a central panel of two sorts of iron, soft iron and steely iron, welding the two together. It is specially noteworthy, he says, that these patterns are deliberately made by the smiths, in contrast to the Eastern ones (which appear automatically, as it were, during the manufacturing process).

Other Arab writers refer to the swords of the Rus. It would appear, according to Zeki Validi, that these are identical with the *Slimanish* swords described by al-Kindi, since another writer, Ibn-Rustah, calls the swords of the Rus *slimaniya*. The anonymous author of the eleventh-century Persian Geography, *Hudud al-Alem*, also refers to these swords. He knows of the blades used by one branch of the Rus, which, he says, may be bent double, and when loosed they go back to their original position. The same description is given by Nasireddin al-Tusi of the swords of the Franks, which he says are of soft iron, but so sharp that iron cannot resist their stroke, and so pliable that they can be bent like paper.

Here we have knowledgeable and detailed descriptions of pattern-welded blades in the Viking Age, written by men who lived at a time when these weapons were still in use. Certainly the Rus must have possessed such swords, and al-Biruni believed that they themselves manufactured them, doing so in imitation of the Eastern patterned blades produced by different methods. It is possible, as Zeki Validi points out, that by the term *Rus* the Arab writers meant the Scandinavians in general, and not merely the Swedish colonists on the Volga.

It is doubtful how far we can accept the statement of al-Biruni that the smiths of the Rus copied Eastern damascened swords. We know that the pattern-welding technique had been known in western Europe for centuries and was practised there until well

into the Viking Age. Possibly knowledge of Eastern swords gave
a new impetus to the production of patterned blades, and led to new
workshops for their production in eastern Europe. It seems unlikely that the Rus found they could not produce damascened steel
because of their climate; but it is quite possible that they failed to
do so because their furnaces were not sufficiently good, or that
they obtained wootz, and were unable to work it successfully;
Belaiev[1] notes that if this steel was hardened by the usual European
methods of quenching and tempering it would break like glass.
There seems little doubt that a large number of pattern-welded
swords were possessed by the Rus, and if some workshop in the
Baltic region produced them it would account for the distinction
made between their swords and those of the Franks. Liestøl (p. 95)
is disposed to interpret al-Biruni's account as based on Scandinavian manufacture of pattern-welded swords, but of this we have no
convincing archaeological evidence up to now.

These Arab writers show the great impression which Teutonic
swords made upon the Moslem peoples. Another Arab, Ibn
Miskawaih, who died about A.D. 1043, records that after the
Scandinavian settlers in one district lost their power,

. . . the Moslems disturbed their graves and brought out a number of
swords, which are in great demand to this day for their sharpness and
excellence.[2]

This last piece of independent evidence as early as the eleventh
century is of considerable interest in view of what the literary
sources have to tell us about the taking of swords from the graves
of dead men. It bears testimony also to the great value set on a
good sword, and to the high reputation which was possessed
by European smiths at this time. There was clearly great demand
for their work, and the Arab writer, Nasireddin al-Tusi,[3] states
that since the export of Frankish swords to the East was forbidden, they could only be smuggled out, and the cost of one of

[1] Belaiev, p. 418.
[2] *Eclipse of the Abbasid Caliphate*, trans. D. S. Margoliouth, p. 140. Cf. N. K.
Chadwick, *Beginnings of Russian History*, p. 53.
[3] Zeki Validi, p. 29.

them was a thousand Egyptian dinar. This is all the more interesting in view of the fact that by this time fine damascened swords from Persia must have been obtainable. The fact that al-Biruni, living in Afghanistan, had such extensive knowledge of their work is in itself no mean testimony to the renown of the Western smiths.

2. ANGLO-SAXON WILLS

A number of Anglo-Saxon wills of the tenth and eleventh centuries are of special interest because of the references which they contain to swords left as bequests to kinsmen or followers, or to the dead man's overlord. These swords are not usually described in much detail, but some interesting terms are used.

A very rich sword is mentioned by a certain Ælfgar in a will of about 958:[1]

> I gave my lord the sword which King Edmund gave to me, of 120 mancuses of gold, and on the belt (on þam fetelse) four pounds of silver.

With this may be compared a sword worth 100 mancuses left by King Alfred to Æthelred, Earl of Mercia,[2] and two smaller weapons, each described as a *handseax* (dagger or knife), mentioned in the wills of Ælfheah[3] and Brihtric,[4] valued in each case at 80 mancuses. The high value of these weapons—120 mancuses is the value of 120 oxen—gives some idea of their richness. This may have depended on the amount of gold on the hilt and the richness of the various accoutrements as well as on the quality of the blade. Indeed, in the case of Ælfheah's *seax* it is specifically stated that the value is based on that of the *lecg*, an obscure word which occurs in another will also, where two *lecga* and one *lecg* are mentioned as separate bequests with no reference to sword or dagger.[5] Bosworth and Toller suggest 'cross-bar', and give 'gift', 'legacy', as alternatives. Whitelock (p. 123) suggests 'sheath', deriving the word from *lecgan*, 'to place'. This is reasonable on etymological grounds, and while a sword scabbard is not very likely to form a separate bequest, since each sword had its own scabbard into which it would fit exactly, a small sheath to hold a knife, either attached to a belt or made to fit on to one, is a possibility. The usual word for a sword scabbard is *sceað*.[1]

It seems doubtful, however, whether the term *fetels* which occurs in the will of Ælfgar quoted above could have a similar meaning. Whitelock suggests 'scabbard', based on OE *fætels*, used for a vessel, sack, bag, or pouch, as when Judith, for instance, carries the head of the dead Holofernes *on þæm fætelse*.[2] But the Dictionary also gives *fetels* with the meaning 'girdle', 'belt', and this is Keller's interpretation of the term in the wills, and of the alternative form *fetel* which is also found;[3] it is confirmed by the cognates *vezzel* (MHG) and *fezzil* (OHG), which have the meaning of a strap for fastening a sword, and ON *fetill*, used of the strap of a sword or shield or leather bag (see p. 188 below). Keller suggests a derivation from a Germ. root **fat*, 'to hold together'.

Keller's list of references shows that the Old English term *fetels/fetel* is found chiefly in wills, one exception being the puzzling compound *fetelhilt* from *Beowulf* (p. 142 below). A derivative *fetelsian* is found, which Keller translates 'to belt'; this occurs in the will of Brihtric and Ælfswith, where two swords are described as *gefetelsode*, and again in the will of Ælfgar.[4] To specify them here as 'in scabbards' would be stating the obvious, and the expression *swyrdes mid fetele* in Æthelric's will[5] seems likely to mean a sword with belt or fittings. The belt or baldric was a valuable part of a man's equipment, and reference may be made to the belt with plates of silver from a Kentish grave (p. 67 above), to the jewelled belt received by young Æthelstan with a sword in a golden scabbard (p. 110 above), and again to a passage from a Latin will of 867 quoted by Gessler in which a golden-hilted sword is mentioned along with a rich baldric (*baltheum unum de auro et gemmis*).[6] *Fetels* need not necessarily mean a belt round the waist, for it might be

[1] Keller derives this from Germ. **skaiðo, *skaiðjo*, 'to separate', based on the idea of the scabbard as a wall separating sword from body and shutting it off from the outside world (p. 183).   [2] *Judith* 127.

[3] Keller, pp. 163–4. See also A. E. H. Swaen, 'Contributions to A.S. Lexicography', *Neophilologus*, xxviii, 1943, p. 42. He too favours the interpretation 'belt'.   [4] Whitelock, pp. 26, 6.   [5] Ibid., p. 42.

[6] *Hist. eccles. Cisoniensis*, Testamentum Evrardi comitis, p. 87; Gessler, p. 136.

a strap worn over the shoulder; the term might also be used for the various complicated straps fastening the scabbard to the belt. The interpretation of the term as 'sword-belt' or 'sword-strap' is borne out by the fact that in all the references collected by Keller the term occurs in association with a sword. In the will of Prince Æthelstan[1] a *fetels* of gold is mentioned as having been made by a certain Wulfric, but with it is bequeathed a sword with a silver hilt made by the same man, who may have been a craftsman in the prince's service.

Wulfric's silver-hilted sword is one of several which were in the prince's possession. There was a 'silver-hilted sword which belonged to Ulfketel' and another with a silver hilt not further specified. Hilts with elaborate decoration in silver and niello were popular in the tenth century, and a number of Anglo-Saxon examples have survived. Among Æthelstan's swords was also one with a *pytted* hilt, suggesting a pattern raised in relief, as on a number of metal-covered hilts of the Viking Age (see Fig. 80), though another possibility mentioned by Jessup[2] is that it was a hilt from which the jewels had fallen. Æthelstan also left a *brand* to his brother Edmund, which Whitelock interprets as a blade without a hilt.[3] Another term in this will describing a sword 'which belonged to Withar' is *malswurd*.

The term *mal/mæl* is often found in poetry in connexion with swords, and will be discussed in detail later; for the moment it is enough to say that it implies ornamental patterns of some kind. Æthelstan's sword may have had a pattern-welded blade[4] or one with an inlaid pattern. Yet another sword bequeathed by the prince to the seneschal Ælfmær is described as *scearde*, and the same term is used of a second *malswurd* left to Ælfnoth, the prince's 'sword-sharpener'. The meaning of *scearde* is probably 'notched',

---

[1] Whitelock, pp. 56 f.

[2] Jessup, p. 140, note.

[3] The use of the term in Old Norse bears this out. See Cleasby and Vigfusson's Dictionary, *brandr* II.

[4] Whitelock points out (p. 172) that this sword was to go to the chaplain, who according to law would not be permitted to wear it. If the *malswurd* in this case was an old pattern-welded weapon, it might be valued as an heirloom rather than intended for practical use.

and Ælfnoth would obviously be a suitable person to inherit a notched blade, since he could render it serviceable again. Finally, there is a reference in the same will to a sword 'on which the hand is marked'. This is of special interest in view of the blade in the British Museum marked with stamps resembling those used for coins. The device known as the 'Hand of God' is familiar in late Anglo-Saxon sculpture and painting, and was used on coins of tenth-century Northumbria as well as on those of King Æthelred II, and a stamp of this kind may well have been used to mark this particular sword (p. 49 above).

3. SOME SWORD TERMS IN *BEOWULF*

Information supplied by contemporary observers like Cassiodorus, the Arab writers, and the makers of wills, of whom we can feel reasonably sure that they saw the actual weapons which they described, is all too rare. However, in Anglo-Saxon heroic poetry we have a rich store of information in the form of descriptions of particular swords and also in elaborate epithets or terms which refer to swords. There is so much material here that it merits separate study, and parallels from Old Norse literature will only be included when they have close reference to the point under discussion. There are many references to swords in *Beowulf*, the only long heroic poem surviving in full from the Anglo-Saxon period. If we set beside this the allusions to swords in fragments of other poems which have come down to us, we are left with the impression that the subject was a popular one with poets and their audiences. It soon becomes apparent that the epithets used of the sword are by no means colourless and conventional.

Before going on to descriptions of individual swords, it is proposed to consider a number of terms found in the poetry, the various compounds formed with *mæl* which have reference to swords. A large number are found in *Beowulf* and a few outside it: *brodenmæl*, in *Beowulf* 1616; *brogdenmæl* in *Beowulf* 1667 and *Elene* 759; *grægmæl* in *Beowulf* 2682; *sceadenmæl* in *Beowulf* 1939; *wundenmæl* in *Beowulf* 1531; and *hringmæl*, in *Beowulf* 1521, 1564, 2037. The term *malswurd* has been noted in an Anglo-Saxon will, apparently denoting a recognized type of weapon, while the Old Norse term *mál* used in connexion with weapons needs also to be considered.

In Bosworth and Toller's Dictionary the meaning of *mæl* is given as 'measure', 'mark', 'sign', 'occasion'. It appears to be in the sense of 'mark' (cf. OHG *mal*, 'mark') that it is applied to swords, implying that the sword in question bears marks of some kind. In *Andreas*, lines 1132–4, the plural form is used, and the sword is described as 'coloured [? or gleaming] with marks of fire' (*fyrmælum fag*). The marks on the blade produced in the forge by the pattern-welding process are what immediately spring to the mind, and this is what I believe was in the minds of the poets when these compounds were employed. This impression is strengthened by a detailed examination of each term.

The term *broden/brogdenmæl* is used in *Beowulf* of one sword only, that found by Beowulf in Grendel's underwater hall. It does not seem likely that the term refers to an ornamented hilt,[1] since in each case it is specifically used of the part which melts and burns away after being plunged into the baleful blood of the monsters, and this part is the blade:

> sweord ær gemælt,   forbarn brodenmæl (1616).
> The sword had melted away,   the *brodenmæl* had burned up.

> þa þæt hildebil forbarn brogdenmæl (1667).
> Then that battlesword, the *brogdenmæl*, burned away.

Brogden is the passive participle of the verb *bregdan*, meaning 'to move to and fro', 'to draw (a sword)', 'to change', 'to weave'. The participle is also used with *beaduserca*, 'war-shirt', and *byrne*, 'mail-coat', as in *beran brogdne beadusercean (Beow.* 2755). In both cases the meaning would seem to be 'to weave', so that *bro(g)denmæl* may be translated 'blade with woven patterns'. There is no doubt that the patterns on a sword-blade do suggest rich woven material; this was appreciated by one of the Arab writers when he compared pattern-welded blades to woven patterns in cloth (p. 115 above).

[1] On this question see Hatto, p. 146, who takes the view that the patterns in question are on the hilt, and Cramp, p. 65, who disagrees.

This is true not only of the herring-bone type of pattern, which has an obvious resemblance to one type of weaving, but also of the curving patterns, which catch the light like designs on silk or brocade. An Old Norse parallel of a more gruesome kind is found in the terms *bloðvarp, iðvarp*, which Falk (p. 20) interprets as an image of a piece of weaving in which the lines of the sword-blade form the woof while the warp is composed of the blood or vitals of the slain. The image becomes more vivid, however, if the sword is pictured as the implement used by the weaver to part the threads that form the woof (in the way in which a weaving 'sword' is employed) and so forces its way through the blood or vitals of the upright warrior.

In the passage from the Anglo-Saxon poem *Elene*, the *brogden-mæl* is found as the equivalent of *heardecg*, a compound which here as elsewhere appears to denote the sword-blade: 'the hard-edged one'. Again the emphasis is certainly on the blade, for Cyne-wulf is describing the fiery sword which guarded Eden and kept Adam and Eve outside:[1]

> Heardecg cwacaþ,
> beofaþ brogdenmæl   ond bleom wrixleð
> grapum gryrefæst.

The hard-edged blade with its woven patterns quivers and trembles; grasped with terrible sureness, it flashes into changing hues.

Here the quivering blade of the angel's fiery sword, whose changing lights and shades and twisting patterns take on a new and terrible aliveness from the palpitating heat, is contrasted with the ominous sureness of the angel's unfaltering hand. It is, as so often in Cynewulf's poetry, the familiar heroic imagery given a new and surprising twist in the Christian context in which he employs it.

Sceadenmæl has generally been taken to refer to a patterned blade. Klaeber translated it as 'ornamented with distinctive and branching patterns, i.e. damascened sword', and he bases this on a comment by Sievers.[2] The latter in a note published in 1910

---

[1] *Elene*, 756 f.
[2] E. Sievers, 'Gegenbemerkungen zum *Beowulf*', *Beiträge zur Geschichte der deutschen Sprache und Literatur*, ed. W. Braune, xxxvi, 1910, p. 429.

connects *sceadenmæl* with OHG *kaskeidanaz werh*, which appears as a gloss for *opere plumario* in Exodus xxvi. 1; *opus plumarium* has clearly the meaning here of brocade work, embroidery, &c. An Old English gloss for the similar term *ars plumaria* is *wyndecræft*, 'the art of weaving', and this brings us back to the compound *wundenmæl*. Sievers has thus laid a direct trail from *sceadenmæl* to *wundenmæl*, both being probably based on patterns resembling those on rich cloth or embroidery, as is *brogdenmæl*. The contexts in which these terms are found do not throw much light on their meaning. *Sceadenmæl* is used of the sword which executes the victims of the wicked Queen Thryth: 'the *sceadenmæl* was allowed to settle the matter'. Here one can only say that such an interpretation as 'blade with branching patterns' is not unsuitable here. *Wundenmæl* is used of Hrunting, the sword taken down by Beowulf beneath the lake, and there is additional indication, as we shall see, that this sword is one with a pattern-welded blade. The words *stið* and *stylecg*, 'hard' and 'steely-edged', are in agreement with *wundenmæl*, and these certainly apply to the blade and not the hilt.

Grægmæl is an expression used of Beowulf's own sword Nægling. It is not described very fully, but may well have been pattern-welded, since it is said to be an ancient heirloom.[1] The term is often translated 'grey-coloured' in the glossaries, but as Hatto (p. 152, note) points out, the Germanic word refers less to colour than to a metallic, silvery gleam, like the pale light of dawn or hoar-frost. It would thus be very fitting to describe the gleaming silvery patterns on the blade.

There is also the expression *scirmæled* found in *Judith* 230; here it is used generally of the swords which the warriors drew from their scabbards to use in battle. This could be translated 'bright patterned blades', but the context is too indefinite to help to establish the interpretation.

So far these expressions can be fitted without much difficulty into a group based on the image of a patterned sword, but with the last compound to be examined, *hringmæl*, some complications arise.

---

[1] Possibly the description 'marvellous wave-sword' may have applied to Nægling; see p. 144 below.

On the basis of the other interpretations it is tempting to take it as
the sword with curved or circling patterns on the blade, like eddies
in water, and this is suggested by Klaeber in his glossary. In
Genesis 99 there is a reference to *hringmæled sweord* occurring like
scirmæled in *Judith* in an account of warriors going into battle,
which is not inconsistent with such an image. In *Beowulf* it is used
first in line 1521 of Hrunting, where the sword is said to chant a
'greedy song of battle' upon the head of Grendel's mother, and
secondly in line 1564 of the sword found under the lake, when
Beowulf is said to draw the *hringmæl* from its scabbard. But there
is also the possibility that *hring* refers to an actual ring on the hilt,
as suggested by the use of the term in the account of the Heatho-
bard episode in *Beowulf*. The sword of the prince of the Heathobards, who had been slain in battle, was tactlessly carried into their
palace, worn by the son of the Danish warrior who had slain him.
This aroused the fury of the Heathobards afresh, and reopened the
old feud. The sword is described (2036 f.) as the

. . . treasure and ancient heirloom of the Heathobards, hard and ring-
patterned (*hringmæl*).

In line 2041, however, it is hard to escape the implication that the
old warrior is looking at an actual ring on the hilt, for the words *ðe
beah gesyhð*, 'who looks on the ring', are used. The sword must
have been in the scabbard, so that only the hilt would be visible,
and patterns on the blade could not be seen. The word *beah*, 'ring',
must refer to the sword, since in this passage it is equivalent to
mece and *iren*: these can only mean 'sword' and could not be used
of a gold or silver ring worn as an ornament. In this case, then, the
use of the term *beah* seems to indicate that the memory of the ring
on the hilt and its significance has survived in this story.

There is no other clear reference to a ring on a sword in Anglo-
Saxon literature known to me, although the term *hringmæl* is found
in other contexts. Two direct references to a ring-hilted sword in
Old Norse poetry are brief and tell us little, except that the ring
was not forgotten, and it was the mark of a sword held in high
repute (p. 180 below). Since the ringed hilts belong to a much

earlier period than that in which the poems were written down (p. 73 above), this is hardly surprising. It seems on the whole improbable that the term *hringmæl* was inspired by a ring-hilted sword. It may be no more than a coincidence (perhaps an artistic one intended by the poet) that *hringmæl* and *beah* occur in the same passage describing the ancient sword of the Heathobards. While both *hring* and *beah* are terms which may be used for a finger-ring, neck-ring, or armlet, *hring* can also be used to describe something which winds or curves. The serpent-like dragon in *Beowulf* is called *hringboga* (2561), while the curving prow of a ship may be *hringedstefna* (32, 1897), as well as *wundenstefna*.[1] This last term seems a satisfactory one without searching for any reference to ring-ornament on ships to explain it. Both the Oseberg and the Gokstad ships, especially the latter with the beautiful slow curve of its prow, so impressive in the hall at Oslo when seen from below, could fairly be described as vessels with curving prows. The term *hring* could be applied similarly to the curving, winding patterns on a sword-blade.

In Old Norse the term *mál* is found, and this also is used with reference to weapons. The sword Gram is described in the *Edda* as *mækir málfár*; this occurs in a passage in the poem *Sigurðarkviða hin skamma* (4), where Sigurd is said to lay the sword between himself and Brynhild:

The hero from the South laid a naked sword, *mækir málfár*, between them.

Mækir is a familiar poetic word for sword (cf. OE *mece*). It seems likely that *málfár* here signifies a patterned sword, for *fár* belongs to the contracted verb *fá*, used with the meaning 'inscribe' (e.g. runes), 'colour', 'dye'. Finnur Jónsson translates 'inscribed with

---

[1] Admittedly the interpretation of *hringedstefna* is difficult to establish with certainty. Bosworth and Toller suggest the spiral or ring-shaped ornament sometimes found on a prow, as on the Oseberg ship, where the prow itself also ended in a spiral; or alternatively one furnished with a ring or hook. Hatto (p. 146) takes it as based on patterns on a prow. But the description in *Beowulf* of the 'ring-prowed ship' refers to a sea-going vessel, like the Gokstad ship. The Oseberg ship with its carved patterns was an elaborately ornamented vessel for use round the coast only, not intended for sea voyages.

patterns' in his edition of the *Edda* for the same term *málfár* when it is used of the sword of the god Freyr in *Skírnismál* (*Fǫr Skírnis*) 23. Skirnir carries this sword with him to the Underworld when he goes to woo the maiden Gerd for Freyr, and he threatens her with the sword:

Dost thou see this sword, maiden, the slender, patterned (*málfár*) sword which I bear in my hand?

Largely on the basis of this passage, it has been assumed that the patterns (*mál*) inscribed on the sword are runes. But there is no real ground for this, and the patterns may well be those in the blade, both here and in the passage referring to Gram. To anyone familiar with the swords of the Anglo-Saxon and Viking periods, the words 'patterned sword' would call up an immediate picture of a pattern-welded blade.

In the Icelandic Sagas certain weapons are said to have *mál* upon them. In *Víga-Glúms Saga* (viii) the spear given by Vigfuss to the hero Glum is described first as a 'gold inlaid spear' (*spjót gullrekit*). When Sigmund has been stabbed with this spear, men notice 'blood in the patterns' (*í málum*). This suggests that the patterns in question were on the spearhead, and decorated spearheads with gold inlay and also with panels of pattern-welding are known (p. 31 above). In *Gísla Saga* (xi) the spear Grasida was made from a broken sword of the same name which had had a particularly fine blade:

Now the broken Grasida was taken, and Thorgrim made a spear from it, and it was ready by the evening. There were patterns (*mál*) on it.

The same spear is later referred to in *Sturlunga Saga*[1] as a *málaspjótr*, for it appears that it was still in use at the battle of Orlygstad (21 August 1238) about 270 years later:

Sturla defended himself with the spear called Grasida nimbly and well; it was a great *malaspjótr*, old and apt to bend. He thrust so vigorously with this that men fell before him continually; but the spear bent and he straightened it out under his feet several times.

---

[1] *Sturlunga Saga*, iv. 26; vi. 17.

It seems very likely in this case that the patterns are those of pattern-welding rather than inlay, the patterns from the centre of the blade of the original sword being visible on the spearhead.

Other uses of the word *mál* in connexion with weapons point definitely to patterns on the blade of the sword and not the hilt. This is clear from verse 1 of *Krákumál*:

> stakk á storðar lykkju
> stáli bjartra mála

I stuck the steel of bright patterns into the coil of the forest (serpent).

Similarly the term *stálamál* in *Hattarlykill* 33b, as well as *mála-jarn* used of Svafrlami's sword in the first chapter of *Hervarar Saga*, connect the patterns with steel (*stál*) and iron (*jarn*) respectively, that is with the blade. In none of these cases is there any suggestion that the patterns may be runes, although Svafrlami's sword like that of Freyr is used to command supernatural beings. The general inference is that while *mál* may be used to refer to patterns of any type on the blade (perhaps to inlaid patterns in gold or silver) it is likely in the majority of cases to be inspired by the welded patterns running down a blade's centre. In no case is there any suggestion that the patterns are on the hilt.

Returning, then, to the use of *mæl* in compound words referring to swords in Anglo-Saxon poetry, it seems reasonable to assume that they arise out of a poetic tradition based on familiarity with pattern-welded swords. By the eleventh century the term *malswurd* (used in the Wills) might be employed for blades with inscriptions or smiths' marks or inlaid patterns, but the possibility that it is used of a pattern-welded sword must be borne in mind. We know now from archaeological evidence how frequent such decoration was among the finest swords made in western Europe over several centuries, and it is hardly surprising to find a term for these memorable and beautiful patterns surviving in the heroic poetry. There is nothing slavishly conventional in these poetic compounds, though lazy translations like 'inlaid' or 'ornamented' swords may give an impression of dullness which the poet does not deserve. The emphasis, as we have seen, is on different aspects of the appearance of the blade, its grey and gleaming surface, its patterns like rich materials woven or embroidered, its winding, branching, curving shapes. As we go on to descriptions of individual swords in Anglo-Saxon poetry, we shall find that the picture is filled in in greater detail.

4. THE SWORD HRUNTING

If we turn to *Beowulf* for descriptions of individual swords, that lent by Unferth to the hero for his adventure in Grendel's mere must have pride of place, for we are told much concerning it:

This sword which Hrothgar's *thyle* lent to Beowulf in his need was by no means the least of powerful allies. That *hæftmece* bore the name of Hrunting; it was among the foremost of ancient treasures. Its edged blade was of iron, gleaming with twigs of venom (*atertanum fah*) and hardened by blood of battle; never yet had it failed any man who grasped it in his hands in warfare. (1455 f.)

. . . He swung his sword of battle with a mighty rush, and his hand did not fail in the stroke, for the sword with curving patterns (*hringmæl*) sang a greedy song of battle upon her head. Then the visitor found that the battle-ray had no power to pierce and do mortal injury. . . . (1519 f.)

. . . The enraged warrior flung down the sword with twisted patterns (*wundenmæl*) and bound ornaments (*wrættum gebunden*), hard and steely-edged, so that it lay upon the earth. (1531 f.)

But although it proved of little use against Grendel's monster mother, Hrunting went back honourably to its owner with words of praise. At its last appearance it was hailed by Beowulf as 'a good friend in battle and mighty in warfare', and we are told that 'he spoke no word of blame against the weapon's edge' (1811 f.). So he gave the sword back to Unferth, and it goes out of the story.

In these descriptions of Hrunting, two of the terms already discussed, *hringmæl* and *wundenmæl*, are used, suggesting that Hrunting was a sword with a pattern-welded blade. The phrase *ecg wæs iren, atertanum fah* seems to confirm this. *Ecg* is in general used not for the edge of the sword only, but for the whole blade,[1] and in this case the reference is to the iron of which the blade is made.

[1] Hatto, p. 148.

Atertanum fah recalls the expression quoted earlier from *Andreas*: *fyrmælum fag*. The adjective *fah/fag* is often used for objects which are bright and shining, such as a boar-helmet (*Beow.* 305) or the gold-adorned roof of Heorot (*Beow.* 927). It can also have the meaning 'dyed', 'stained', 'variegated', as is shown by examples given by Bosworth and Toller. A man slain by the sword is *blodfag*, 'stained with blood', while the waters of Beowulf's lake are *waldreore fag*, 'stained with slaughter-blood', and the phrase *super basiliscum* in Psalm 91 is translated *ofer fagum wyrme*, the adjective here referring to the variegated colours of a serpent.[1] The adjective then can refer either to brightness or to colour.

The expression *atertanum fah* seems to mean 'gleaming (or dyed, coloured) with venom-twigs'. As to the nature of these twigs, many suggestions have been made, and it is surely possible for the poet here to have deliberately created a phrase which is rich in association, implying more than one image at the same time, as do the more effective compound words and descriptive phrases elsewhere in Anglo-Saxon poetry. 'Twigs of venom' is an excellent kenning for serpents, and would be an imaginative way of describing the serpentine patterns on the blade which caught the fancy of Cassiodorus long before; these are both bright and gleaming, and in a sense they may be said to colour the blade. It is possible that the other adjective *fah*, 'hostile', was also at the back of the poet's mind. Moreover, the sword patterns may be said to resemble twigs as well as serpents, and both resemblances have been stressed in the sword kennings in Old Norse skaldic verse. There is a further possibility that *tan* was a technical term known in the smithy; this is suggested by the Old Norse term *eggteinn*, which Falk (p. 17) takes as the metal strip forming the cutting edge welded on to the core, and connects with the Anglo-Saxon phrase. The process of building up a pattern-welded blade is now

---

[1] Similarly Mittner (*Wurd*, Bibliotheca Germanica vi, 1955, p. 152) notes the association between *fag* and the colours of a serpent's skin, and quotes a parallel from *Heliand* 1878: *nadra thiu feha*. Cf. also an example given in the Supplement to Bosworth and Toller's Dictionary: *Hwites heowes and eac missenlices on hringwisan fag* given as a translation for *candido versi colore in modum ranarum*, where colour and not brightness must be intended.

known to have consisted of twisting strips of metal which, as Anstee's work has shown, bear a striking resemblance to twigs. This may partly explain the remarkable popularity of the word *teinn* in Old Norse sword names and kennings.

In addition, there is the association of weapons with poison, found constantly in heroic literature. Some commentators have seized on this as the whole meaning of the term, and sought to explain it by the use of poisonous acids in the process of manufacturing the blade. It is true that acids were almost certainly employed during the etching process, and these would be of great importance in bringing out the patterns (p. 28 above). This may give additional meaning to the phrase 'twigs of venom'. We may compare a description of Sigurd's sword Gram from a poem in the *Edda, Brot af Sigurðarkviðu* (19):

> eldi vóru eggiar útan gǫrvar
> en eitrdropum innan fáðar.
>
> The edges without were wrought by fire
> and dyed within with poison drops.

Here the outside edges, hardened in the furnace by fire, are distinguished from the central panel, which is imagined as being dyed or patterned (*fá*, 'inscribe', 'paint') with drops of poison, an idea no doubt based on the etching process, which emphasized the colours and patterns in the centre of the blade. This description, however, is not as many-sided in its implication as the vivid, economical Anglo-Saxon phrase, which is like a good metaphysical conceit in its effectiveness.

It is most unlikely that references of this kind are to be understood as referring to poisoned weapons. It is true that we find phrases like *ættryne ord*, 'poisoned sword-point', in *Maldon* (47), or descriptions like this of a sword in the *Fornaldar Sǫgur*:[1]

. . . as smooth as a mirror, and it seemed to him that poison dripped from its edges,

but such poison is more likely to have resided in the deadly keenness of the blade than to have been added to the sword before battle. It would have been unnecessary and extremely difficult, as

[1] *Hálfdanar Saga Eysteinssonar*, xvi.

Genzmer has pointed out,[1] to put poison on a sword. There are references in the literature to poisoned weapons used for assassination; the ruthless Frankish Queen Fredegund twice used knives 'cut with deep channels and smeared with poison' to remove inconvenient fellow rulers,[2] and we have an incident described in Bede's History,[3] when Cwichelm, King of the West Saxons in the seventh century, sent a messenger with a 'two-edged weapon dipped in poison' to murder King Edwin of Northumbria. But these are the methods of assassins and not of warriors. There are two adequate reasons for associating weapons and poison: one is the use of acid in the making of the sword, and the second is the continual association in poetry between swords and serpents. There is satisfaction to be gained from the image of a gleaming, silvery sword darting like a snake to leave its deadly imprint on the victim, while the serpentine patterns which formed the hall-mark of a good blade in early times strengthen this connexion.

Hrunting is also said to be 'hardened in the blood of battle'. This idea occurs again in *Njáls Saga* (cxxx), a work which is full of heroic cadences. Flosi asks concerning Kari, the only survivor of the burning, 'Had he any weapons?' The reply is:

He had the sword *Fjǫrsvafnir*, and one edge of it was blue with fire; and Bardi and I said that it must have become soft; but he replied that he was going to harden it in the blood of the sons of Sigfuss or the others who did the burning.

Since quenching played so essential a part in the making of a blade (p. 18 above), there is no need for fantastic explanations like that of dragon's blood suggested by Neckel[4] to elucidate an image of this kind. Blood here is pictured as the liquid used to harden iron. Indeed, if the effect of dragon's blood were similar to that of the Grendel pair, the result would be to melt the blade rather than to harden it, and neither in Scandinavian nor Germanic legend does Sigurd or Siegfried harden his sword in the blood of Fafnir.

---

[1] F. Genzmer, 'Haben die Germanen vergiftete Schwerter verwendet?' *Arkiv f. Nordisk Filologi*, lxviii, 1953, pp. 179 f.

[2] Gregory of Tours, *Historia Francorum*, iv. 36, p. 160; viii. 29, p. 349.

[3] *Historia Ecclesiastica*, ii. 9.

[4] G. Neckel, 'Sigmunds Drachenkampf', *Edda*, xiii, 1920, pp. 208 f.

But the image as it stands is quite consistent: swords in battle are constantly likened to fire, flaming torches, and the like, and Hrunting itself is called *beadoleoma*, 'Battle Light', so that the idea of the blood shed by the sword acting as the liquid which cools the glowing metal is a natural and satisfying one for those knowing the basic methods of working iron.

Possibly the term *scurheard* applied to Hrunting may refer to the same process of quenching in blood. It is found again in *Beowulf* 1032 f., where the helmet given to the hero is said to be so hard that

> . . . the terrible survivor of the files[1] (*fela laf*), showerhard, could not injure it.

Here the 'survivor of the files' is the sword, and this is a good description, in view of the important part played by the file in the blade's making. The hardening showers seem unlikely to be those of battle, for though a shield might be imagined 'hardened' by showers of spears or arrows, the image can scarcely fit a sword, which is the weapon of attack. Probably the reference is to some process connected with the sword's making. Bosworth and Toller suggest that *scur* here and in *Judith* 79 is based on the idea of a shower of blows falling on the anvil; this is a possible interpretation, since the effect known as 'work-hardening' is familiar to metallurgists. If the reference is to quenching, it suggests some process by which the liquid is poured on to the heated metal instead of the metal being plunged into the static liquid. Rapid cooling by means of a stream of falling water would in fact be extremely effective. The phrase is found in *Judith*, and the term *scurheard* occurs in *Andreas* 1132, so that it is not confined to *Beowulf*.[2]

The exact type of ornament described as *wrættum gebunden* is

---

[1] Klaeber emends the plural verb (*meahton*) to *meahte*, to agree with the singular *laf*. See his note (pp. 169–70) and also Chambers's sensible comment on p. 53 of his edition of *Beowulf*.

[2] This seems to count against Wrenn's suggestion (p. 81) that *scurheard* is in imitation of *regnheard*, *regn* having originally had the significance of magic or divine power, but later having been confused with *regn*, 'rain'. It seems unlikely that the term would be used more than once in so unintelligent a way.

hard to determine with certainty. *Wræt* is a word which could be used of any curious or beautiful piece of craftsmanship, and is twice employed to describe treasures in the dragon's hoard (*Beow.* 2771, 3060). It might refer to something fastened to a sword (like the pyramid strap-ends) or to twisted ornament (metal wires, niello work, or inlaid patterns) on the hilt. Apparently a contrast with *wundenmæl*, the twisted patterns on the blade, is intended, and therefore one would expect it to refer to the ornamented hilt, so that a picture of the whole weapon is given.

Perhaps the most difficult of all the terms used of Hrunting is that which introduces it, *hæftmece*, a compound word not found elsewhere. Bosworth and Toller and Klaeber translate 'hilted sword', and *hæft* (neuter) is used elsewhere in both poetry and prose with the meaning 'hilt', 'handle'. There is, however, nothing in the description of Hrunting in the poem to suggest any special characteristic of the hilt which would explain such a term. The word *hæft* (masc.) is also found in *Beowulf* and elsewhere with the meanings (1) 'captive', (2) 'fetter'.[1] This might imply that the sword was fastened down in its scabbard in some way, but again the text gives no support for this. Complications are increased by the appearance of a similar term, *heptisax*, also unknown elsewhere, in the story in *Grettis Saga* of the hero's adventure with underwater giants which closely resembles the story of Beowulf's descent into the lake (p. 139 below). But while in *Beowulf* the word *hæftmece* is used of the weapon which Beowulf takes down into the lake with him, *heptisax* in *Grettis Saga* is the name given in a verse to the weapon used by the giant against Grettir. The saga-teller goes to some pains to explain that this is a knife fastened to a wooden shaft, as though it were an unfamiliar term needing some explanation. Such a weapon was undoubtedly known in Merovingian and Carolingian times,[2] and Keller (p. 45) identifies it with the *stafsweord* which appears in Old English glossaries; it was a kind of pike, a suitable weapon for a giant to use. The similarity of the two

---

[1] See Keller, p. 168, and cf. examples given in Bosworth and Toller.

[2] M. Jähns, *Handbuch einer Geschichte des Kriegswesens*, Leipzig, 1880, p. 260, Taf. xxviii.

terms suggests that a partially remembered sword with special characteristics featured in an earlier form of the story than that recorded in *Beowulf*, and this influenced the Icelandic version, but it is by no means a wholly satisfactory solution to the problem. To consider it further, however, it is necessary to consider the other sword which appears in the story, the one taken from the giants' dwelling under the lake.

5. THE SWORD FROM THE LAKE

This sword is described in lines 1557 f. as

... an all-conquering (*sigeeadig*) weapon, ancient sword of giants (*eald-sweord eotenisc*), doughty of edge, a treasure among warriors. It was a most excellent weapon, but too huge for any other man to bear to the battle-play: a trusty and splendid sword, wrought by giants (*giganta geweorc*). The champion of the Scyldings grasped the *fetelhilt* and drew the sword with its curving patterns (*hringmæl*).

Later, after Beowulf has slain Grendel's mother and cut off the dead Grendel's head with the sword, we learn more concerning it (1605 f.):

The sword, weapon of battle (*wigbil*), began to dwindle away into war-icicles (*hildegicelum*) on account of the blood shed in the fight (*heaðoswate*). This was a marvel indeed, for it melted away wholly, even as the ice does when the Father who governs times and seasons loosens the bonds of the frost and slackens the chains on the waters. . . . The blade with its interwoven patterns (*brodenmæl*) had now melted and burned away, such was the heat of the blood and so poisonous was that strange being who had perished there.

Thus it was that this blade perished beneath the lake, and it was the hilt only which Beowulf carried up to Hrothgar. There is some further description of the sword: Beowulf describes it to the king as a 'beautiful and ancient sword of mighty size' (1662–3) and alludes again to the *brogdenmæl* 'which burned away as the blood gushed forth' (1667). As Hrothgar examines the hilt we learn more about this part of the weapon in lines 1694 f. First it bears an inscription:

Likewise also on the *scennum* of bright gold, in runic symbols rightly inscribed, was set down and recorded for whom that sword, noblest of blades, was first made, with its hilt of twisted work and its serpentine colours (*wyrmfah*).

The adjective *wyrmfah* at the end of this description must refer either to the blade or to the sword as a whole, and not to the hilt as some have thought, since the words *sweord* and *iren* are used in agreement with it, and these can hardly apply to the hilt alone.[1] The contrast between the twisted work of the hilt and the twisted patterns of the blade would be fully in accordance with the style of the poem, and is likely to be deliberate, *wyrmfah* referring to the blade with its rich colours and serpentine patterns.[2] There is little doubt that this sword is to be regarded as pattern-welded; it is twice called *brogdenmæl* and once *hringmæl*, emphasizing the curving patterns of the blade.

The runic inscription on the hilt apparently gave the name of the first owner, the man (or giant?) for whom the sword was made. Whether the poet knew the name, or whether he was merely assuming that runes on a hilt were likely to give the owner's name, is a question to which we are not likely to find an answer. The phrase *hwam þæt sweord geworht* is slightly ambiguous, but it seems improbable that *hwam* is a dative of agency, referring to the maker, 'by whom the sword was made'; this is not in accordance with Old English usage. The Gilton hilt may be quoted as an example of one on which runes appear to give the owner's name, but in no known case except a late Scandinavian one (p. 80 above) is the name of the maker recorded in this manner.

This hilt is called *wreopenhilt*, and such a term is not difficult to explain from what we know of hilt decoration. It might be used of any of the hilts with interlacing ornament dating from the sixth century and later: the Cumberland hilt with tiny twists of gold filigree, the Windsor pommel with exquisite and delicate inter-

---

[1] See Cramp, p. 67, who takes *wyrmfah* to refer to the blade.

[2] The closest known parallel to *wyrmfah* is the phrase *wyrmlicum fah* in the poem known as *The Wanderer* in the Exeter Book. It seems to describe serpentine or interlacing ornament on a ruin of some kind, part of a hall or possibly a memorial cross or pillar, and a hall with such ornament is shown on the Egil panel of the Franks Casket. But the phrase may refer to colour (see Kershaw, p. 167).

lacing, or the Abingdon and other hilts of later date with panels of interlacing alternating with figures and leafwork: Rosemary Cramp (p. 67) gives the Snartemo hilt from Norway as a possible example. Girvan's choice of one particular hilt of about A.D. 800 (from Fetter Lane)[1] hardly seems justifiable in this case. We cannot even assume as he does that 'the cross-pieces were occupied by the runes', as these could have been either on the pommel or on metal rings at the end of the grip. Girvan claims that *wyrmfah* should apply to a hilt of the Fetter Lane type, but we have seen that this is more likely to refer to the patterned blade. It is in fact scarcely possible to base any sound argument for dating the sword on this description, detailed although it may appear to be, for up to this point it remains general rather than particular.

A passage of description occurring earlier in the poem, however, gives a different picture, suggesting that there were special traditions about the appearance of this hilt, and that the poet had met with a detailed account of it in some earlier version of the story. It is clear incidentally from lines 1687 f. that the hilt could not have resembled the one from Fetter Lane. It appears that not only the name in runes but something else was inscribed upon the hilt:

Hrothgar . . . examined the hilt, the ancient heirloom on which was recorded the beginning of ancient strife (? *on ðæm wæs* or *writen fyrnge-winnes*), when the flood of the surging ocean destroyed the race of giants, and they endured terrible sufferings. That race was estranged from the eternal Lord, and the Ruler gave them final requital by the rushing waters.

The hilt, then, in addition to the runic inscription bore some recognizable allusion to the destruction of giants by water. It has been suggested that this is a picture,[2] but no hilt of which we have knowledge from the Anglo-Saxon or Viking period has any pictorial representation of this kind. We know that runes could be inscribed on a hilt, but nothing of the complexity suggested here—resembling the lines on the Franks Casket describing the stranded whale—has yet been found. The term *writen*, however, suggests an inscription of some kind, perhaps on the *scennum* of gold, like

[1] R. Girvan, *Beowulf and the Seventh Century*, London, 1935, p. 39.
[2] For example, Cramp, p. 66.

the runes said to give the owner's name. The exact significance of the term *scennum* is not determined, and it does not occur else-where. Falk (p. 30) relates it to Germ. **skanjo*, MHG *schene* (mem-brane), and to ON *skán* (crust). On these grounds he interprets it as the 'skin' or covering fitted over the tang of a sword. On early hilts the tang was probably covered by wood with an outer cover-ing of skin or leather, and the name for this may have been transferred to the metal plates which formed more elaborate hilt-coverings in later times. Similar terms are found in Old Norse, for *véttrim* (covering strip?) and *valbǫst* (foreign covering?) were used for some part of the sword-hilt, and we are told in an Edda poem that runes could be placed on these (p. 179 below). It is usually assumed that the metal rings often placed at either end of the grip are to be identified with the *véttrim*, and on a Norwegian sword of the late Viking Age it was on these that runes were placed (p. 80 above). Unfortunately it does not seem possible to get any nearer to the precise meaning of *scennum* or the place which these plates of gold occupied on the hilt.

But even if we assume that the allusion to the destruction of giants is in the form of an inscription, the nature of such an inscrip-tion is puzzling in the extreme. Klaeber and others[1] have assumed that the reference is to the wicked destroyed in the Biblical Flood, and that the giants are those referred to in Genesis vi. 4. Such a subject, however, is a very peculiar one to be selected. As far as I know, it was never chosen to be illustrated in early manuscripts or on stone carvings, and it does not appear as a recognized subject of Christian illustration. A twelfth-century manuscript in the British Museum, Nero C. IV, shows some of the dead floating in the water beside the Ark, but there is no suggestion that these are giants. Nor does it seem a likely subject to be described by an inscription on a sword. It is true that there was evidently a non-Christian tradition in the north of giants drowned in a flood, referred to by Snorri[2] when he expands the story of the creation

---

[1] See notes in Klaeber's *Beowulf*, and O. F. Emerson, 'Legends of Cain espe-cially in Old and Middle English', *P.M.L.A.* xxi, 1906, pp. 892 f.

[2] *Gylfaginning*, viii.

of the world given in *Vafþrúðnismál* 35, and states that the race of frost-giants was drowned in the blood of Ymir, and only one escaped. But we have no evidence for such a legend being known to the Anglo-Saxons, and it is not very likely that it could have inspired the passage in *Beowulf*.

But a possible explanation of this strange choice of subject is suggested by the version of the story of the hero's descent into the water in *Grettis Saga*, lxvi. Here again an inscription is carved in runes, and the strange term *Heptisax* is used of a weapon,[1] recalling *hæftmece* in *Beowulf*. Heptisax is the name given to the weapon of the giant whom Grettir meets under water, and Grettir, using his famous short sword, cuts the giant's weapon from its shaft. Later on Grettir leaves in the church a bag of bones he has brought up from the giant's cave and with it a piece of wood carved in runes, a *rúnakefli*, on which two verses are said to have been 'excellently carved'. Could this possibly be the wooden shaft of Heptisax? The saga does not tell us what became of the giant's weapon after Grettir destroyed it, but the coincidence of the strange term, the separation of the giant's weapon from its hilt (as in *Beowulf*), and the reading of runes on it after the battle is over (again as in *Beowulf*) is certainly striking, all the more so because there is so much difference in the two accounts.

The verses given in the saga and said to have been written in runes are therefore worthy of attention. They run as follows:

Gekk ek í gljúfr et døkkva
gein veltiflug steina
við hjǫrgœði hríðar
hlunns úrsvǫlum munni.
Fast lá framan at brjósti
flaugstraumr í sal Naumu
heldr kom á herðar skaldi
hǫrð fjón Braga kvánar.

Ljótr kom mér í móti
mellu vinr ór helli;
hann fekksk heldr at sǫnnu
harðfengr við mik lengi.
harðeggjat létk hǫggvit
heptisax af skepti;
Gangs klauf brjóst ok bringu
bjartr gunnlogi svarta.

I went into the dark chasm; the torrent, rolling down the stones, gaped with wet cold mouth against the sword-warrior (endower of the roller of the sword-storm). The rushing stream thrust vigorously against my breast in the hall of the troll-wife (Nauma). The wrath of the

---

[1] *Hepti* is the term used for a hilt without a double guard: see p. 178 below.

whirlpool (Bragi's wife)[1] came down exceeding hard on the shoulders of the skald.

The hideous friend of the giantess (Mella) came against me out of the cave. Very powerfully he struggled against me for a long while. I caused hard-edged Heptisax to be cut from the shaft. The bright flame of battle clove the breast, the black chest of the giant (Gangr).

A point which is worth noting is that the content of these verses and the passage in *Beowulf* summarizing what is recorded on the hilt resemble one another fairly closely. Both tell of surging water and the destruction of giants. It seems unlikely that the verses in *Grettis Saga* are the genuine work of Grettir himself. Boer in his edition of the saga suggested that they might have been added by someone acquainted with some form of the *Beowulf* story, and pointed out that originally the tale of Grettir and the troll-wife probably had a different ending, in which she was turned into stone outside the hall when day broke; such a tradition is in fact referred to in chapter lxv of the saga and said to be a version known to the men of Barðardale. Guðni Jónsson in his 1936 edition of the saga gives reasons for doubting the verses to be genuine, because of rhymes which indicate a later (probably thirteenth-century) date.[2] But this does not necessarily detract from the interest in the content of the verses themselves, which is considerable. They describe Grettir's descent into rushing surging waters, down into the 'hall of the giantess', his struggle with a giant there, the cutting of Heptisax from its shaft, and the slaying of his adversary with a sword. It is not clear either from the verses or the prose account with what weapon he actually slew the giant, but the prose account refers to a sword hanging up in the cave which the giant tries to reach, and the introduction of this into the story is quite pointless unless it was used in some way. As it stands, the account of Grettir's under-water adventure could not have been derived

---

[1] Apparently a kind of pun on the name *Iðunn*, wife of Bragi, and *iða*, whirlpool.

[2] See preface, pp. xl, liii, &c. Mr. Peter Foote, to whom I am grateful for some help on this point, suggests that 'it would not be unwise to conclude that the prose account and the verses could have been written together'. We may notice, however, that the prose account has a reference to a sword hanging in the cave not given in the verses.

direct from the incident in *Beowulf*, but it seems to indicate some version of the same story as a source, and one which gave considerable detail.

Klaeber's assumption that the passage is a strange and somewhat pedantic reference to the destruction of giants by the Flood, based on the Book of Genesis, becomes more reasonable if the poet was comparing this with the destruction of the giant race to which Grendel and his mother belonged. He was clearly anxious to give these monsters a respectable Biblical background; we are told that they were of the race of Cain, and that as Cain's descendants they were 'estranged from the Eternal Lord'.[1] They met their end under the rushing waters, and the blood set flowing by the sword dyed the lake crimson, so that to equate them with the giants destroyed in the Flood would require no extraordinary leap of the imagination on the poet's part. It is the more probable if there was an earlier version of the story in which the runes (as in *Grettis Saga*) referred specifically to the giants under the lake and their destruction.

We are still left, however, with the problem of why runes should be inscribed on the hilt at all. In *Grettis Saga* the inference is that the words were carved by Grettir himself and left in the church as a record of his achievement. Could Beowulf himself similarly have cut runes on the hilt, recording his struggle with the giants, before he presented it to the king? It is not impossible, but one is bound to say that there seems no such inference in the poem. Another possibility is that the hilt bore some prophetic inscription in runes, emphasizing the fact which we know from the poem, that it was the only weapon which could kill Grendel's mother and cut off Grendel's head. As it stands, the Biblical interpretation so warmly supported by Klaeber seems obscure and purposeless, but if we regard it as a slight twisting of an earlier non-Christian tradition connected with the sword, given by a poet well acquainted with Genesis, it becomes more understandable. Confusion over the two swords—Hrunting and the sword of the giants—which come into the story has rendered the problem more complex.

[1] *Beow.* 107–8, 1258 f.

An additional minor problem connected with the sword from the lake is the meaning of the term *fetelhilt*, which is said to be grasped by Beowulf when he pulls down the sword hanging from the wall (1563, 1662). Klaeber, Keller, and others interpret this term as 'belted hilt', and it will be remembered that *fetel(s)* was interpreted as a belt or baldric in the Anglo-Saxon Wills (p. 119 above) or alternatively as the straps attached to the scabbard. A hilt would not normally be fastened to a belt, but here *fetel* might denote some fastening which secured the sword in its scabbard; alternatively the scabbard might have been fastened to a sword-belt, so that the sword had to be pulled loose from the belt when Beowulf drew it. Suggestions that the term could refer to a ringed hilt do not seem to me convincing.[1] A point perhaps worth making is that in a number of stories where a sword is obtained from a supernatural being or won by the hero in the Other World, it is secured in some way so as to seem impossible to draw. Well-known examples of this are the sword Excalibur, which only Arthur could pull loose from the stone, and the sword Gram, fixed in a tree-trunk in the hall of King Volsung by Odin himself, which only Sigmund could pull out. It is thus possible that this unique term *fetelhilt* is not a descriptive one but one arising out of a traditional element in the story, though its significance is no longer apparent in the poem as we have it.

6. OTHER SWORDS IN ANGLO-SAXON POETRY

Hrunting and the sword from the lake are described in considerable detail in *Beowulf*. Several other swords are mentioned, but less attention is paid to their appearance and workmanship. Beowulf's own sword, which he took to Denmark and presented to the sentinal of the coast when he left for home, is merely said to be an 'adorned sword' (*hyrsted sweord*) and the choicest of blades (672–3). In his old age he bore the sword Nægling. This is called an 'ancient heirloom, exceeding keen of edge' (2563–4),[2] and also

---

[1] For example, Wrenn's Glossary; also S. Pfeilstücker, *Spätantikes und Germanisches Kunstgut* (Kunstwissenschaftliche Studien xix, 1936, p. 202).

[2] The MS. reading *ungleaw* has recently been defended by Wrenn in his

incge lafe (2577). This last term still awaits convincing elucidation.[1] A suggestion made long ago by Thorpe in his edition of the poem remains the most tempting: he interpreted it as *Incges laf*, 'heirloom of Ing'. Ing is mentioned in the Anglo-Saxon Runic poem, and evidently had some special connexion with the Danes, who are twice called in *Beowulf* 'Friends of Ing' (*Ingwine*).[2] If he were viewed as the divine founder of the Danish royal line, then his name might well be associated with a royal ancestral sword, handed down within the family of the Danish kings. We know that a Danish sword, described as 'a famous treasure-sword' (1023), was indeed presented to Beowulf by Hrothgar as a reward for his great service, and it is conceivable that this was Nægling. We are told that Beowulf handed it along with the other gifts to his lord, King Hygelac, but it could have returned to his possession later, after Hygelac's death. This would not be inconsistent with a later passage concerning Nægling, when in lines 2499 f. Beowulf says:

. . . as long as this sword endures, which many times, both early and late, has stood me in good stead, ever since before the eyes of the host[3] I became the slayer of Dæghrefn, champion of the Franks.

This has led to the assumption that Beowulf obtained the sword Nægling from Dæghrefn, in the battle in which Hygelac was slain. But in this case we are faced with the difficulty which has puzzled Klaeber and others, namely, why the sword is mentioned at all when Beowulf expressly says that he did not fight Dæghrefn with

edition of *Beowulf*. Some previous editors have accepted the emendation *unslaw*, 'of undulled edge'.

[1] It is linked with the interpretation of *icge gold* in line 1107. Klaeber suggests a possible connexion with *æce*, the adjective given by Hempl as an interpretation of the first part of the Chessel Down runic inscription (p. 100 above), but both this adjective and the link with *icge* are dubious. Du Bois (*Englische Studien*, lxix, 1934–5, pp. 321 f.) derives both words from Ing's name, and suggests that he was a phallic deity whose symbol was the sword, but there is insufficient evidence to establish such a theory.

[2] Presumably the term is based on the *Ingvaeones* of Tacitus, the group of Germanic tribes who claimed descent from the mythical founder *Ingw* (ON *Yngvi*). See Wrenn, introduction, pp. 56–57, and Chadwick, *Origin of the English Nation*, pp. 216 f., 276 f.

[3] *for dugeðum*: this alternatively might mean 'through my valour'.

the sword but killed him with his hands. But we are told that Beowulf prevented the Frankish warrior from plundering the body
of his leader Hygelac and carrying off the necklace which the king
wore.[1] He would presumably at the same time have saved the
king's sword, and could have carried it as his own from that time;
he would have had the right to do so, since he succeeded Hygelac
as ruler of the Geats. The passage becomes more comprehensible
if Beowulf is remembering the time when his lord was slain and he
inherited the wonderful sword which he saved from the hands of
Hygelac's slayer.

There is little doubt that Nægling, a name which lived long in
heroic story, had memorable traditions associated with it, now for
the most part lost. Concerning its appearance, we are told that it
had a burnished edge (*ecg brun*), and that its blade was ancient
and gleaming with patterns (*gomol ond grægmæl*, 2577–8, 2682).
Though we may not be sure of the origin of this sword, we know
its end in the poem: it was shattered against the head of the dragon
when Beowulf's life as a warrior was ended, even as Sigmund's
sword was shattered on the field of battle by Odin. There is
nothing in the epithets used to give an exact picture of the sword,
but its age is stressed, and it seems to have a pattern-welded blade.
This impression is strengthened if we accept the passage beginning
at line 1488 as referring to Nægling. When Beowulf was about to
descend into the lake, he directed that if he did not return, the
treasures given him on the previous night by Hrothgar should
be sent to his lord, King Hygelac, while the 'ancient heirloom,
the marvellous wave-sword, hard of edge' (*wrætlic wægsweord,
heardecg*) should be given to Unferth, presumably in return for
Hrunting. Klaeber suggests that this is the sword which had been
given to him by Hrothgar; it can scarcely be a command to return
Hrunting to its owner, since Beowulf had no guarantee that this
sword could ever be retrieved if he lost his life in the lake. The
description in any case is an interesting one. *Wrætlic*, with its

---

[1] *Beow.* 2503 f. It would seem from lines 1210 f. that in the end other Frankish
warriors succeeded in carrying off armour and necklace. This makes it even
more puzzling why Beowulf should look back to the fight with Dæghrefn at all
unless he gained possession of Nægling as a result of it.

suggestion of the skilful and the marvellous, is a fitting epithet to use of a fine sword, and the reference to waves is a new variation on the theme of the patterns on the blade, seen now not as serpents, twigs, or woven work, but as movements in water. Falk (p. 19) instances *vægir* used to describe a sword with undulating patterns, and *blóðiða*, 'blood-eddies', used of sword-blades in Old Norse, while the resemblance to water had been noticed by the Arab writer al-Kindi (p. 115 above).[1]

The other sword used in the battle with the dragon was that of Wiglaf. It is not given a name, but we are told that it had belonged to the Swedish Prince Eanmund, and it is described as an 'ancient sword of giants' (2616). It was 'gleaming and plated' (*fah and fæted*, 2701), the plating evidently referring to the hilt. If we take the passage from line 2828 as referring to this sword and not to Nægling, it had 'iron edges, hard and notched in battle (*heaðoscearde*), survivors of the hammer'. An old sword is likely to have received many notches, and it seems probable that the manuscript reading *scearde* and not the duller emendation *scearpe*, 'sharp', is correct. The term *scearde* was used in one of the Wills to refer to a sword (p. 120 above).

The sword of Eofor the Geat used against the Swedish King Ongentheow is also said to be 'ancient work of giants', and is called a 'broad sword' (2978-9). Of Ongentheow's own sword, carried to Hygelac in token of victory, we are told only that it is 'hard and hilted'. There seem to be no special traditions as to appearance and workmanship where these swords are concerned. The two references to the 'work of giants' are perhaps worth noticing here, however, and may be compared with two phrases in the description of the sword from the lake, *ealdsweord eotenisc* and *giganta geweorc* (p. 135 above). The hilt of this lake sword is called *enta ærgeweorc*, 'ancient work of giants' (1679), while the helmet of Ongentheow the Swedish king is called *entisc helm* (2979). Attempts have been made to explain the adjectives *entisc, eotenisc* by reference

---

[1] Cf. also from *The Destruction of Dá Derga's Hostel* (W. Stokes, *Revue Celtique*, xxii, 1901, p. 189): 'The slender stream of water which thou sawest whereon the sun shines, and its trickle down from it, this is the flickering of his sword.'

to the Antes or Anti, a tribe in the Caucasus mentioned by Jordanes who were fighting against the Goths at the end of the fourth century, on the grounds (though there is no real evidence for this) that they were famed for their weapons and armour.[1] Klaeber was puzzled by the term 'giants' in the various phrases given above, since he held that the giants of Germanic tradition were not makers of weapons, and he suggested that it was based on the reference to biblical giants on the sword-hilt recovered from the lake. But there is evidence that Weland the Smith was pictured, sometimes at least, as a giant, and that he was presumed to come from giant stock. His name has lingered on in folk tradition both in England and Denmark, in association with the early stone burial chamber on White Horse Hill, 'Wayland's Smithy' (called in eighteenth-century accounts 'Wayland Smith'),[2] and with a rocky island near Alletop in Denmark.[3] It may be noted that the same phrase as that used of swords is employed for the ancient stone tomb within the mound where the dragon dwelt, which is called *enta geweorc* in *Beowulf* (2717), for ancient ruins in *The Wanderer* and *The Ruin*,[4] for a stone highway and stone columns in *Andreas* (1235, 1495). Such a phrase could hardly be explained in these passages as references to the Anti or to biblical giants, but would not be out of place as references to supernatural weapon-smiths like Weland, Regin (called *jǫtunn*, 'giant', in the *Edda* poem *Reginsmál*), Albrich of the *Nibelungenlied*, and others.[5] The phrase 'work of Weland' is used of the sword Mimming in *Waldere*, and again to describe Beowulf's splendid mail-coat (455), while another mail-coat is called *Wielandia fabricia* in the tenth-century Latin epic *Waltharius* (965).

---

[1] By Olrik and others. See Klaeber, 'Altenglische wortkundliche Randglossen', *Anglia*, Beiblatt XL, 1929, pp. 21 f.

[2] See C. R. Peers and R. A. Smith, 'Wayland's Smithy, Berkshire', *A.J.* i, 1921, pp. 183 f., for full references.

[3] P. Maurus, 'Die Welandsage in der Literatur', *Münchener Beiträge zur romanische und englische Philologie*, xxv, 1902, p. 25.

[4] Kershaw, p. 165.

[5] References to giants and to supernatural Germanic smiths have been discussed in detail in my article 'Weland the Smith', *Folklore*, lxx, 1958, pp. 145 f.

Other incidental references to swords are found in *Beowulf*. In 1285 f. we read of

. . . the bound sword (*heoru bunden*), beaten by the hammer, the blade stained with blood and doughty of edge.

Klaeber suggests that *heoru bunden* might mean a sword bound with a gold ring, but it seems more likely that the sense is the same as in the phrases *bunden golde* (1900), *brugðinn golli* in Old Norse (p. 177 below), and *auro ligata* in the account of the ninth-century Anglo-Saxon sword presented to the Pope (p. 110 above). It seems most likely to refer to the gold-adorned hilt, although a reference to a scabbard encircled with bands of gold ornament is just possible.

On the whole it would seem that references to swords in *Beowulf* are general ones, so that it would hardly be possible to identify any particular weapon, or a weapon in the style of any particular period, from these passages. Swords are thought of essentially as precious heirlooms with richly ornamented hilts. In one case there is a definite allusion to runes on a hilt, and in another a doubtful allusion to a ring-hilted sword. There seems, however, to be a clear tradition of swords with pattern-welded blades, and it is these which inspire the most imaginative and vivid descriptions. Several of the swords are said to be old, and the work of giants. Although the descriptions tend to be general, they are by no means vague or inaccurate; on the contrary they imply considerable detailed knowledge of swords and their appearance.

No single poem adds much to the information given in *Beowulf*, since the other heroic poems are little more than fragments. It is likely that *The Fight at Finnsburg*, had it survived in entirety, would have told us much about swords, since what is left tells of the defence of a hall and desperate fighting. As it is we have a fine imaginative description of the fight (35–36):

> The sword-light shone out
> As if all Finnsburg were aflame.

In the other heroic fragment, *Waldere*, the subject of swords is again in the forefront. Unfortunately the significance of the two passages which have survived and their exact place in the story of the hero Waldere are so problematical that almost every term used in the two sword-descriptions gives rise to long discussion and argument.[1] This does not concern us at the moment, as there is not a great deal about the appearance of the swords. One point, however, which would be of service for the better understanding of the poem is the interpretation of the terms *syncfæt* and *stanfæt*. The *syncfæt* is said to have been refused by Guthere together with a sword as an offer of peace:

> He refused the sword and *syncfæt*, abundance of rings.

The question is whether *syncfæt* is to be taken as a chest or receptacle for treasure, distinct from the sword, or whether there is some closer connexion with the sword, and the term signifies a rich scabbard or some receptacle in which a sword can be kept. Similarly in the other passage *stanfæt* is mentioned in connexion with a sword:

> ... that other which I possess, hidden (? *stille*) in a *stanfæt*. I know that Theodric himself intended to send it to Widia, and much treasure along with the sword. ...

The literal meaning of *fat/fæt* is 'vessel' (cf. NE *vat*). There seems no warrant, apart from the *Waldere* passages, for taking it to mean 'chest'. *Stanfæt* presumably indicates a vessel of stone, and whether it is the same as the *syncfæt* (treasure-vessel) depends on whether the sword hidden away is Mimming or another, and also on who is presumed to be speaking about the sword in the stone vessel. A parallel word in Old Norse suggests that some kind of cask or tub-like receptacle was actually used for storing swords and other weapons. In skaldic verse a sword is called 'fish of the *kęr*', and *kęr* is used elsewhere for vessel in much the same way as *fæt*. A mythical sword, Lævateinn, mentioned in one of the *Edda* poems, is securely hidden away in the '*kęr*' of Segjarn, secured by nine sure fastenings' (*Fjǫlsvinnsmál* 26). Again in *Guðrúnarhvǫt* 7 we are told that Gudrun chooses helmets and mail-coats for her sons in the storeroom out of such vessels (*ór kérom*). We know very little about the conditions under which valuable swords were

---

[1] See notes in F. Norman's edition, Methuen's Old English Library, 1933.

stored when not in use, but the use of a special word in both Anglo-Saxon and Old Norse suggests that some particular kind of receptacle was used for arms, and it is possible that the reason for this was that they could be immersed in wax or fat and kept free from rust in this way.

References in the Christian poems *Genesis, Andreas, Elene,* and *Judith* have already been noticed, because the terms are related to those used in *Beowulf. Andreas* (1180 f.) has also a vivid metaphor describing the way of the sword:

> Let the track of the weapon, the hard-edged blade (*iren ecgheard*), cut its way through the house of life, the treasure-hoard of the doomed.

In *Exodus* (492 f.) too there is a fine imaginative image of the unloosening of the waters of the Red Sea upon the doomed Egyptians:

> God's handiwork fell upon that fatal road from the high heavens; the guardian of the flood smote the foamy-bosomed sea, that unavailing wall, with an ancient sword.

An ancient weapon, as we have seen, is in full accordance with heroic tradition, and at the same time a fitting symbol for the eternal power of the Almighty, the Ancient of Days.

The poem on the Battle of Maldon stands out from other Anglo-Saxon narrative poems as the detailed account of a conflict fought in Essex in 991, which could have taken place only a short time before the poem was composed. The impression given by the poem is that it is the work of an eye-witness, or at least that it was inspired by a first-hand account of what took place there. The battle in the main is fought out with spears and arrows, but swords are used by the Anglo-Saxon leader Byrhtnoth and some of his warriors, and are employed as a second line of defence when hand-to-hand fighting becomes necessary. It is interesting to have this account of what must have been a contemporary weapon, the sword of Byrhtnoth, but unfortunately only fairly vague terms are given. It is said to be 'broad and bright-edged' (*brad ond brunecg*), 'ornamented' (*gerenod*), and *fealohilte* (lines 161 f.). The last phrase is difficult to determine with certainty, the adjective *fealu* being used of various indeterminate colours, yellow, brown, pale red, or yellowish-green: it suggests a bright hilt without striking ornamentation.[1] In fact it is not possible from this poem to get a clear picture of this sword or of any other weapon used in the battle. No swords are mentioned by name, and most references are very general ones, ranking sword with spear and shield as weapons of war, 'ancient swords' (47) being, for instance, ironically offered to the Vikings for tribute. Such adjectives, unlike the ones used in *Beowulf*, appear to be static and traditional ones, although this is far from being a dully conventional poem.

The *Battle of Brunanburh*, a poem commemorating another tenth-century battle, has again only incidental references to swords. It is by the 'edges of the sword' that Æthelstan and his brother won glory:

... They clove through the shield-wall and hewed through the linden-wood defences with hammered blades (*hamora lafum*),

and they hewed down the fugitives 'with blades grindstone-sharp' (*mecum mylenscearpum*). One cannot draw conclusions from so little material. It may have been the deliberate policy of the composer of this vigorous, triumphant declaration of victory to use only active epithets for the sword, the clash of hammers and movement against the grindstone helping to build up a general picture of effort and speedy victory; more leisurely descriptions of wondrous workmanship would be out of place here.

Outside the field of narrative poetry there is not much additional information about the sword. In the *Cotton Gnomes* the statement is made that the place of the sword, the 'goodly iron', is on the lap (*on bearme*). This could refer to the sword held by king and leader, who may be seen in a number of Anglo-Saxon illuminated manuscripts of the eleventh century sitting on his throne or high-seat with a sword upright in his lap, supported by right or left hand (Fig. 116).[2] In later manuscripts the king is

[1] See L. D. Lerner, 'Colour Words in Anglo-Saxon', *M.L.R.* xlvi, 1951, p. 247. He says of *fealu* that its significance is 'intense rather than pale or dark', and 'the brightness which almost obscures hue'.

[2] For example, Ælfric's Paraphrase of the Pentateuch (B.M. Claudius B. IV, fols. 59, 69, 73); similar scenes may be found on the Bayeux Tapestry.

usually shown holding a sceptre while his sword-bearer has the sword. The sword lay in the lap of the Norwegian king, the hilt pointing forward, when his liegemen came to take the oath on entering his service (p. 76 above). Again, when Beowulf received the family sword from Hygelac together with a gift of land in recognition of his great achievement, we are told that it was 'on his lap' that the sword was placed.[1]

In the *Exeter Gnomes* we find the statement: 'Gold is fitting on a man's sword', and this is well borne out by surviving hilts and scabbards with rich ornamentation, as well as allusions to swords decorated with gold in Anglo-Saxon wills of the tenth and eleventh centuries. From another strange poem, *Solomon and Saturn*, we find one of the few references in the literature to the cutting of runes upon a sword.[2] Here it is said of the Enemy (the Devil):

He writes upon his weapon a great number of deathmarks (*wællnota heap*), baleful letters (*bealwe bocstafas*); he cuts them on his sword (*bill forscrifeð*), on the sword's glory (*meces mærðo*). Therefore no man must draw out the blade of his weapon (*wæpnes ecgge*) thoughtlessly, pleasing though its beauty may be to him, but always he must sing the Paternoster when he draws his sword, and pray with glad heart (*mid blisse*) to the Palmtree, that it may give him both life and skill of hand (*feorh ond folme*) at the coming of his enemy.

The cutting of runes, as the baleful letters referred to here must be, is here identified with the devil, and condemned by Christians. But the warning against lightly drawing the sword (found again in Old Norse sources, p. 166 below) and the need for a ritual before battle, is here found retained in a Christian setting; there can be little doubt that it reflects pre-Christian practice. It would be of value to know exactly what is meant by 'the sword's glory'; from other references to runes and from what we know of surviving inscriptions, some place on the hilt would seem most likely: perhaps on the pommel.

This passage serves as a useful reminder of how much swordlore

---

[1] *Beow.* 2194. There is evidently special significance in the action of Hunlafing in placing a sword on the lap of Hengest (*Beow.* 1142-5). See Wrenn, p. 207. Unfortunately the relationship between the two men here is problematical.   [2] *Solomon and Saturn*, ed. Menner, i. 161 f., p. 89.

is likely to have existed and is now lost to us. There are further problems in the interpretation of certain riddles from the *Exeter Book*, which appear to have the sword as their theme, and which merit study in detail.

7. SWORD RIDDLES

The first riddle to be considered is no. 20 in Krapp and Dobbie's edition of the *Exeter Book*, and 21 in Tupper's *Riddles of the Exeter Book* and Wyatt's *Old English Riddles*. It runs as follows:

I am a wondrous creature, shapen in strife, dear to my lord and beautifully adorned. My coat of mail is of gleaming colours, while a bright wire lies round the death-jewel (*wælgim*) which a ruler gave to me, he who in his journeyings (*widgalum*) sometimes himself guides me to the battle. Then do I carry treasure throughout the bright day, smiths' handiwork of gold throughout the dwellings. Often do I slay a living creature (*gæstberend*) with weapons of battle (*compwæpnum*). The king decks me out with treasure and silver and honours me in the hall; he does not grudge me words of praise, but tells of my qualities (*wisa*) before the company there as they drink mead. He keeps me in confinement, but at times he lets me come forth and be at large when I am wearied with travel and bold for the combat. Often in the hands of his friend (*æt his freonde*) I have done severe injury to others; I am outlawed far and wide, accursed among weapons (*wæpnum awyrged*). No cause have I to believe that a son will take mortal vengeance for me upon the slayer, if any enemy should assail me in battle. Nor will the family from which I sprang be increased by any child of mine, unless I, giving up my lord, can leave the possessor who gives me rings. If I obey my lord and do battle as I have done hitherto at my prince's pleasure, my fate henceforth is to give up the begetting of children. I may not enjoy the love of a wife, for he who formerly laid bonds upon me denies me that joyous sport: therefore I must enjoy the treasures of heroes as a bachelor. Often, proud of my adornments (*wira*), I give anger to a woman, frustrate her desire; she speaks an evil word to me, clasps her hands and chides me with words, crying out bad things: but for this kind of conflict I care nothing.

The two solutions which have been suggested for this riddle are *sword* and *hawk*; the interpretation *sword* has been generally accepted, but it cannot be denied that *hawk* fits almost every point made in the riddle extremely well, so that it is hard to choose between them. In particular, the passage where the speaker compares himself to a bachelor, denied the joys of wife and children, appears to apply better to the falcon bred for hunting than to the sword. If the *gæstberend* slain by the speaker means 'soul-bearer', then a sword must be intended, but if it merely stands for a living creature it could signify the birds the hawk has slain. It is likely that the riddle-maker intended deliberately to mislead his audience by the ambiguity, a trick familiar to crossword-puzzle enthusiasts.

If, however, we consider the interpretation *sword*, the opening line with its reference to a creature 'shaped in strife' becomes significant. Tupper has pointed out that it is similarly employed of the bow, in another riddle, while the harsh treatment which the blade receives while it is being made in the smithy is alluded to in a second riddle quoted below. The mail-coat, said to be gleaming and coloured (*bleofag*), can clearly not be the scabbard, as some have suggested, since one does not take off a mail-coat before battle; such a false analogy would soon be challenged by a critical audience. But the adjective is an excellent description of a sword-blade, and particularly of a pattern-welded blade with its changing lights and hues. It is in agreement with descriptions of such blades in heroic poetry, and one might see a further connexion between the *hringmæl*, a blade with curving patterns, and the ringed mail-coat. Wires are mentioned elsewhere in connexion with swords, and probably refer to the hilt: the allusion might be to filigree work, to raised decoration of various kinds, to wires bound round the grip, or to the twisted wire between the divisions on some pommels. The 'jewel of death' is puzzling (but even more so if the *hawk* solution is accepted); the inference might be that an ornamental stone or charm has been set in the hilt. There is also gold upon the sword. Sometimes the sword slays living men, and it is praised and honoured in the hall. It is kept confined in a scabbard, except when taken out and used in battle. If *æt his freonde* means 'in the hand of his friend' then, presumably, the sword is sometimes used by one of the friends or followers of the lord who owns it. The most puzzling passage is the lament that it has no wife and child and can have none unless it leaves its lord's service. The idea of the sword as a bachelor warrior is well enough, but it is worked out in such detail here that one would expect some special meaning behind it. Two possibilities are that if a sword no longer remained in service it might go back to the armoury with other weapons, and perhaps it might go into the smithy and be reforged as a new weapon. Since the sword is a recognized phallic symbol, it is also possible that we have a double entendre here, as seems also the case in another riddle quoted below. Finally the sword, in the pride of its ornaments, provokes a woman and 'frustrates her desire'. This is easier to understand and supports the *sword* solution better than the *hawk* one, for the woman would be provoked because the sword could take her man away from her side, and she might also grudge the ornaments and gold bestowed upon its hilt and scabbard. Some have thought that the riddle's abrupt ending means that it is incomplete: Wyatt, however (p. 79), believed the sudden climax to be intentional, and certainly there is humour in the sardonic close: 'For *this* conflict I care nothing'—since the sword, essentially a man's weapon, has no time for womanish tantrums and abuse, a point which would no doubt be appreciated by a largely masculine audience in the hall.

The second riddle, 70/71, is fragmentary, but here there seems little doubt that the favourite interpretation, *sword*, is correct. Here it is interesting to find what seems to be a reference to the actual making of the blade, about which there is all too little information in the literature. It runs as follows:

> I am possessed by the rich man, and clothed in red. Once I was a hard, high field, the place of brilliant plants (*stið ond steap wong, stapol wæs iu þa / wyrta wlitetorhtra*); now I am the survivor of cruel treatment, of the fire and the file, firmly confined and adorned with wire. Sometimes the bearer of gold weeps because of my touch, when I must destroy. . . .

There is some doubt as to where the riddle ends, and several more lines probably belong to it: from these the words *hringum gehyrsted*, 'adorned with rings', and *dryhtne min*, 'my lord', can be made out from the manuscript.

The explanation given for the first part of this riddle has been to take the 'hard high field' to refer to iron in the earth. But a different solution is suggested by the word *wlitetorht* which does not merely mean 'beautiful' but has the idea of brightness and radiance, and this gives a more effective and telling meaning to the passage. If the iron is the piece from which the blade is forged, a hard, flat piece raised high upon the anvil and beaten by the hammer so that brilliant sparks, like flowers, are seen to spring from it, we have a fine imaginative picture. Moreover, it leads on naturally to the use of the fire and the file, referring to the working and filing down of the sword-blade. The red worn by the sword can be explained by red gold, or jewels like the popular garnet set in the hilt, while no doubt the secondary meaning of red blood is also hinted at here. Once more wires are mentioned as part of the decoration, and the idea of confinement within the scabbard stressed. The 'bearer of gold' is presumably a woman, who weeps because she is bereaved by the action of the sword.

It seems likely that Riddle 79, which has puzzled the commentators, has also some connexion with a sword, though here it appears to be the sword in its scabbard. It runs:

I am the shoulder-companion (*eaxlgestealla*) of the prince, the warrior's comrade, the associate of a king, dear to my lord. Sometimes a fair-haired lady, an earl's daughter, noble as she is, lays her hand upon me. She has me, who grew in the forest, in her lap. Sometimes I ride on a proud horse at the head of a troop (*herges on ende*). Hard is my tongue. Often I am given to a poet as a reward for his words after a song. I have fine qualities and I am dark in colour. Say what I am called.

The allusion to the forest can be explained by the fact that the scabbard was usually formed of wood. The hard tongue, a point which has ruled out several other interpretations of the riddle, is very fitting as a description of the sword within the scabbard. The sword is the companion of warriors and princes, it is worn on horseback, and it is frequently given as a gift to a poet in return for his work. For this last point there is plenty of evidence in saga literature, as, for example, the advice given to a young Viking ruler in

Dublin, who was uncertain how to reward a poem which a visiting poet had recited in his praise:[1]

Other kings as a reward for a poet give rich treasures such as a good sword or fine gold rings.

Both the blade itself and the wood or leather of the scabbard could be described as dark. The description 'shoulder-companion' is an excellent one for the sword in its scabbard, since this was often worn high on the shoulder; thus the word used, which had for the Anglo-Saxons the significance of 'right-hand man' (and is so used by Hrothgar of his thane Æschere in *Beowulf* 1326), is an excellent one. The only point which does not seem immediately explicable is the allusion to the high-born lady: is she thought of here as helping to arm her lord, or is it an allusion to the setting of a hand on the hilt of a sword when taking an oath, as brides in Germany in the eleventh century and later were apparently accustomed to do?[2] Some kind of ceremonial is implied in the sword on the lap of the lady (p. 150 above) and probably there is a double entendre here as well.

It is instructive to compare these three riddles with two by Anglo-Saxon scholars, composed in Latin. Two by Tatwine and Aldhelm have been published by Wright[3] and are easily accessible. They run as follows:

1. Armigeri dura cordis compagine fingor,
   cuius et hirsuti extat circumstantia pepli,
   pangitur et secto cunctum de robore culmen,
   pellibus exterius strictim qui tegmina tute
   offensam diris defendunt imbribus aulam.

I am formed with a hard body and a warrior's heart, surrounded by an enveloping hairy robe; this is fixed at the top with cut wood, and on the outside these coverings defend the dwelling securely with skins, when attacked by hostile showers.

(Tatwine's *De Ense et Vagina* (Sword and Scabbard).)

---

[1] *Gunnlaugs Saga Ormstungu*, viii. Another instance is given on p. 187 below.
[2] See Davidson, 'The Ring on the Sword', *Journal of the Arms and Armour Society*, ii, 1958, pp. 216–17, and 'The Sword at the Wedding', *Folklore*, lxxi, 1960.
[3] In the Appendix to *Anglo-Latin Satirical Poets*, ed. T. Wright, Rolls Series, 1872, pp. 532, 552..

2. De terrae gremiis formabar primitus arte,
   materia trucibus processit cætera tauris,
   aut potius putidis constat fabricata capellis.
   Per me multorum clauduntur lumina letho,
   qui domini nudus nitor defendere vitam.
   Nam domus est mihi constructa de tergore secto,
   nec non et tabulis quas findunt stipite rasis.

First I was skilfully formed from the lap of earth, and the rest of my material came from savage bulls or else consists of what is made from stinking goats. Through me the lights of many are extinguished in death. Naked, I strive to defend the life of my lord. For I have a home framed from cut leather and also from smoothed planks which men cleave from the tree-trunk.

(Aldhelm's *De Pugione vel Spata* (Dagger or Sword).)

It will be seen that there is a wide difference in the treatment of the subject in Latin and Anglo-Saxon riddles, and that here at least there is little reason to suspect that the native poet has been inspired by Latin models. The riddles of Aldhelm and Tatwine are products of the study, not of men who were familiar with the sword as a weapon. They are intellectual descriptions of the sword and scabbard, not pictures of the weapon against the background of the life of the time. Above all, the weapon appears static, and is not in constant movement, as in the Anglo-Saxon riddles. More attention, especially in Tatwine's riddle, is given to the scabbard than to the blade inside it. Aldhelm's verse is the more interesting one (Tatwine's may have been composed in imitation), and closer to native poetry in two points which he makes: that the sword extinguishes the lights of many lives, and that it defends the life of its lord. These, however, are obvious points, and they are lifeless metaphors in comparison with the vivid images of the outlaw slayer, the shoulder companion, the creature whose touch causes women to weep. Technically they add nothing to our knowledge of the sword, although the description of the scabbard formed of thin pieces of wood, enclosed outside in leather made from the skins of cattle or goats, is interesting corroboration of archaeological evidence. Possibly the allusion to bulls is also based on a hilt of horn.

From this wealth of evidence about the sword in Anglo-Saxon times, which tells us much concerning its form and appearance and how the poets delighted to describe it, we shall now pass on to the evidence to be gained from Old Norse poetry and prose.

8. THE SWORD-BLADE IN OLD NORSE LITERATURE

In Old Norse literature, evidence concerning the sword is scattered over a much wider field than in Anglo-Saxon literature, and the sources vary in date from the tenth to the thirteenth century. Concentrated and detailed accounts of individual swords such as we find in *Beowulf* are lacking, but nevertheless the sword plays a continual and important part, and there is much to be learnt concerning it. The earliest material comes from the skaldic poets, some of whom lived before A.D. 1000. Their poems are mainly in the form of short verses, and the diction is extremely complex, allusive, and rich in mythological associations. The sword is described indirectly by means of 'kennings' or condensed metaphors, which replace the simple noun *sword*: it is alluded to in such phrases as the 'fire of the helm', the 'ice of battle', or the 'candle of Hild (the Valkyrie)'. The treatment of the sword in these kennings is of importance for our understanding of how it was used as a symbol in literature, but this aspect will not concern us here, and the kennings will only be used, therefore, when they appear to have some bearing on the construction of the sword or its use as a weapon. The *Edda* poems, which are later than *Beowulf* in their present form, are known to contain early material. Unfortunately, although they include heroic stories about kings and warriors, references to the sword are relatively few. The prose sagas have a good deal of material, not in the form of detailed sword descriptions, but in accounts of the part which the sword played in the lives of the Norwegian kings and their followers and of individuals in Iceland. From these there is much to be learnt of the appearance and the qualities of the swords mentioned. Many swords bear names, and some have a history which covers the lifetimes of several men, and appear in more than one saga. While some of this material is certainly derived from early traditions of the Viking Age, we must be prepared for it to be mingled with customs and traditions of the thirteenth century as well, and cannot assume without good reason that it goes back to Anglo-Saxon times. The same is true of the material from the first nine books of the Latin history of Saxo Grammaticus, Danish antiquarian and scholar, who took much interest in stories of duels and fighting with the sword. Saxo in the twelfth century had access to many heroic stories and poems now lost, and often produced versions of tales differing from those in Old Norse sources. He sometimes appears to do strange things with his material, but his information is of considerable interest, and since at the time when he wrote the sword was still a weapon in everyday use, he is unlikely to mislead us about it to any serious extent. With this preliminary caution, then, I propose to use his evidence whenever it seems relevant. In this section we are concerned with all that can be learnt of the quality, appearance, and origins of the sword from the evidence of Old Norse literature, and each part of the weapon will be considered in turn, beginning with the blade.

There is little information in Old Norse sources about the forging of a sword-blade. The most detailed if slightly fantastic account comes from *Thiðriks Saga*, compiled in Norway in the thirteenth century but containing some early material from both German and Scandinavian tradition. This saga has much to tell concerning three famous swords, Nægling, Mimming, and Ekki-sax, and the making of one of these, Mimming, is described. First Velent the smith made a sword in seven days, and tested it by cutting a piece of felt floating in the river. The king who had ordered the sword was well satisfied, but Velent said (ciii–civ, pp. 98 f.):

'It will have to be better before I have finished.' . . . Then Velent went to the smithy and took a file and filed the sword down to dust. He took the filings and mixed them with meal, and then he took poultry (*ali-fugla*),[1] starved them for three days, and took the meal and gave it to the birds to eat. Then he took the birds' droppings and brought them

[1] The alternative version has 'geese and hens'. See *Thiðriks Saga* (Bertelsen), p. 99.

to the forge and worked out all the soft parts of the iron; and from it he made a sword which was not as big as the first one.

The king was very pleased with this second sword, but Velent said:

'Lord, this is a good sword, but it must be better still.' He said he must make it half as good again. . . . Then Velent went to his smithy and filed the sword to pieces, and carried out the same process as he had done before. And when three weeks were passed, Velent had made a shining sword, inlaid with gold and with a fair hilt. . . . It was of convenient size, although those he had made before were longer.

This sword the king was very eager to possess, but Velent carried it off again on the plea that he had to make belt and accoutrements for it, and he rapidly made a far inferior sword which resembled the other in appearance and gave this to the king.

There is no suggestion of any knowledge of the pattern-welding process here, but the picture of the smith filing down the blade and working out impurities is likely to be based on some knowledge of sword-making; we know that the file was of very great importance, and although the blade would not be filed down to dust, as here, a surprisingly large portion of it would be filed away (p. 27 above). It may not be irrelevant that this information comes in a saga containing much German tradition, since Germany was one of the areas where good swords were made.

The incident of the birds is interesting from a technical point of view. One possible explanation for such a tradition is that the smiths used the birds' droppings as a source of nitrogen. Examination of a sword of the Iron Age showed that it contained nitride needles, and Coghlan[1] interpreted this as evidence that the iron had been heated 'with some ammonia-bearing fuel such as animal dung'; it may be noted that bird excrement is very rich in ammonia. The suggestion was recently made in an American scientific

[1] H. Coghlan, 'Etruscan and Spanish Swords of Iron', *Sibrium*, iii, 1956–7, p. 168. It may be noted that Anstee used a paste of pigeon droppings, flour, honey, olive oil, and milk when he heated the rods which formed the centre of his blade (Appendix A, p. 220).

journal[1] that since fowls like to peck at bright particles of a certain size, they might devour the tiny bits of good steely iron lying round the smithy. If the smith encouraged them to do this and then removed the contents of their stomachs after they had been killed, he might have a primitive but effective means of sorting out such particles for further use. Such a complex method, however, does not seem likely to have appealed to the smith, although Salin (after a practical experiment with a duck) thinks that it may possibly have been used to free iron particles from slag.[2] It is surprising to find that the idea of feeding iron filings to birds is found also in Asiatic sources,[3] and ostriches—well known for their partiality for bright metallic objects—are mentioned more than once in this connexion. Zeki Validi also quotes al-Biruni in the eleventh century for the statement that he has heard tales of the Rus cutting the steel for their swords into small pieces and mixing it with meal to give to ducks and geese. This independent piece of evidence, considerably earlier in date than *Thiðriks Saga*, implies that either the story of Weland or the practice on which the story was based was known among the Scandinavians at a much earlier date than that of the prose saga as we have it.

A reference to the use of charcoal for treating the edges of swords comes from Saxo Grammaticus,[4] and one would like to have the source of his story. He tells us that the hero Starkath was disgusted at the weakness of King Ingild:

Resenting that a youth of such great parts should have renounced his descent from his glorious father, he hung on his shoulders a mighty mass of charcoal, as though it were some costly burden, and made his way to Denmark. When asked by those he met why he was taking along so unusual a load, he said that he would sharpen the dull wits of King Ingild to a point by the use of charcoal.

---

[1] C. Balhausen, 'Notions concerning the Wieland Saga', *Powder Metallurgy Bulletin* (New York), vii, 1956, pp. 69–72. Summarized in *Folklore*, lxix, 1958, p. 193; see ibid., p. 272, for comment.

[2] Salin, iii, p. 96, note. He quotes an interesting analogy—the feeding of small olive-like fruits to camels so that the stones can be procured after the camels have eaten them; the oil obtained from crushing the stones is used for watches.   [3] Zeki Validi, p. 23.

[4] Saxo, vi. 199, Elton's translation.

This can only be a reference to case-hardening, alluding to the method of hardening the edge of a sword so that it can be sharpened (p. 25 above).

A riddle in *Hervarar Saga* (xi) refers to the process of forging a sword in the smithy, for the bellows are thus described:

Two lifeless ones, without breath, were boiling a leek of wounds.

The point of this lies in the use of the word *sjóða*, 'to cook', 'boil', since the same verb has the technical meaning 'to weld', while 'leek of wounds' is a kenning for sword.[1] The bellows are without soul or spirit (*andalausir*), since they are inanimate, and in this sense are without breath, although they are filled with wind.

A brief reference to sword-making is found in the account of the sword Ekkisax in *Thiðriks Saga*.[2] This sword is said to have been made by the dwarf Albrich:

He hid it down in the earth before it was completed. He searched also through nine kings' realms before he found the water in which he could harden it.

The burying of iron in the earth has been alluded to earlier, and may have been done deliberately by the smiths so that inferior parts would rust away (p. 17 above). We have many other references to the importance of the right liquid for the quenching of steel (p. 19 above).

There are two accounts in the sagas of good steel from a sword being used again to make a new weapon when the first was broken. In *Gísla Saga* a very fine sword was broken in battle, and remade as a spear (p. 127 above). The sword Gram of the hero Sigurd the Volsung was also said to have been reforged by Regin the Smith out of the broken pieces of the original sword given to Sigurd's father by Odin himself. When Sigmund died on the field of battle, Odin shattered his sword with a blow from his spear, but the pieces were carefully kept by Sigmund's widow and given to

---

[1] For example, *ímunlaukr*, 'leek of battle', *randar laukr*, 'leek of the shield', and *saralaukr*, *benlaukr*, 'wound-leek'. De Vries (*Z. f. d. A.* lxxxv, 1954, p. 105) suggested that the *itrlaukr*, given to Helgi in the Poetic Edda as a symbol of his investiture as a ruler, is really a sword. For list of 'leek' kennings, see Meissner, p. 152.   [2] *Thiðriks Saga*, clxxv, p. 179.

Sigurd. He asked Regin to reforge them for him, because the swords made for him were not satisfactory, and although Regin was angry, he did as Sigurd demanded:[1]

. . . and when he carried it from the hearth, it seemed to the smith's boys as if the edges burned with fire; then he bade Sigurd take his sword, saying that he knew not how to make a sword if this one failed. Sigurd cut at the anvil and sliced it in two to its base, but the sword neither shattered nor broke; he praised the sword greatly, and went to the river with a strand of wool and threw it up stream, and it was cut in two when it touched the sword; then Sigurd went home satisfied.

The test of the cutting of the strand of wool may well be based on actual practice, and it recalls the test of a good damascened blade mentioned by Belaiev (p. 424), that of being able to cut a gauze handkerchief in two in mid-air. In the story of the making of Mimming from *Thiðriks Saga*, referred to above, the test has become that of cutting through a thick piece of felt in the river. The cutting of the anvil is found elsewhere; it was said to have been the test used by the hero of the Estonian epic, the *Kalevipoeg*, when he bought a sword from a Finnish smith.[2] The first sword he tried broke against the anvil, the second cut deep into it, but the third clove it to the ground. A similar tradition is attached to the sword of a tenth-century Norwegian king, Hakon the Good:[3]

King Athelstan gave Hakon the sword with guard and grip of gold; yet its blade was of even greater worth. With it Hakon cut a millstone to the centre, and ever afterwards the sword was called Quernbiter (*Kvernbítr*); this sword was the best that ever came into Norway, and Hakon had it till the day of his death.

It is interesting to find that this good sword was connected with the Anglo-Saxon king whose name, as we have seen, is already associated with more than one sword (p. 110 above). Could this have been another of those fine swords with gold-ornamented hilts of native workmanship? It is known that more than one of these reached Norway about this time (p. 70 and Fig. 42). As to the cutting of the millstone, this sounds like a literal interpretation

---

[1] *Vǫlsunga Saga*, xv; cf. *Skáldskaparmál*, xl.   [2] Kirby, pp. 43 f.
[3] *Heimskringla, Háralds Saga Hárfagra*, xli.

of the sword's name by Snorri; a good sword might conceivably cut into the steel top of a wooden anvil, but could hardly slice a millstone. The word *kvern* can, according to Vígfusson, be used metaphorically for an eddy in a river, and it is just possible that a pun of this kind lies behind the name. The sword was evidently famous as a cutting weapon, and the description of it in *Hákon-armál*,[1] a tenth-century poem composed on Hakon's death, refers to the sword cutting through water:

Then did the sword in the hand of the hero pierce armour, Odin's raiment, as if swept through water.

This is reminiscent of the other test of a good blade, that of cutting a strand of wool floating down the river.

A different test of a blade, for pliability, occurs in *Svarfdœla Saga*. Although it comes in the second chapter (a late addition) it is of interest:

Then Thorolf took off his own sword and gave it to him; it was a good treasure and well ornamented. Thorstein received the sword and drew it forthwith. He took the point (*blóðrefill*) and bent it between his hands so that the point came up to the hilt. Then he let it spring back, and it had lost all its elasticity (*var þá ór allr staðrinn*). Then he gave back the sword to Thorolf and bade him get another and stronger weapon, 'for this switch will not do for me'. Thorolf took the sword and judged it to be spoilt.

A similar test of a blade was made of the weapon presented to the Emperor Louis by envoys from Scandinavia (p. 113 above). It is found again in the story from the *Kalevipoeg* referred to earlier:

He picked out the longest and bent it into a hoop, when it straightened itself out at once.

Again in an Irish saga the sword of Cuchulainn is said to have undergone this test:[2]

If the point were bent back to its hilt, it would stretch back again like a rapier.

---

[1] Kershaw, p. 104, verse 6.
[2] *Decision as to Cormac's Sword*, translated Stokes and Windisch, 59, *Irische Texte*, iii, p. 199.

It may be remembered that Arab writers stressed the flexibility of the swords of the Franks and Rus (p. 116 above).

The disadvantage of a blade made from iron not sufficiently flexible is vividly illustrated in *Eyrbyggja Saga* (xliv). Steinthor of Eyre, a man with the reputation of being one of the three finest fighters in Iceland, went out one day prepared for a fight, and it was noticed that he was carrying a new sword:

It is said that he had a fair shield and helmet, and was girded with a splendidly adorned sword; the guard was white with silver and the grip bound with silver, with a gilded edge.

But when the battle began . . .

Steinthor was at the head of his party, and he hewed with both hands, but the elaborate sword was of little use (*en sverð þat it búna dugði eigi*) when it came against a shield, and he often had to straighten it out under his foot.

His enemies did not omit to remind him of that humiliating experience next time they met (xlv):

Thorleif *kimbi* remarked when he saw Steinthor draw his sword: 'So you are still using the silver hilt, Steinthor? But I can't tell whether you are still using the same soft blade (*deigr brandr*) that you had in Alptafirth last autumn.' 'I am in hopes', replied Steinthor, 'that you will have found out whether I have a soft blade or not before we part.'

From the account of Steinthor's doings in the fight which followed, when his sword never failed him during some extremely tricky work on slippery ice (p. 203 below), the saga-teller probably intends us to assume that a new blade had been fitted to the fine silver hilt.

We are also told of another famous champion of Iceland, Kjartan in *Laxdœla Saga* (xlix), that he was let down by a soft blade at a moment of crisis. He was caught in an ambush without his good sword, the one which Olaf Tryggvason had given him with the counsel to keep it always with him, and the one which he carried was so soft that he too was said to have straightened it with his foot. This was the reason why that battle proved Kjartan's last. A similar fate befell Helgi Droplaugarson when he was attacked while carrying a borrowed sword (p. 204 below).

As to the appearance of the blade, there is little information, and not much to suggest that pattern-welded swords were still in use at the time of the sagas. But the memory of these swords had not wholly faded. It seems probable that the famous Skofnung was such a blade. In the story in *Kormáks Saga* (ix) of how young Kormak borrowed it from its owner Skeggi for a duel, he received careful warning as to how it must be treated:

'You will find it difficult to manage,' said Skeggi. 'There is a small bag with it, and this you must leave alone. The sun must not shine on the pommel; and you must not bear the sword unless you are about to do battle; and when you come to the place of battle, sit down by yourself and draw it. Pull out the blade and blow on it; and then a little snake will creep out from beneath the hilt. Turn the sword and make it easy for him to creep under the hilt.'

This suggests sword ritual before battle, and incidentally nothing could be better planned to induce an impetuous young man to treat a precious blade with care and respect. But Kormak scorned such precautions and ignored the careful instructions:

He took no precautions to keep the sun from shining on the hilt, but girded it outside his clothes and tried to draw it; this he could not do until he set his foot on the hilt. The serpent came, and was not treated as it should have been, and the luck of the sword was broken and it came groaning from the scabbard.

This allusion to the serpent becomes more comprehensible in the light of a passage from *Thiðriks Saga*,[1] where the sword Ekkisax is described:

The blade (*brandr*) is well polished and marked with gold, and if you set the point down on the earth, it seems as if a snake runs from the point and up to the hilt, gleaming like gold. But if instead you hold it upwards, then it seems as if the same snake runs from the hilt and up the point, and it moves as if alive.

The idea of a serpent creeping along the blade would arise naturally out of the serpentine appearance of the band of pattern running along a pattern-welded sword, and the moisture of the breath would bring this out more clearly. The same idea probably

---

[1] *Thiðriks Saga*, clxxv, pp. 179 f.

lies behind the description of the sword promised to young Helgi in a poem in the *Poetic Edda*, *Helgakviða* (9), of which we are told first that it had a ring on the hilt (p. 180 below), and secondly:

> along the edge lies a blood-hued serpent,
> and on the *valbǫst* a snake twines its tail.

The *valbǫst* will be discussed later as a part of the hilt, but the blood-coloured serpent must belong to the blade itself, since it is said to lie along the edge of the sword. The varied shades of a pattern-welded blade have been mentioned (p. 29 above), while the association with blood is also fitting for a blade which has seen use, and it is likely that this is the basis of the description rather than an inlaid pattern in gold. We may compare the Anglo-Saxon expression *wyrmfah*, emphasizing the colour of a patterned blade and the resemblance to a serpent (pp. 130, 136 above), and the description of the sword Gram, similarly said to be coloured in the centre of the blade (p. 131 above). Other references to blades which have patterns (*mál*) have already been discussed.

Some of the recorded Old Norse sword names in Falk's list may have been inspired by pattern-welded blades. *Miðfáinn*, 'ornamented' or 'coloured in the centre', suggests such a sword, and Falk (p. 52) suggests a possible derivation for *Hrotti*[1] from Germ. *hrungt*, based on wrinkled or wavy patterns on the blade. Other names which suggest a patterned blade are *Fiskhryggr*, 'Fishback', the sword of King Magnus Erlingsson, since the central panel of such a blade has a striking resemblance to a fish's back seen from above[2] (and the herring-bone pattern moreover resembles a fish's skeleton), and *Veigarr*, which Falk compares with the term *veigaðr*, used to describe rich brocaded cloth. A name recently discussed by Liestøl (pp. 71 f.) in connexion with pattern-welding is *Refill*, the name of the sword of Regin the Smith in the account of the dragon-slaying given by Snorri. The word *refill* is used of woven tapestry

---

[1] Another suggested derivation for the Old English sword name *Hrunting* and ON *Hrotti*, which are related, is from *hrindan/hrinda*, 'to thrust'; see Klaeber and Falk.

[2] Falk took *fiskr* to mean 'muscle' here, but this does not make very satisfactory sense.

or embroidered pictures, and particularly of a narrow piece of weaving against a background of plain work (cf. mod. Norw. *revle*). This would account for the name *refilstígar* which is given to winding paths through a wood, and it would make *refill* a good name to describe the narrow band of pattern-welding between the plain edges of a sword.[1]

There is little indication in the sagas of the length of swords. The sword Laufi (*Lǫvi*) in Saxo (ii. 56) is said to be 'of wonderful sharpness and unusual length'. Elsewhere Saxo tells us (viii. 258) that certain followers of Harald of Denmark 'had their bodies covered by little shields and used very long swords'. The opposite picture is given of a band of sword comrades in *Hálfs Saga* (x), of whom it is said that their laws commanded

. . . that none of them might have a sword of over an ell long, so that they were forced to get to close quarters; they used a sax because a bigger wound could be inflicted.

In *Kormáks Saga* (xiv) the hero accuses Bersi of having a sword too long to be used in a duel, 'longer than the law allows', but unfortunately the law as recorded in the sagas does not specify what length was permissible. There is a tradition in *Vǫlsunga Saga* that Gram was seven spans (over 5 feet) long, but this evidently fits in with the picture of Sigurd as a giant, here and in *Norna-Gests Tháttr*.

Throughout the literature we are given little information concerning the origin of swords. Many of them are said to be of supernatural origin, forged by the dwarfs or else given by Odin, if their origin is mentioned at all, and even Velent, the smith of *Thiðriks Saga*, is himself a partly supernatural being. In the Icelandic sagas, swords are often said to have come into Norway or Iceland from abroad, as gifts or trophies, but again no details are given as to where they are thought to have been made. In *Sturlunga Saga*[2] we heard of a sword *Brynjubítr* which was brought into Iceland

---

[1] *Refill* is sometimes used by archaeologists for the medial hollow in a Viking blade, but there is no early instance of this use. *Blóðrefill* in the sagas is used for the point of the sword, but Liestøl shows that there is reason to think from the use of the term in poetry that it originally applied to the whole blade.

[2] *Sturlunga Saga*, K. IV. 19; O. VII. 37; p. 318.

from abroad, and obviously caused much stir in the neighbour-hood:

Thorvard . . . had the sword called *Brynjubítr*: Sigurd the Greek brought it from Constantinople. Svein Jonsson of Vidiness had it and struck mighty blows with it (*hjó stort með*). The sons of Sighvat, Tinn and Sturla, wanted to purchase the sword, but were unable to buy it. However Thorvard was persuaded to lend the sword to Sturla.

No further details are given about the sword; it is possible that it had an Eastern damascened blade. According to saga tradition, one of the famous swords, Dragvendill, the weapon of Egill Skalla-grimsson, came into Scandinavia as a gift from Gusi, the king of the *Finnar* or Lapps. Gusi gave it to the Norwegian hero Ketill *hæng*; he passed it down to his son Grim, and later Grim gave the sword to Thorolf Kveldulfsson, Egill's uncle.[1] It is likely that some weapons were forged in the far north, for in the Finnish *Kalevala*, the epic pieced together from oral poems of the Finns, Ilmarinen, the 'great primeval craftsman', set about the forging of iron, and the process is described in detail. He collected his ore from swamps and marshes, carried it home and heated it in the furnace, using bellows and hammering it on the anvil until it was as soft as dough. Then he shaped it into spears, axes, and tools. But since he needed harder weapons, he prepared to quench his steel. He prepared ashes and lye, but when he tasted the mixture he was not fully satisfied, and called to the bee to bring him honey. The story goes that he was cheated by the hornet, which brought him a poison made of snakes and toads, so that the iron was poisoned in the quenching, and this explains the evil which weapons have brought into the world. This account shows considerable knowledge of the making of weapons, and it is possible that good swords were made in the Baltic regions, as the Arab writers seem to imply. From Estonia we have a detailed account of a visit to a smith and the purchase of a sword of outstanding value,[2] and again the smith is said to be a Finn. The sword was bought by the hero of the epic,

---

[1] It passed to Thorolf's brother Skallagrim after his death, then to Skalla-grim's son Thorolf, who gave it to Arinbjorn, a kinsman of his wife. Arinbjorn later returned it to Egill, Thorolf's brother and the hero of the saga.

[2] Kirby, pp. 42 f.

the Kalavide. He tried several weapons which the smith brought to him, but found he could break all in pieces with his strong hands, while the smith looked on and swore. Some better swords were then brought out, but he blunted the best of these when he tried it on the anvil. Finally, the smith said he had one sword worthy of the hero, but the price of this was enormous: it included gold, silver, cattle, horses, wheat, barley, and rye, the third of a kingdom, and the dowry of three maidens. It had been ordered by the Kalavide's father, and the smith and his sons had worked on it for seven years. This sword the hero took with joy. It is perhaps significant that no such account as this of the purchase and testing of a new sword is found anywhere in Old Norse literature.

In poetry the adjective *Valskr* is occasionally used of a sword, and this has been taken as based on the memory of swords coming from Valland, the land of the Franks.[1] The Arab writers, it will be remembered, refer to 'Frankish' swords. In the poem on the Battle of Hafsfjord composed in the ninth century, the adversaries of King Harald are said to carry 'western spears and swords from Valland' (*vigra vestrœnna ok Valskra sverða*).[2] The sword Gram is called *Valskr* in the Eddic poem *Oddrúnargrátr* (18), and again we find in an eleventh-century poem by Sigvat Thordarson:[3]

> Sverð bitu Volsk.
> The swords from Valland bit.

The same adjective is in use in the twelfth century, since the blade wielded by King Magnus in the *Magnúsdrápa* is called *valsk*.[4]

Other such adjectives applied to swords are rare. Not very much weight can be placed on the phrase *ensis teutonicus* in Saxo;[5] Olrik (p. 105) suggested this was a mistranslation of *sax*, but it is hard to believe that a Dane like Saxo, so familiar with the old literature, could make such an error; the same problem arose over the significance of *ensis Saxonicus* in William of Malmesbury (p. 110 above). One reference to a Norwegian sword (*norrænt*

---

[1] Another possibility is that the term has arisen from a tradition going back to Roman times (see Kershaw, p. 185). A 'southern spear', presumably meaning a spear made in the south, is mentioned as the weapon of a Viking in the poem on the Battle of Maldon, 134.   [2] Kershaw, p. 90.

[3] *N.I.S.*, B 1, p. 214.   [4] Ibid., p. 408.   [5] Saxo, ii. 60, p. 73.

sverð) in *Eiriks Saga viðfǫrla*[1] is probably only meant to emphasize the nationality of the hero, who brings his own sword into the strange Oriental paradise described in the saga.

Two qualities of the blade which are continually emphasized in the sagas are its cutting power and its durability as an effective weapon. It is usually said of an outstanding weapon that 'it never fails in the stroke', as is declared of the famous Tyrfing which dominates *Hervarar Saga*. Of this same sword it is declared in *Qrvar-Odds Saga* (xiv) that 'it never halted in its stroke for either iron or steel which might come in its way'. The power of a blade to cut through all obstacles is once more emphasized in Saxo's account of the sword used by young Offa in his duel:[2]

The king had a sword of extraordinary sharpness, called Skrep, which at a single blow of the smiter struck straight through and cleft asunder any obstacle whatsoever, nor would aught be hard enough to check its edge when driven home.

Evidence for the terrible cutting strokes which a sword could deal in battle (p. 197 below) shows that such statements were not as wildly extravagant as might at first seem.

In many cases outstanding swords mentioned in the sagas can be traced through several generations, often being handed down within one family. Egill's sword, Dragvendill, may be quoted as an example of this, and we have seen that according to *Sturlunga Saga* Gisli's spear, made from an old sword, was still in use about 270 years after the time when it was reforged as a spear (p. 127 above). Another instance is the sword Ættartangi. This according to *Vatnsdœla Saga* was obtained from a Norwegian sea-captain by Ingimund, by a trick. It passed to his son Jokull, to Jokull's son Bardi, and then to Bardi's daughter, who was the mother of Grettir the Strong. In *Grettis Saga* (xvii) we are told how the same sword is passed on to the young Grettir by his mother when he leaves home:

'This sword belonged to my grandfather Jokull and to the men of Vatnsdale in former days, and it brought them fortune and victory.'

Grettir uses the sword until he wins a sax from a burial mound

---

[1] *Fornaldar Sǫgur*, iii, chap. 3.   [2] Saxo, iv. 115, Elton's translation.

which he prefers to it; we last hear it mentioned as in the possession of his brother Atli (xliii). This sword was obviously recognized as a family weapon, since when the old man Ingimund died in *Vatnsdœla Saga*, the eldest of his sons took the estate, the second the family ship, the third the office of temple priest, and the fourth, Jokull, the sword Ættartangi; Jokull, however, insisted that Thorstein should carry the sword at law meetings, where presumably he represented the family. It has been pointed out that the name of the weapon, *Ættartangi*, must mean 'Sword [lit. tang] of generations',[1] a good name for a sword which was handed down from one generation to another.

Perhaps the most interesting of these long-treasured swords is one which did not remain within one family: the sword Skofnung, said in *Hrólfs Saga kraka* to be 'the best of all swords which have been carried in the Northern lands' (xxx). There is a firmly established tradition that this sword was taken out of the burial mound of King Hrolf of Denmark by Skeggi of Midfirth, one of the early settlers in Iceland. This is told in *Landnámabók*,[2] where we are told of Skeggi:

. . . he was chosen by lot to break into the mound of King Hrolf *kraki*, and out of it he took Skofnung, the sword of Hrolf, and the axe of Hjalti, and much treasure beside. But he did not get Laufi, because Bodvar was going to attack him.

The story is also alluded to in the twelfth-century poem *Íslendinga-drápa* (21):

The battle-bold raiser of the storm of swords [warrior] went into the howe of the generous Kraki to the grasper of the corpse-bramble [sword-warrior], after Skofnung.

The best-known story about Skofnung is how it was borrowed from Skeggi by Kormak. That headstrong young man, however, ignored the instructions he had been given (p. 166 above), and

---

[1] Falk, p. 64, and Gwyn Jones, notes to translation of *Vatnsdoela Saga* (Princeton University Press), p. 135.

[2] *Hauksbók*, 140, p. 57. In *Sturlubók* there is a slightly different version (174, p. 180), and we are not told why he did not get Laufi (Bodvar Biarki's sword). The reason given in *Thorðar Saga hræðu* is that he was unable to bend Bodvar's arm.

when he returned the sword, there was a nick in the blade. Several verses said to have been spoken on this occasion have been recorded in the saga, among them Kormak's own version of the affair:[1]

Skeggi brought me no strong-edged death-wand for the slaying. There is no elasticity in the serpent of the strand of the belt-sapling [i.e. serpent of the shield, sword]. Skofnung bit Hviting in two at the hilt. I have broken a hollow [?] jag in the notched staff of the belt.

Skeggi was understandably annoyed at this damage to his valuable sword, for the saga evidence as a whole leads us to assume that Kormak's criticism concerning its flexibility was unfounded: 'Just what I thought would happen', he is reported to have said. We are told that Kormak had made the damage worse by trying to resharpen the edge before returning it:

They sharpened the notched edge of Skofnung, but the more it was sharpened the bigger the notch seemed.

At a period early in the eleventh century, according to *Laxdœla Saga* (lvii), Skofnung was in the possession of Skeggi's son Eid, who by then was an old man. He too was asked to lend his sword, and he handed it over to Thorkell Eyjolfsson, in order to slay the outlaw Grim who had killed Eid's son. But after they met and fought, Thorkell made friends with Grim, and he never returned the sword to its owner. He still had Skofnung when he sailed over Broadfirth on his last voyage, and when the ship went down, part of the timber, with the sword fixed in it, was washed ashore on an island afterwards known as Skofnung's Island (lxxvi). It was recovered, and borne by Thorkell's son Gellir, and when Gellir was an old man he still carried it when he set out on a pilgrimage to Rome. But on his way home from Rome he was taken ill in Denmark and died there. *Laxdœla Saga* (lxxviii) records:

He died and rests at Roskilde. Gellir had taken Skofnung with him, and it was not recovered afterwards: it had been taken out of the howe of Hrolf *kraki*.

Roskilde, where the Christian kings of Denmark were buried in the cathedral, was not far from the site of Hrolf's palace, so that

[1] *Kormáks Saga*, xi, verse 31, *Is. Forn.* viii, p. 242.

according to this tradition Skofnung went back to the place from which Skeggi had originally taken it.

The various references to Skofnung in the different sagas are quite consistent, and it is agreed that it was a sword of outstanding quality, that certain taboos were connected with it,[1] and that it came out of a burial mound. Gordon (p. 225) rejected this tradition of Skofnung's origin on the grounds that Hrolf's burial place was not likely to be remembered after three centuries and also that a sword would be of no value after lying so long in the earth. But there is evidence for oral traditions about burial mounds and their occupants surviving in Scandinavia for hundreds of years, when they were tombs of kings;[2] again, if the sword were carefully waxed and oiled in a stout scabbard it seems quite probable that good quality pattern-welded steel would be as good as ever when repolished and sharpened, provided that the grave-chamber was dry and conditions for preservation good. A number of swords from the Middle Ages have survived in excellent condition without special treatment, while the sword of Henry V from Westminster Abbey and others from knights' tombs at Königsfeld which go back to the fourteenth century would still be serviceable today if burnished and resharpened.[3]

There seems no valid reason to reject such traditions of the long history of certain swords, preserved as carefully as genealogies. This is well illustrated by a story told of the sword of King Olaf the Holy, the sword *Hneitir*. According to tradition this sword also was taken from a burial mound, and was originally the property of an earlier King Olaf called *Geirstaðarálfr*, but had been given to the second Olaf at birth when he received his name.[4] The Christian king had it all his life, and at the Battle of Stiklestad, where he was killed in 1030, he is said to have dropped it on the

---

[1] Besides those already mentioned (see p. 166 above) it is said in *Thorðar Saga hræðu* that it must only be taken from the scabbard when it is to be put into use, and in *Laxdæla Saga*, lvii, that it must not be drawn when a woman is by.

[2] I have given some examples in 'The Hill of the Dragon', *Folklore*, lxi, 1950, p. 174.   [3] I owe this observation to R. E. Oakeshott.

[4] *Flateyjarbók*, ii. 7, p. 7. For the tradition that the second Olaf was the first reborn, see Ellis, pp. 138 f.

ground when he received a fatal wound. It was found by a man from Sweden who was taking part in the battle:[1]

He had broken his sword, and he took up the sword Hneitir and fought with it. . . . He got away to Sweden, and went home to his property. He kept the sword all his life and his son after him, and so one after another of his kinsmen took it, and always it followed that as each possessed the sword he told the next the sword's name and also whence it came.

A descendant of this man came to Constantinople and entered the Emperor's bodyguard, but he found that every night the sword disappeared from under his pillow and was found some distance away. The Emperor heard of this, and also whose the sword had been, and he purchased it for three times its value in gold. Thus it came about that the sword was placed over the altar in St. Olaf's Church in Constantinople. This story was told by Einarr Skulason in the poem *Geisli*, recited in Trondheim Cathedral in 1153. We see from this that each kinsman who inherited the sword learnt its name and history when he did so, so that the memory of its origin was preserved during the century which elapsed between the battle fought in 1030 and the discovery of the sword in Constantinople.

The literary evidence for the keeping of a good sword in use over the lifetimes of several men is a testimony to the value of a fine blade that had been kept in good condition. One of the swords mentioned in an eleventh-century will as a bequest from the Atheling Æthelstan to his brother is said to have belonged to King Offa, a king of Mercia who died in 796.[2] This sword must have been at least two hundred years old by the time of the will, although we do not know its condition.

It is clear that one of the duties of a king was to keep a stock of sharp swords in readiness for time of need. In the account of the last battle of King Olaf Tryggvason we find that when he

---

[1] *Heimskringla, Hákonar Saga Herðibreiðs*, xx.
[2] This is the sword which Akerman suggested might have been the Hunnish sword presented to Offa by Charles the Great. See p. 109 above, and p. 120 for other swords mentioned in Æthelstan's will.

noticed his men's swords were not cutting well, he took instant action:[1]

> . . . He shouted 'Are you being lazy with your swords? I see they don't bite for you.' A man replied: 'Our swords are blunt and badly nicked.' Then the king went down into the forehold and opened the high-seat chest, and out of it he took many sharp swords, and gave them to the men.

It has been pointed out by Bruce-Mitford[2] that the presence of the great ceremonial whetstone in the Sutton Hoo treasure ship no doubt emphasizes this function of the king as 'giver and master' of swords. It had never been used for sharpening, but it reminds us that the keeping sharp of weapons for his men was one of the king's duties, and a 'sword-sharpener' (*swurd hwita*) was among the officers in Prince Æthelstan's household in the eleventh century (p. 120 above). That the sharpening and polishing of the blade was an expert's task is brought home to us by a passage in the Welsh *Mabinogion* (p. 122) in the tale of Culhwch and Olwen, when Cei gains possession of the sword of Wrnach the Giant by claiming to have such knowledge. Wrnach said:

> 'For some time I have been seeking one who should polish my sword, but I found him not. Let that man in. . . . Why man, is this true which is reported of thee that thou knowest how to furbish swords?' 'I do that', said Cei. The sword was brought to him. Cei took a striped whetstone from under his arm. 'Which dost thou prefer upon it, white-haft or dark-haft?' 'Do with it what pleases thee, as though it were thine own.' He cleaned half of one side of the blade for him and put it in his hand. 'Does that content thee?' 'I would rather than all that is in my dominion that the whole of it were like this.'

A story from *Droplaugarsona Saga* (ix) shows how such things were managed in Iceland:

> Thorbjorn was the name of a man who was a house-servant of Groa, and he was skilled with weapons (*gerði vel við vapn*). Helgi Droplaugarson asked him to see to his sword (*gera til sverð sitt*) while he went down to the firth. Thorgrim found another sword for Helgi.

This was the reason why, when Helgi was attacked, he was

---

[1] *Heimskringla, Óláfs Saga Tryggvasonar,* cix.   [2] *Sutton Hoo,* p. 16.

unable to defend himself as well as if he had had his own weapon. Thorbjorn's job was the resharpening of Helgi's sword, for later on Grim says: 'See if you can get hold of the sword which Thorbjorn whetted.'

Finally, it is worth noticing that a number of Old Norse sword names appear to have been inspired by the appearance or the characteristics of the blade. Those which suggest a pattern-welded blade have already been mentioned. We may add to these others from Falk's list: *Hvítingr* and *Lýsingr* (*Hwytingus* and *Lysingus* in Saxo), both alluding to the gleam of the blade; *Afspringr*, which must refer to its flexibility; *Skǫfnungr*, probably from *skafa*, 'to scrape, polish', based on the high polish of a blade, and *Skyggðir* and *Snyrtir*, which have a similar meaning; *Grásíða*, 'Greysides', referring to the steely gleam of the blade; and names based on its cutting-power, such as *Eggumskarpi*, *Hvati* ('sharp'), *Langhvass* ('long and sharp'), and *Hneitir* (from *hneita* 'to wound'). The last is said to have been the name given by Olaf the Holy to his famous sword 'because he thought it cut more keenly than other swords'.[1]

9. THE HILT IN OLD NORSE LITERATURE

Concerning the hilt of the sword, there are many allusions to elaborate hilts on weapons owned by kings and great men. King Olaf the Holy's sword Hneitir had a hilt 'ornamented with gold' (*gulli búnu*), according to Snorri's account in *Heimskringla*.[2] The same phrase is used for the hilt of the king's sword in Sigvat's poem on the king's death,[3] and in Einarr Skulason's poem *Geisli* the same sword is described as 'marked with gold' (*hjǫrr gulli merkr*, 44). The sword Gram in *Brot af Sigurðarkviðu* 19 is said to be *brugðinn gulli*, 'bound with gold'; this probably refers to the use of gold wire to cover the grip or other parts of the hilt (see p. 147 above). References to silver hilts are also frequent. The followers of Harald Fairhair are said in *Hrafnsmál* 11 to have swords 'bound with silver' (*sverðum silfrǫfðum*). The poet Sigvat calls his own sword which was given to him by King Olaf when he entered his

---

[1] *Fornmanna Sǫgur*, iv. 58.
[2] *Óláfs Saga Helga*, ccxiii. [3] *Erfidrápa Óláfs Helga*, 16.

service 'silver-hilted' (*silfri hjaltat*).[1] Steinthor's sword with the soft blade described in *Eyrbyggja Saga* (p. 165 above) was said to have a silver guard and pommel-bar, a grip bound with silver (*vafiðr silfri meðalkaflinn*) and edged with gold (*gyldar listur á*); these gold 'edges' to the grip were probably gold rings at either end (p. 59 above).

This last detailed description of a hilt illustrates the different terms used for the various parts. The grip is *meðalkafli, kafli* signifying a rounded piece of wood; though this part of the hilt might be covered with metal, metal wire, and so on, it was usual for the tang to be protected by wood under the covering (p. 58 above). The bars above and below the grip (guard and pommel bar, sometimes described as upper and lower guard) were called *hjǫlt*, and could be differentiated as *eptra hjalt*, the upper hilt, and *fremma hjalt*, the lower hilt. The term *hepti* might be used for the simple hilt of a knife or dagger without guards,[2] but the plural term *hjǫlt* is commonly employed for the hilt of a sword. Similarly the Anglo-Saxon term *hilt* could be used for the whole hilt, but a plural term *hiltas* is also found. It may be noted that the singular form is more frequent in *Beowulf*, the only use of the plural being in line 1574. The plural form, however, remained in use, and still occurs in Elizabethan times, as when Brutus says in *Julius Caesar* (v. 5): 'Hold thou my *swordhilts* while I run on it.'

The terms *véttrim* and *valbǫst* are also used for parts of the hilt, and probably refer to some part of the covering of the tang. In Vígfusson's Dictionary the interpretation given to *véttrim* is 'lid-ridge', from *vétt* meaning the lid of a chest or shrine; by this he means apparently the ridge running down the blades of many Viking Age swords. There is little doubt that this interpretation is based on a passage in *Kormáks Saga* (ix), where Kormak fights a duel with Bersi and the sword Skofnung breaks Bersi's sword Hviting. The prose account runs thus:

. . . tók Skǫfnungr af . . . dinn af Hvíting fyrir framan *véttrimina*.

The missing word was usually taken as *oddinn* (point), so that the

---

[1] *N.I.S.*, B1, p. 245, v. 27.
[2] Falk, p. 10. Cf. the puzzling term *heptisax* in *Grettis Saga*, p. 139 above.

meaning would be 'Skofnung took off Hviting's point at the *véttrim*'. But Falk (p. 29) suggested as an alternative *brandinn* (blade). This would mean that the place at which Hviting broke was not near the point but at the top, immediately below the hilt; and in this case the *véttrim* could be taken to be the band of metal encircling the hilt either above or below the guard. For a sword to break at a point just below the hilt would not be surprising: it was a point of weakness, but such a break might be repaired, as Hviting was repaired later. It may be noticed that in the parallel incident in *Gunnlaugs Saga*, when Gunnlaug breaks the sword of his opponent but like Kormak is wounded by the point cutting his hand, the break comes just below the hilt: *ok brast sverðit þegar sundr undir hjǫltum* (xi).

The word *véttrim* occurs in sword kennings. In *Geisli* 47 the sword is called 'snake of the *véttrim*' and elsewhere 'tongue of the véttrim' (*Magnúsdrápa* 8).[1] If the blade is thought of as issuing out of the ring of metal by the guard like a snake from its hole or a tongue from a mouth, this would explain the kenning satisfactorily. We do not know what is the exact distinction between the terms *véttrim* and *valbǫst*, though both were evidently part of the hilt, and we are told in *Sigrdrífumál* 6 that they are both places on which runes should be cut:

> Cut them on the hilt of your sword,
> some on the *véttrim*,
> and some on the *valbǫst*.

Possibly the *valbǫst* was the ring at the other end of the grip, below the pommel, on which runes were actually carved on a hilt of a sword in Oslo Museum (p. 80 above). It is the *valbǫst* round which a snake is said to be twined in a sword given to the hero Helgi (p. 167 above). The term also occurs in sword kennings, in both singular and plural forms. In *Geisli* 43 the sword is called the 'glory of the *valbǫst*', while again in *Runhenda* 6 blood is the 'Rhine [river] of the *valbastar*'. Egill Skallagrimsson calls the sword the 'fire of the *valbastar*'.[2] These do little to clarify

---

[1] *N.I.S.*, Bı, pp. 439, 406.   [2] Ibid., pp. 438, 446.

the issue, as in the first and last case the *valbǫst* appears to stand for the hilt as distinct from the blade, though Egill's use of the plural term would be consistent with its being used for the two rings on the grip. In the other instance, the kenning for blood as river of the *valbastar* would seem to signify that it stands here for the sword in general. Falk interprets *véttrim* and *valbǫst* as 'covering strip' and 'foreign covering' respectively. The Old English term *scennum*, referring to some part of the covering of the hilt, also remains obscure (p. 138 above).

Another term for the covering of the hilt is *oman*,[1] which Falk (p. 23) derives from the root **wem*, 'to wind'. This could be based on leather binding or gold and silver thread wound round the grip. In *Thiðriks Saga* (clii) Hiltibrand removes *hjǫlt ok oman* from the sword Mimming and puts them on to his own sword which he wishes to substitute for it: here the terms could stand for 'guard and grip' or possibly 'hilt and covering'. It may be remembered that it was not too difficult to change the hilt of a sword, particularly if the pommel was left untouched.

There are two references to a ring on the hilt in poems in the *Edda*, although none appears to have survived in the prose literature. In *Helgakviða Hjǫrvarðsonar* (8–9) the Valkyrie who gives a name to the young hero promises him a sword, the best of those that lie on *Sigarsholmr*:

> Hringr er í hialti,   hugr er í miðio,
> ógn er í oddi,   þeim er eiga getr.

> A ring's in the hilt,   valour midway,
> and fear in the point,   for him who wins it.

This is poetic language, not exact description, but it seems to imply that there is some special significance in the ring, making it something more than a mere ornament, since it is mentioned along with the abstract qualities of valour and the power to inspire terror.

---

[1] Vígfusson gives 'boss' for *oman*, basing this on the occurrence of the term in the account of the touching of the king's sword (see p. 76 above), but the reference in this passage could be to the hilt just as well as to the pommel or boss. Falk points out that in another description of the ceremony the term appears to be equivalent to *meðalkafli*, 'grip'.

The second reference is found in a description of Gram, the sword of Sigurd the Volsung, in the shorter *Sigurðarkviða* (68). It is, however, only found in one manuscript and has been rejected by most editors, since if included it gives an irregular first line to the stanza. According to this reading the sword is called *malmr hringvariðr*, 'ring-mounted [or -defended] metal'. Although these references do not give us much material, it may be noted that both Helgi and Sigurd are rulers and leaders of men, so that there is nothing to contradict the idea that the ring is a symbol on the leader's sword.

Horn and bone are mentioned in the sagas as possible coverings for a hilt. The sword Footbiter in *Laxdœla Saga* (xxix, lxxvii) was said to be

... a great weapon and a good, with the hilt formed of walrus ivory (*tannhjǫlt*); there was no silver on it. .... The grip was bound with gold.

The same play on the idea of a biting sword is found in the sagas of the kings, where the sword of Magnus Barefoot is called 'Legbiter',[1] and this also has an ivory hilt:

... with guard of walrus-ivory, and the grip bound with gold, the best of weapons.

Hornhjalti, a sword mentioned in *Gull-Thóris Saga* and *Halfdanar Saga Eysteinssonar*, and said to be 'much adorned with gold', is presumably from its name to be pictured as a sword with a hilt of ivory or horn. Falk (p. 27) notes the Old Irish term *claideb dét*, 'tooth sword', in this connexion. A number of references to swords with ivory hilts in the Irish sagas have been collected by O'Curry,[2] and in some cases it is said that there was also gold on the ivory.

An interesting addition to a sword was that possessed by the famous Skofnung, which was said to have a 'life-stone' which 'went with it'. It is not clear whether this was actually fastened to the sword in any way. It may have been inside the little bag which Kormak is told to leave alone, and which appears to have been

---

[1] *Heimskringla, Magnus Saga Berfœtts*, xxiv.
[2] E. O'Curry, *Manners and Customs of the Ancient Irish*, 1873, ii, p. 316.

attached to the scabbard (p. 166 above). In *Laxdœla Saga* (lvii) this stone is again mentioned:

> If a man gets a wound from the sword [i.e. Skofnung] the wound will not heal unless the life-stone that goes with the sword be rubbed on it.

Here it is implied that the stone is separate from the sword itself, or at least could be detached from it if necessary, since when Thorkell wished to heal a wound which Grim had received from Skofnung

> ... he took Skofnung's stone and rubbed it on, and tied it on to Grim's arm, and immediately it took all the smarting pain and swelling from the wound.

Similarly Bersi had a 'life-stone' which went with his sword Hviting and was apparently not kept with sword or scabbard but in a bag round his neck. One day when he was swimming a man snatched it from him in the sea, so that he would be prevented from winning a duel; and after that his wounds were slow to heal. Meanwhile, however, the stone had been washed ashore, and it was brought to the wounded man so that his wounds were healed by it.[1] The purpose of this stone was apparently to bring victory to the wearer as well as to cause quick recovery from wounds received in battle. Such accounts suggest that in these cases we may have a late survival of the practice of attaching beads or balls to the scabbard of a sword, for which there is plenty of archaeological evidence; unfortunately, examples from the Viking Age are lacking to confirm this.

In the *Fornaldar Sǫgur*[2] a reference to 'life-stones' seems to indicate something of a different kind, small enough to be kept inside the pommel-bar:

> Life-stones were shut into the pommel-bar (*í eptra hjalti*) which drew poison and swelling from wounds, if they were scraped into them.

In the same saga the hero, Hrolf, cures his wounds by using these 'stones':

> He took the life-stones and scraped along the edges (*skefr í stúfana*), and immediately he took the soreness from the wounds.

---

[1] *Kormáks Saga*, xii, xiii.   [2] *Gǫngu-Hrólfs Saga*, iii and xxv.

This passage seems to allude to the later practice of keeping charms (necessarily of minute size) inside the pommel of a sword, as relics appear to have been kept in Christian times. There is no early evidence for this. In one story from the Irish sagas the hilt of a sword is opened to reveal the name of the owner hidden inside.[1] The expression 'wound-fingers' (*benknúar*) is found among a list of parts of a sword given in the *Thulur*, and Falk (p. 27) suggests that this is the pommel, used to heal wounds in the way described above. Some pommels resemble the fingers of a hand, and an extreme example on a sword found near Florence is shown by Laking.[2] The 'death' or 'slaughter' stone mentioned in the Anglo-Saxon riddle for which no explanation has been found might possibly denote some kind of charm (presumably not beneficent in this case) in the hilt of the sword (p. 153 above).

There are scattered references to Christian relics in the hilt, the earliest being the account of the sword given to the Anglo-Saxon King Æthelstan in the tenth century (p. 111 above). In *Karlamagnús Saga* the holy relics in Roland's sword are mentioned:[3]

In thy hilt is the tooth of the Apostle Peter, and some of the blood of the holy Bishop Blasius, and some of the hair of the holy Bishop Dionysius. It would not be right that thou shouldst come among heathen men.

This passage evidently comes from the *Chanson de Roland* (2344–9):

Ah, Durendal, how fair art thou, how very holy! In the gilded pommel there are many relics: a tooth of St. Peter, blood of St. Blaise, hairs of my lord St. Denis, and part of the robe of Blessed Mary. It is not right that pagans should possess thee.

Elsewhere in the same poem (2503–8) Charlemagne himself is said to have mounted in the golden pommel of his sword Joyeuse the point of the holy lance with which Christ was wounded on the Cross, and there are a number of other references to such relics in the hilts of swords in the French romances.[4] It is doubtful, how-

---

[1] 'The Decision as to Cormac's Sword', *Irische Texte*, iii, Stokes and Windisch, 62–64, p. 200.   [2] Laking, i, fig. 27.
[3] *Karlamagnús Saga* (ed. B. Vilhjálmsson, 1950), iii. (8), 36, p. 841.
[4] I am grateful to Dr. David Ross for information on this point.

ever, whether this custom ever became prevalent among Anglo-Saxon and Scandinavian warriors.

A number of references in the sagas make it clear that in Viking times at any rate the sword was sometimes secured by a loop over the wrist, so as to keep it ready for instant use in time of danger without the necessity of drawing it, and at the same time to keep the hand free. It is stated in *Egils Saga* (lxv) that this was the method of carrying a sword before a duel:

> In order not to have to draw their swords at the place of fighting, it was the custom of those who fought a duel (*hólmganga*) to have the sword fast to the arm, and then it was ready when wanted.

Accordingly Egill had a shield before him and a halberd in his hand, 'but the sword Dragvendill he fastened to his right arm' (*festi hann við hœgri hǫnd sér*), and his opponent was apparently equipped in the same way (lvii). Gunnlaug, fighting a duel with a berserk, wore a second sword fastened by a loop to his wrist, the loop being round the grip (*lykkju um meðalkafla*).[1] The same procedure was adopted on other occasions when the sword was to be kept ready for instant use, as when Grettir was hunting a bear:[2]

> He had a cord (*hǫnk*) on the hilt of the sax, and slipped this over his wrist; he did this because he thought he could better manage to do what he planned if his hand were free.

Again when Egill was looking for an enemy:[3]

> ... when he saw where Berg-Onund was, he drew his sword; and there was a cord (*hǫnk*) on the hilt, and he slipped it on to his arm and let it hang there. He took a spear in his hand. ...

It is possible that the cord used in this way was the same as that which fastened the sword into the scabbard when it was not needed. This fastening is mentioned in a passage in *Gísla Saga* (xxviii) in the vivid story of the avenging of the death of Vesteinn by his young son at the Assembly. Thorkell (who had killed him), a man rather proud of his appearance, was sitting with his sword in his hand, when two young boys got into talk with him:

> The elder said 'Who is that most distinguished man sitting near us?

---

[1] *Gunnlaugs Saga*, vii.   [2] *Grettis Saga*, xxi.   [3] *Egils Saga*, lvii.

I have never seen a handsomer and nobler-looking person.' 'I am obliged to you for your words,' said he; 'I am called Thorkell.' The boy said 'That sword which you are holding in your hand must be a fine treasure. I wonder if you would let me see it?' Thorkell replied 'That is an odd thing to ask. Still I will show it to you all the same,' and he passed it to him. The boy took the sword and turned slightly and unfastened the peace-bands (*friðbǫnd*) and drew the sword. And when Thorkell saw this, he said 'I never gave you leave to draw the sword.' 'I did not ask you for leave,' said the boy, and he raised the sword and struck at Thorkell's neck with it, so that it cut off his head.

The same expression 'unfastened the peace-bands' is found in *Sturlunga Saga*[1] when an attack is made at night, and Gizur and Groa are surprised in bed:

Groa seized the sword *Brynjubítr* and unfastened the peace-bands and gave it to Gizur. Thereupon he drew the sword.

It is clear from this that the bands have to be undone while the sword is still in the scabbard.

There are several allusions to the hilt of the sword which show that it was used for the swearing of a solemn oath. It is sometimes assumed that this was on account of the tang and guard giving the hilt the form of a Christian cross, but evidence collected by Grundt-vig[2] from early literature, going back to the time of Ammianus Marcellinus, shows that the weapon oath was used among the Teutonic peoples long before they became Christian, and there is little doubt that the swearing on the hilt owed a good deal to pre-Christian practice. The Norwegian Court Law of the thirteenth century describes how the man entering the king's bodyguard touched the hilt of the king's sword while he swore loyalty to him (p. 76 above). According to Saxo, this was also the custom among the men of King Hrolf. When Wigg was offered his life after the death of his king, and handed a sword as a sign that he accepted service with the conqueror, we are told[3] that he

refused the point and asked for the hilt, saying first that this had been Rolf's custom when he handed forth a sword to his soldiers. For in old

---

[1] *Sturlunga Saga*, K. IX. 3; O. VII. 257; ii, p. 196.
[2] S. Grundtvig, *Om de gotiske folks vábened*, Copenhagen, 1869–70, pp. 44 f.
[3] Saxo, ii. 7, Elton's translation.

time those who were about to put themselves in dependence on the king used to promise fealty by touching the hilt of the sword.

In this case the sword touched was apparently the one to be given to the new liegeman; possibly Saxo here is drawing on a custom of his own time, but the giving of swords certainly went back to an early period, and it has been suggested that the rings on the hilts of swords of the sixth and seventh centuries were intended to be used when the oath of fealty was sworn (p. 77 above). Another reference to the importance of touching the hilt of a sword offered by the lord is found in Snorri's account of the trick played by the Anglo-Saxon king Æthelstan on Harald of Norway, when he sent him a rich sword and scabbard as a gift.[1] The messenger handed the golden hilt to the king, and when he took it he was told:

Now you receive this as our king wished, and you must be his thane now that you have accepted his sword.

Such customs must have given an added importance to the hilt. When the king ceased to provide his retinue with swords, according to Sveno in the time of Canute,[2] it was proclaimed that men who were admitted to the king's bodyguard must bear two-edged swords with hilts inlaid with gold, and men made such haste to obtain them that 'the sound of the sword-smith's hammer was heard through all the land'. Evidently the gold-hilted sword was a mark of a certain status[3] and the ornament on the hilt—the part of the sword which could be seen when in the scabbard—was something more than mere decoration.

10. THE SCABBARD IN OLD NORSE LITERATURE

We know from the sagas that a scabbard was normally given with every sword. It was unusual for the poet Hallfred to receive one, as he did, without a scabbard, and a good deal of interest was caused by the fact. The king was rewarding his good but trouble-

[1] *Heimskringla, Háralds Saga Hárfagra,* xxxix.
[2] *Lex Castrensis,* ii. Larson (p. 158) quotes this as a reliable tradition, probably dating back to about 1018.
[3] Cf. definition of a *ceorl* in *Norðleoda laga* (Whitelock, *E.H.D.* i, p. 433), 'Even if he prospers so that he possesses a helmet and a coat of mail and a gold-plated sword, if he has not the land, he is a *ceorl* all the same.'

some skald for a poem which he had composed, but Hallfred had angered him a little, so he gave him a rich sword, saying:[1]

It will be difficult for you to keep, because there is no scabbard for it; and you must keep it like this for three days and nights, so that no harm comes to it . . . it is well fitting that a troublesome poet should have a troublesome gift.

Afterwards the king relented, because Hallfred fulfilled his appointed task and composed a poem 'with a sword in every line'. In the course of this he pointed out:

There will be nothing lacking to the sword if there may but be a scabbard for the sword.

When in *Laxdœla Saga* (xlvi) Kjartan's sword disappeared through the malice of Gudrun and finally was found hidden in a bog without its scabbard, Kjartan 'wrapped it in a cloth and laid it in a chest'. Occasionally in the graves a sword found without a scabbard is said to have been wrapped in cloth (p. 11 above). Indeed a scabbard must be thought of as a necessity, not a luxury. Gessler (p. 141) noted that in the *Lex Ripuaria* (xxxvi. 11) a sword with a scabbard is valued at 7 solidi, but one without at only 3.

The usual term for scabbard in the literature appears to be *umgerð/umgjorð*. This is used for the complete scabbard. A less frequent term is *skálpr*, which seems originally to have had the sense of 'bag', 'cover', and probably refers specifically to the leather sheath. Sometimes the terms *skeiðir*, *sliðrar*, or *spænir* are used: these are in the plural because they refer to the two wooden sides of the scabbard, which had to be covered in leather or some other material. It can be seen from *Thiðriks Saga* that some distinction was made between the various terms, for Velent says in one version[2] when he has completed the sword Mimming:

I am going first to provide the sword with *umgerð* and *spænir*.

In this case the term *spænir* probably stands for the wooden framework and *umgerð* for covering and adornments. In the main text given by Bertelsen the version is slightly different:

ek skal búa fyrst at fetlum ok umgerð allri.

---

[1] *Hallfreðar Saga*, vi.   [2] *Thidriks Saga*, cvii, p. 101.

The meaning of *fetill* in Old Norse is 'strap', and presumably 'sword-belt' by extension of meaning. Falk (p. 35) takes it as the strap hanging from the shoulder to which the scabbard is attached. In *Thiðriks Saga*, clxxv, we find a description of a rich scabbard:

The whole scabbard (*umgerð*) is covered with red gold, and all the straps (*fetlar*) are overlaid with gold and ornamented with fine buckles (*goðum sylgjum búnir*) and set with precious stones.

When the king held his sword out to his followers for them to take the oath, as described in *Hirðskrá* (p. 76 above), he was directed to place the sword with the hilt away from him, and to turn the *fetils sylgunni*, presumably the buckle of the strap, in such a way as to let his right hand come on top of it. He would be sitting in his high seat at the time, with the sword, still in its scabbard, upon his knee. Beside this we may set another helpful passage from *Háttatál*,[1] in which Snorri explains how to build up a consistent poetic image, and gives as an example the picture of the sword as a snake. The poet is told

. . . at kalla sverðit orm . . . en slíðrirnar gǫtur hans, en fetlana ok umgjørð hama hans.

. . . to describe the sword as a serpent, and the sides of the scabbard (*slíðrirnar*) as his path (i.e. along which he crawls), and the straps and covering (*fetlana ok umgjorð*) as his skin.

From this Snorri goes on to elaborate the image of the sword leaving its scabbard when battle comes, and abandoning it, as the serpent leaves behind his old skin. He speaks of the sword coming eagerly from its 'strap-skin' (*fetilshamr*), which must be the scabbard and its straps. Similarly the kenning for sword, *fetilstingi*, is 'pin of the strap'. This is in agreement with the interpretation of *fetel* as 'belt' or 'baldric' in the Anglo-Saxon wills (p. 119 above).

---

[1] *Prose Edda*, ed. F. Jónsson, p. 152.

III

THE USING OF THE SWORD

Who can separate a man and his sword? One is worth
nothing without the other.   *Kalevipoeg*

BEFORE leaving the subject of the sword in Anglo-Saxon
and Viking times, it is necessary to deal briefly with its use
in fighting, the end for which it was designed. The fighting
described in the heroic poetry and in the Scandinavian sagas is
almost always fighting on foot, and for the greater part of the
period with which this study is concerned, the sword in north-
western Europe was the weapon of the warrior on the ground and
not of the man on horseback. It is true that the long sword of the
Romans was a cavalry weapon, and Veeck (p. 124) believed that
the large number of swords found in Alamannic cemeteries from
the Migration period were the weapons of mounted warriors, and
that later on fewer swords were buried because the Alamanni had
taken to fighting on foot. A great deal of attention has been paid to
this question by Oman in his *History of the Art of War in the Middle
Ages* and by Lot in *L'Art militaire et les armées au moyen âge*.[1]
There is no doubt that the Germanic tribes who came into contact
with the East became proficient on horseback at a fairly early date.
The Romans began the swing-over from infantry to cavalry in the
fourth century, influenced largely by the needs of the Persian wars,
and before long this change was reflected in the formation of
mounted forces by Goths, Lombards, Gepidae, Heruli, and
Alamanni. The Franks were, however, fighting chiefly as foot-
soldiers in the fifth and sixth centuries, and it was not until the
eighth century that they adopted the use of cavalry on a large
scale, while the Anglo-Saxons were still slow to make use of
cavalry in the eleventh century, and the Scandinavians—fighting

[1] Cf. also Hoffmeyer, pp. 151 f.

to a great extent from ships—never came to rely on horses to any great degree. It is hardly surprising then that the literature shows us the sword as the weapon of the man on foot. The use of the long sword as a cavalry weapon must have been restricted to a limited area of Europe during the Anglo-Saxon period. Outside this area it was nevertheless widely used, as may be seen from the evidence of certain Anglo-Saxon cemeteries, and we know from the accounts of battles given in the literature that it was used by men fighting on foot.

A scene in which a sword is used against a man on horseback can be seen on the plate from the helmet found in the Sutton Hoo ship-grave, but this scene, which is closely paralleled by a brooch from the Alamannic cemetery at Pliezhausen, is one of those which Holmqvist believes to be non-Germanic in origin and to be based on scenes from Coptic and late classical art;[1] in any case it may be noted that the mounted man's weapon is a spear and not a sword. The mention of a war-horse in *Beowulf* puzzled Oman, and he suggested that it might be due to continental influences. But the Anglo-Saxon wills and references to *heriot* in the laws remind us that horses with their trappings formed a recognized part of a warrior's equipment in addition to sword, spear, and shield. The passage in *Beowulf* runs as follows (1037 f.):

Upon one of [the horses] rested a saddle, wondrously adorned, richly ornamented; this was the battle-seat (*hildesetl*) of the high king, when Healfdene's son was minded to indulge in the play of swords.

An explanation is offered in the detailed account of the fighting at Maldon in East Anglia in 991, given in the poem composed not long after the battle (p. 149 above). Here the English force arrived on horseback, but dismounted from their horses before the fighting began, and were drawn up in their ranks to form a 'shield-wall' to await the enemy's attack. At the opening of the poem[2] it is stated that they were commanded to leave their horses and advance; but their leader, Byrhtnoth, did not dismount at once, since he needed

---

[1] Bruce-Mitford, p. 47 and plate vii.
[2] *The Battle of Maldon* (ed. Gordon, Methuen's Old English Library), lines 18 f.

his horse to carry him quickly to different parts of the field in order to encourage his men and inspect the line of battle:

He rode round giving orders (*rad ond rædde*) and instructed the warriors how they should stand and hold their position.

Finally he dismounted among his bodyguard, and from that time he appears to have fought on foot like his men. He first used a spear and defended himself with his shield, and only when he was attacked by a Viking at close quarters did he draw his sword from its sheath to defend himself. Evidently his horse was not far away, since after he had been cut down by the enemy and the cowards among his followers began to take flight, we hear that it was on Byrhtnoth's horse that Godric rode away (190 f.):

He leapt upon the horse which had been his lord's, upon the trappings (*geræde*) where it was not right that he should be.

There are allusions to 'trappings' in Anglo-Saxon wills in which horses are mentioned as part of a heriot: for example:

. . . six swords and six horses with trappings, and as many spears and shields . . .

are mentioned in the will of Ælfheah the ealdorman.[1] Ælfheah leaves this to his lord, and it seems likely that a horse with trappings is one with a fine saddle, harness, and accoutrements, such as were worn by the horse which Hrothgar presented to Beowulf, and that these were the marks of a horse ridden by a leader, a man who would also possess a sword. This may explain the careful distinction in the wills between horses with saddles or trappings and those without.[2]

It can be seen from the poem on the Battle of Maldon that most of the fighting in a battle of the late tenth century was with spears and bows, the sword being used by the leaders for close fighting; and this is in general agreement with other accounts of battles in the literature.[3] Comparatively little is said of bows and arrows,

---

[1] Whitelock, p. 22.

[2] For example, in the will of the Ealdorman Æthelmær (Whitelock, p. 26): 'eight horses, four with trappings and four without'. I owe this suggestion to Miss Rosemary Cramp.

[3] Examples collected by Gessler (pp. 147 f.) from continental sources confirm this.

here or elsewhere, although they were certainly in use, and axes, not mentioned in the description of fighting at Maldon, were used by many of the Teutonic peoples both for throwing and for close fighting, and were a favourite weapon of the Vikings.

Certain Greek and Latin historians give some account of the equipment of the Teutonic peoples at a period of which the poets and saga-writers known to us are not likely to have received reliable information. Procopius, writing in the sixth century,[1] describes the army which in the year 539 was led by King Theodibert into Italy. He tells us that there were only a few horsemen, who surrounded the king, and who carried spears. The greater part of the force was formed of infantry, armed with swords, axes, and shields. The method of fighting was to hurl the axe against the shields of the enemy, and then to leap forward and attack with the sword. This would seem to imply a whole force provided with swords, but it is unlikely that the long two-edged weapon is meant here, and the term probably includes short swords and daggers. In the *Strategicon*, dated about 580,[2] it is stated that 'Franks, Lombards and the like' are lovers of single combat, 'on horseback or on foot', but that

. . . should they find themselves in a confined place, the horsemen, should there be any among them, dismount and fight on foot.

It is also said that they use shields, lances, and swords (*spatha* or 'long sword' is the word used here). They fight according to families and not in regular troops,

. . . so that if it come about that their friends fall, they expose themselves to danger to avenge them. . . . They charge swiftly with much spirit, both foot-soldiers and horsemen, as if they were of a single mind, and quite without the slightest fear. They do not obey their leaders well. Headstrong, despising strategy, precaution, or foresight, they show contempt for every tactical command, especially the cavalry.

This account vividly reveals the disadvantages of the Teutonic tribes as allies, while at the same time it suggests, from a new

---

[1] Procopius, *History of the Wars*, vi. 25.

[2] See F. Lot, *L'Art militaire*, Paris, 1946, pp. 43, 85. I have made use of his translation.

viewpoint, the characteristic courage and individuality and loyalty to comrades which we should expect from a knowledge of their heroic poetry.

Beside this may be set the seventh-century description of the Franks left by Agathias. He tells us[1] that their arms are very simple, so that for the most part they can do their own repairs; few wear helmets or mail-coats, and few have horses:

Fighting on foot is for them a familiar custom, in which they are extremely well practised.

For weapons he mentions the sword, which is worn on the thigh, the shield on the left side, the double axe—a favourite Frankish weapon—and the barbed spear.

Such accounts of fighting among the Teutonic people rule out the idea of the sword as an exclusively cavalry weapon. They confirm the idea gained from the grave-finds, that the sword was used as one of several weapons throughout the history of these peoples, and that the long sword, with which this study is mainly concerned, was worn by the leading men only. But this is by no means to detract from its importance, since we are told more than once that the Teutonic peoples were lovers of single combat, and battles were often lost or won by close fighting between two adversaries; moreover, as at Maldon, the death of the leader usually proved the turning-point. The evidence of the literature suggests that the importance of the duel, fought on foot between adversaries armed with swords, was very great, and continued to be so until late in the Viking Age. It is largely from the various descriptions of single combat which have survived that we can learn something of the technique of swordsmanship.

As early as the time of Tacitus, in the first century A.D., there appears to have been a custom among the Germanic tribes which is closely linked with the use of a duel to decide the issue between two peoples. He says:[2]

... There is yet another kind of auspices used to forecast the issue of serious wars. They somehow or other contrive to secure a captive from

---

[1] *History of the Emperor Justinian*, ii. 5.
[2] *Germania*, x, Mattingly's translation.

the nation with which they are at war and match him against a champion of their own, each armed in native style. The victory of one or the other is taken as a test case.

Anderson in his commentary[1] on this passage suspected some misconception on Tacitus' part: 'Victory might hearten the tribe that staged the duel, but what would result from defeat?' But such an objection might be made to any consultation of omens before battle. Grönbech is probably nearer the correct interpretation of such a custom when he points out[2] that it is not merely based on an attempt to discern the will of the higher powers, but rather is to be seen as the testing of the strength and 'luck' of one individual (representing his tribe) against another; if the 'luck' was found to be not sufficiently potent, then no victory could be expected in battle.

By the time of Procopius, it would seem that the duel was an accepted method of reaching a decision when two armies were ready to fight. He tells us in his *History of the Wars*[3] of a Goth called Valaris, who

... rode his horse out before the rest of the army and took his stand in the open space between the armies, clad in a corselet and wearing a helmet on his head; and he challenged all the Romans, if anyone was willing to do battle with him.

In this case the men were on horseback and the weapon used was the spear. Paul the Deacon has another example,[4] when the Langobards found their way blocked by an unidentified tribe called the Assipitti. The latter had a great champion:

They offered him alone to fight for all. They charged the Langobards to send any one of their own they might wish, to go forth with him to single combat upon this condition, to wit: that if their warrior should win the victory, the Langobards would depart the way they had come, but if he should be overthrown by the other, then they would not forbid the Langobards a passage through their own territories.

The Langobards successfully met this challenge, owing to the intervention of 'a certain person of servile rank' on their side, but

[1] *The Germania of Tacitus*, edited J. G. C. Anderson, Oxford, 1938, p. 82.
[2] Grönbech, ii, p. 219.
[3] Procopius, vii. 4. 21; translation from Loeb edition, p. 187.
[4] Paul the Deacon, *History of the Langobards*, i. 12, from Foulke's translation, p. 20.

unfortunately this story, which has every sign of being a good one, was not told in any detail by Paul, and we are not even told what weapons were used.

Such duels have inevitably played a part in heroic literature. The challenge to single combat was one which the ruler himself had to be prepared to meet, as is shown by another story recorded by Paul the Deacon,[1] that of Cunincpert and Alahis. Alahis tried to avoid a duel with the king on whom he was about to make war:

> And when they were already near so that both lines were joining to fight, Cunincpert again sent a message to Alahis in these words: 'See how many people there are on both sides! What need is there that so great a multitude perish? Let us join, he and I, in single combat and may that one of us to whom God may have willed to give the victory have and possess all this people safe and entire.'

In just such a spirit does Offa fight against his father's enemies, in a story which the Anglo-Saxons remembered with enthusiasm and of which we have a detailed account in Saxo (p. 199 below). Another battle fought by two champions between two opposing armies is described in the *Hildebrandslied*, a fragmentary poem in Old High German probably from a Langobardic poem of about A.D. 650. For this the combatants were clad in armour and armed with spears, linden shields, and swords, and they were apparently on horseback at the opening of the fight. They began by hurling spears, and then they 'strode forward' to fight with swords, for it was as a combat between two swordsmen that the main battle was to be fought out. Unfortunately the poem breaks off before much can be learnt of the fighting.

Other accounts of close fighting between two men armed with swords, however, provide us with more detail. A fight at close quarters between the Swedish king Ongentheow and two brothers is vigorously described in *Beowulf* (2961 f.):

> Then was the grey-haired Ongentheow brought to bay by the point of the sword, so that the mighty king was forced to submit to the will of Eofor alone. [First] Wulf son of Wonred smote at him wrathfully with his weapon, so that the blood spurted out from the veins on his forehead

[1] Ibid. v. 41, p. 248.

at the stroke. Yet was the old Scylfing in no wise daunted, but quickly dealt out a worse return for that murderous blow, when the mighty king turned on his adversary. The brave son of Wonred had no chance to deal a counter-blow at the old man, for Ongenthiow cut through the helmet he wore, and he had to give way and fall to the earth covered in blood; yet he was not doomed and he survived, though the wound had touched him close. Then when his brother lay low, the valiant thane of Hygelac let his broad blade, his ancient sword of the giants, strike against the wall of the shield, shattering the helmet which giants made; and then the king, the people's guardian, fell with a mortal wound.

It is clear from this passage that such fighting was largely a matter of blow and counter-blow, the helmet and shield acting as a defence against the cutting strokes of the sword, brought down upon the head of the adversary. Such a battle is not likely to go on for long, a point which is explained by Saxo[1] in describing such sword combats:

For of old, in the ordering of combats, men did not try to exchange their blows thick and fast; but there was a pause, and at the same time a definite succession in striking; the contest being carried on with few strokes, but those terrible, so that honour was paid more to the mightiness than to the number of the blows.

In dealing such blows, the sword was usually employed as a cutting weapon. Gessler (pp. 144 f.) has collected a large number of brief references from continental literature between the eighth and eleventh centuries, and notes that in two-thirds of the cases it is clear that a cutting stroke is described. The favourite strokes seem to be the cutting of the head from the shoulders, the cutting off of arm or leg, and a slicing stroke down through the head. In many cases the wound was dealt in spite of armour. Salin quotes two striking instances of the cutting blow,[2] though there is surely no need to assume, as he does, that it could only be dealt with a scramasax and not with the long two-edged sword. The first is that dealt by Theodoric to Odovacar, the King of the Ostrogoths in 493, a horrible blow indeed as described by the seventh-century historian John of Antioch,[3] since it was struck at a defenceless man,

---

[1] Saxo, ii. 56, p. 68; Elton's translation.   [2] Salin, iii, p. 54.

[3] John of Antioch, *Fragmenta Historicorum Graecorum*, ed. Didot, Paris, 1874, v, p. 29.

while his hands were seized by two soldiers pretending to make a petition to him. Since Theodoric's guards hesitated, the king drew his own sword and raised it to strike Odovacar:

> ... He leaped upon him and dealt him a blow with his sword upon the collar-bone. . . . It was a killing blow, and the weapon pierced Odovacar's body down to the hip: it is said that Theodoric exclaimed 'In truth, the wretch has no bones!'

The other reference is from Ammianus Marcellinus, who in an account of a fourth-century battle of the Goths with the Romans,[1] refers to the Goths cutting at the enemy with their swords so that the blade cut through the head and 'horrible indeed, the severed halves hung down on either shoulder'. It seems unlikely that this was done with the short sword resembling the Roman *gladius*; it is the cutting stroke from above, characteristic of the *spatha*, which is described here, and it is the difference from the Roman method of using the sword when fighting on foot that accounts for the horror and amazement reflected in the account.

The possibility of such blows with long swords is confirmed by examination of the skeletons of the men who perished at Visby in Gotland in 1361.[2] The multiple wounds on the armoured skeletons bring home to us the fierceness of hand-to-hand fighting—not from horseback—in which swords and axes were used. One man had both lower legs cut off, 'probably by a single blow'; in several cases the steel coif worn on the head had been cut to pieces and the blows had penetrated the bones of the cranium, while in other cases part of the skull was cut away. In some cases repeated wounds had been dealt, although a single one would be sufficient to cause death. Ingelmark comments: 'It is almost incomprehensible that such blows could have been struck', and he remarks that they show the berserker rage which must have overcome the warriors. The damage which could be done by the sword was also stressed by France-Lanord, commenting on the state of skeletons from Ala-mannic cemeteries.[3]

---

[1] *History*, xxxi. 7, at the Battle of the Willows, A.D. 376.

[2] Report by E. Ingelmark (Anatomical Inst. University of Uppsala) in *Armour from the Battle of Visby, 1361* (Kungl. Vitterhets Hist. Antik. Akademien, Stockholm).　　　　　　　　　　[3] France-Lanord 1, pp. 19 f.

There are occasional references to thrusting strokes. Gessler instances the account in *Beowulf* of Sigemund's slaying of the dragon, when the sword is said to pierce 'the wondrous serpent' and to penetrate the wall behind. Another instance might be added from Beowulf's account of the swimming-match (555–6) when he slew the sea-monster:

However it was granted me to reach the monster with my sword-point, with my sword of battle.

In both cases the circumstances were clearly outside the usual conditions of single combat.

Saxo, who shows interest in swordsmanship, tells us a little about training for the fighting of duels. His hero Gram, in youth,[1]

. . . taught by the fencers, trained himself by sedulous practice in parrying and dealing blows.

This apparently formed part of his education while he was fostered by Roar. Saxo also refers[2] to the training of the king's men during a period of peace:

To save the minds of his soldiers from being melted into sloth by this inaction, he decreed that they should assiduously learn from the champions the way of parrying and dealing blows. Some of these were skilled in a remarkable manner of fighting, and used to smite the eyebrow on the enemy's forehead with an infallible stroke; but if any man, on receiving the blow, blinked for fear, twitching his eyebrow, he was at once expelled the court and dismissed the service.

Such a technique is perhaps what is referred to by the hero Beowulf, when he explains in lines 679 f. why he does not choose to attack Grendel with the sword:

I will not destroy him with the sword and take his life, though I might do so with ease. He does not know of those brave practices (*goda*) of striking back at me and hewing at the shield, famed though he is for deeds of violence.

When attacked by those who use witchcraft or attack in unfair numbers, a hero is evidently permitted to use wrestling tactics,

---

[1] Saxo, i. 12, p. 18; Elton's translation.
[2] Ibid. vii. 250, p. 301.

as Beowulf did, or any available weapon such as a club, like Halfdan and Gram in Saxo's stories,[1] but the inference is that for a duel with an adversary whom he respects, the sword must be the chosen weapon.

It is interesting to note how many single combats Saxo includes in the early books of his Danish History. Nearly all his heroes fight duels: Biarke, Rorik, Horwendil, Frode, Starkad, Helgi, Halfdan, and Ole, among others. It is clear from his descriptions that they fought according to well-established custom and rule, and that in practically every case the battle was fought with swords. How far these battles are based on genuine early material from lost heroic literature is not easy to determine, but his evidence certainly deserves consideration. One of his most interesting duels is that fought by Prince Uffe (Offa), and we know that the tradition of this particular combat is an early one, since it is referred to in the Anglo-Saxon poem *Widsith* (38–40),[2] in which it is said that Offa won for his people the right to hold their territory 'with his sword alone'. But the only account of the fighting which has survived in any detail is that in Saxo.[3] Here the battle takes place on an island in the river Eider, while the king and the rest watch from a bridge. The *Vitae duorum Offarum* gives an account of Offa leading a great army against the enemy, and this is almost certainly a confused tradition, though the crossing of a river and the slaying of two of the enemy by Offa agree with the earlier accounts. Saxo states that Offa fought against two opponents in order to wipe out the disgrace brought on the Danes by the slaying of the King of Sweden by two of their race, 'for the ancients held it to be unfair and also infamous for two men to fight against one'. We may remember, however, that no criticism seems to be levelled against the two men who fought Ongentheow in *Beowulf* (p. 195 above), while Saxo himself gives an account of another battle on an island of one man against two, a battle also mentioned in *Landnámabók*.[4] The criterion may be whether the two opponents meet the other

[1] Ibid. vii. 219, p. 264; i. 17, p. 22.
[2] *Widsith*, edited R. W. Chambers, Cambridge, 1912, p. 203.
[3] Saxo, iv. 115–16.   [4] Ibid. vii. 254.

man in turn, one taking his companion's place once he has fallen (as in the fight with Ongenthiow) or whether they both attack at once, which would be obviously unfair.

Saxo states that Offa's victory was due to the force of the tremendous blow dealt with his sword Skrep:

> Wermund asked on what particular part he had dealt the blow. The retainers answered that he had gone through no one limb but the man's whole frame.

Having dealt with the first, he kills the second opponent by a similar cutting blow, but this time apparently turns his sword so that the other cutting edge comes into use:[1]

> He turned the other edge of his sword to the front, fearing that the thin side of his blade was too frail for his strength, and smote with a piercing stroke through the prince's body.

Another duel between Froger[2] and Frode suggests that there were strict rules governing the layout of the duelling ground, as in the Icelandic duels described in the sagas, although the planning of this is different. Froger offers to instruct Frode in fighting, and he

> . . . marked off on the ground two square spaces with sides an ell long opposite one another, meaning to begin by instructing him about the use of these plots.

The practice indicated here, with each combatant taking up his stand in a marked square, suggests a possible explanation of an obscure phrase in the Anglo-Saxon poem *Waldere*: *mæl ofer mearce*.[3] A translation of the passage in which it occurs, where the heroine is encouraging Waldere before a battle, runs as follows:

> Never, my friend, shall I utter words of reproach against you, telling how I saw you cravenly give way before any man in the play of swords, or fly to the wall to save your life, though many foes were hewing at your mailcoat with their weapons. But ever you sought to press forward,

---

[1] '. . . gladio quod tenuem quis laminam suis imparem viribus, formidaret, in aciem alteram verso, penetrabili corporis seccione transverberat' (*Gesta Danorum*, ed. Holder, 1886, iv. 35, p. 116).

[2] Saxo, iv. 118, pp. 144–5; Elton's translation.

[3] Edited F. Norman (Methuen's Old English Library 3), lines 12–22, pp. 36 ff.

forcing battle across the boundary (*mæl ofer mearce*), so that I feared for your fate, lest you pursued the fight too fiercely over to the other man's position (*ætstealle oðres monnes*) in accordance with the plan of battle (*wigrædenne*).

The speaker is not in fact describing a duel here, but the conditions under which the battle was fought cause it to resemble a duel, since Waldere was attacked in turn by one foe after another in a narrow opening in the rocks, and fought what might be regarded as a series of single combats with the enemy who were pursuing him.[1] Terms which belong to the duel would thus be suitable in this context, and it seems possible to take the term *mearc*, 'boundary', the exact significance of which has remained obscure, as the marked-out square in which the swordsman takes his stand. The *ætsteall* would then be the opposite position taken up by his opponent, a suggestion which is strengthened by the resemblance to the German fencing term *Anstand*, which has been pointed out.[2] Finally, the puzzling word *wigræden* could refer to the ground marked out for the duel, and possibly also to the rules under which the duel is fought. The meaning of the passage would then be as follows: Waldere has shown no lack of courage, either in single combat or on the battlefield when faced with many opponents; the speaker herself can testify to this from her own observation during the fighting which has just taken place. Rather he has pressed forward too impetuously to the attack, like a rash and daring fighter in a duel, who is not content to remain in his own square, but continually attacks his opponent's position as speedily and fiercely as the rules of the combat allow, running the risk of losing his own life by his extreme daring.

In the fights of which we have descriptions in the literature, the sword is normally wielded in one hand. But a good swordsman might be capable of using both hands with equal dexterity, as occasion demanded; Grim in *Droplaugarsona Saga* (xv), for instance,

[1] Assuming that the battle went as described in the tenth-century Latin epic *Waltharius*, since the account in the Anglo-Saxon poem is lost. See Norman, op. cit., p. 8.

[2] Mullenhoff compared it with the German *Anstand, Antritt*. Trautmann also suggested that fencing terms were being used here. See *Z.f.d.A.* xii, 1865, p. 268, and *Bonner Beiträge zur Anglistik*, xvi, pp. 184 f.

carried two swords against a man who was thought to have the power to blunt weapons, and we are told:

Grim could fight equally well with both hands; he brandished a sword in his left hand, but with the right he struck at Gauss and cut off his leg above the knee.

Saxo too has a detailed account of the transference of a sword from one hand to the other:[1]

Halfdan attacked Grim, cutting through the meshes on the edge of his cuirass, as well as the lower part of his shield. Grim wondered at the deed, and said, 'I cannot remember an old man who fought more keenly', and, instantly drawing his sword, he pierced through and shattered the target that was opposed to his blade. But as his right arm tarried on the stroke, Halfdan, without wavering, met and smote it swiftly with his sword. The other, notwithstanding, clasped his sword with his left hand, and cut through the thigh of the striker, revenging the mangling of his own body with a slight wound.

In such battles the sword is normally used along with the shield, on which the fighter must receive the strokes of his opponent while he has his sword ready to deal the return stroke before his opponent's weapon is disengaged. Thus two-handed fighting with the sword is something exceptional. In one instance given by Saxo,[2] Asmund 'gripped his hilt with both hands, and, fearless of peril, swung his shield upon his back and slew many'. But this was because he was desperate and cared no more for his life after the death of his son, as he declares in the poem which Saxo quotes:

. . . My eager love of him driveth me to my death, that I may not be left outliving my dear child. In each hand I am fain to grasp the sword; now without shield let us ply our warfare bare-breasted, with flashing blades.

Similarly we find in *Vatnsdœla Saga* (xxix) that when things are going badly in a battle for the men of Vatnsdale, Jokull uses both hands on his sword:

. . . Jokull said, 'I can't boast of Ættartangi's bite.' 'It is the same way with us too,' said Thorstein, 'and yet our men are getting wounds.'

---

[1] Saxo, vii. 223, p. 269; Elton's translation.
[2] Ibid. i. 26, p. 32.

Jokull was foremost of all, and he hewed with both hands. He was a very powerful man and of great courage; his strokes were hard enough to do injury, yet the sword did not bite.

Jokull on this occasion had been taken by surprise and had no shield with him, as often happened in the fights described in the Icelandic Sagas. But the Icelanders used shields if they could, as may be seen from Steinthor's battle referred to below. It must have been a grim affair to fight a duel without a shield. In one described in the tale of Thorstein *Stangarhǫggr* (p. 205 below) both men fought until their shields were cut to pieces, but one of them then fetched two more shields from the house: 'I should prefer not to have to stand up to any more of your strokes without a shield', he remarked dryly.

The Icelandic sagas contain many accounts of battles in which the swordsman has been attacked by enemies without warning and has had to defend himself as best he can, without rule or ceremonial. Some of these battles are described in such detail that the tradition of a brilliant piece of sword-play seems to have been carefully preserved. Such was the fight on the ice between Steinthor and his friends against the sons of Thorbrand, of which a magnificent description is found in *Eyrbyggja Saga* (lv). The sons of Thorbrand defended themselves on a skerry, a lump of rock rising out of a frozen river:

. . . And when they had been contending against each other for a good while, Thord Hawkeye made a run at the skerry and hurled a spear at Thorleif *kimbi*; for he was ever in the forefront of the battle. The missile struck Thorleif's shield, and Thord was so busy defending himself that he lost his footing on the sheet of ice and fell on his back, and slid backwards off the skerry. Thorleif *kimbi* sprang after him, and was going to slay him before he got on to his feet again, but Steinthor ran up and defended Thord with his shield, and with his other hand he hewed at Thorleif *kimbi* and cut off his leg above the knee. At the same time another man cut at Steinthor's middle, and as he saw this he leapt into the air and the blade came between his legs: performing all three actions at one and the same instant.

It is hardly surprising in view of this that Steinthor was said to be one of the three finest fighting men in Iceland.

Another vivid account of skilful swordsmanship is that of the last battle of Helgi Droplaugarson in *Droplaugarsona Saga* (x), fought with a borrowed sword because he was caught without his own weapon:

Then Hiarrandi made a furious attack on Helgi Droplaugarson, and cut at him fiercely many times, and no fewer nor less forceful were the strokes of Helgi, but the sword which Helgi had did not serve him well. . . . Then did Helgi show his skill in fighting (*vigfimi*), and he threw up shield and sword, and caught the sword in his left hand, and cut at Hiarrandi and struck his thigh; the sword went through to the bone but would go no further, and glanced off behind the knee, and this wound put him out of the fight.

But important though these unregulated battles were, the duel fought according to certain rules and on a limited field was also of great significance, and continued so until the early eleventh century, leaving a considerable mark on the saga literature of Iceland. The official duel, fought at the public assembly or at some other recognized spot, was known as the *hólmganga*. In *Kormáks Saga* (x) there is a reference also to the *einvígi*, single combat fought with any weapon and without elaborate rules, for Bersi says to Kormak:

You are young and inexperienced, and there are difficult rules for the *hólmganga*, but none at all for the *einvígi*.

Commentators have found no confirmation for this, but common sense suggests that two men occasionally chose to fight out a quarrel without going through the rigid system of the *hólmganga*, and the term *einvígi* no doubt signified such an informal combat. Gwyn Jones (p. 216) has suggested that some of the duels which took place in Norway, and which according to the descriptions in the sagas were fought with no great regard for rules, are examples of *einvígi*. We have one delightful account of an informal fight, conducted none the less according to certain accepted rules, in the *Thorsteins Tháttr Stangarhǫggs*,[1] which is worth examining in detail, because it gives a clear picture of a duel fought with swords outside the *hólmganga* system.

[1] *Þorsteins Þáttr Stangarhǫggs*, ed. Jóhannesson, *Austfirðinga Sǫgur*, Ís. Forn. xi, 1950, pp. 69 f.

It is the story of two men, Thorstein and Bjarni, neither of whom was quarrelsome or anxious to fight, but who became involved in a quarrel through the rudeness of one of Bjarni's servants, and through the egging-on of Thorstein's peppery old father, who had been a great fighter in his youth, and who though now poor was very proud. Finally, Bjarni reluctantly came over to Thorstein's farm and challenged him:

> Thorstein, today you must come and fight with me (*til einvigis ganga*) on the hill in the meadow here.

Thorstein at first said he was unwilling, but in the end he came out with his weapons, and they fought with swords until their shields were cut to pieces. Bjarni then said he was thirsty, and Thorstein told him to go down to the brook and drink. He laid down his sword, and Thorstein picked it up and examined it. For a second time they fought, and each found the other a good opponent. Then Bjarni said that his shoe was undone, and Thorstein told him to tie it up; meanwhile he went into the house and brought out two fresh shields and a sword for Bjarni, which, he said, would be less blunt than the one he had been using. He remarked at the same time that he would be very willing to break off the fight and come to terms. Bjarni, however, said they must go on, but Thorstein refused to strike the opening blow:

> Then Bjarni cut Thorstein's shield clean away, but Thorstein hewed through Bjarni's shield in return. 'That was a mighty stroke', said Bjarni. 'Yours was just as good', replied Thorstein.

Again Thorstein offered to come to terms. They were now once more unprotected by shields, and as Bjarni was about to strike he thought better of it, and declared that he now considered himself fully compensated for anything which Thorstein had done against him. The end of the story was that Bjarni put in a man to manage the little farm for Thorstein's old father, and took Thorstein into his household, and they remained close friends all their lives.

Here, surely, we capture the very atmosphere of the *einvigi*. We see it is a serious duel, brought about by a challenge from a man who considers himself to have been wronged. It cannot end until either one man is incapacitated or the challenger is willing to come to terms. The implication here is that had the men gone on fighting without their shields one at least would have been seriously wounded and possibly killed. The challenger chooses the spot for the fight, and there is a certain amount of formality, for they strike in turn, the challenged man apparently having the right to strike the first blow each time they recommence, unless he renounces it as Thorstein did. Bjarni is twice permitted to have a break in the fighting, and new shields can be provided when the first are destroyed. The difference between such a fight as this and the rules and formalities of the *hólmganga* is clear, however, if we compare this account with the famous description of a duel in the tenth chapter of *Kormáks Saga.*

Here we are told that a *feldr* or cloak (Magnússon suggested 'rug') is to be fastened down with loops at the four corners to form a square, and secured to the ground by pegs. Each side of the square is five ells long (2½ yards), and it is enclosed within three further squares, each larger than the previous one, so that the gap between one square and the next is a foot in width. At the corners of the outermost square stand four poles called 'hazels' (*hǫslur*), so that the field of battle is sometimes called a 'hazelled field'. Each combatant has three shields, held by a supporter. He uses each in turn, and when all have been hacked to pieces the two men come into the central square and there do battle with swords alone. The challenged man has the right to strike the first blow, and if either is wounded so that blood falls on the cloak he is declared to have lost the fight. If a man puts one foot outside the hazelled boundary it is counted against him, and if he puts both feet outside he is held to have run away. The man who loses the fight must pay a ransom of an agreed sum of money, which varies in different accounts in the sagas and no doubt did vary between different districts. According to *Egils Saga* (lxiv) a man who ran away could be forced to come back and fight out the battle to a finish.

There are a number of accounts of the *hólmganga* in other Icelandic sagas, of which those in *Egils Saga, Víga-Glúms Saga,* and *Gunnlaugs Saga* are perhaps the most interesting. They have been discussed in considerable detail by Wagner[1] and Gwyn Jones.[2] It is evident that there is general agreement between the accounts, though some variation in detail, and it may be generally accepted that they are based on what was an established custom in the Scandinavian north in the late Viking Age. Certain problems are raised by the accounts of duels in the sagas. The term itself seems to have originated in Iceland, where 'to go to the island' (*ganga*, 'to go', *hólmr*, 'island') came to mean 'to fight a duel', because the most famous site for these official duels was the island in the river beside the General Assembly or Althing at Thingvellir. Other islands, however, are mentioned in the sagas, in both Iceland and Norway,[3] while there is the story of Offa's fight on an island given in Saxo, although this may not be an early tradition. The obvious advantage of an island was that it gave a limited area from which the combatants could not retreat, and where they could not be interrupted. In *Egils Saga* a duel at Vors in Norway is said to be fought inside a ring of stones, and it is interesting to note that the Icelandic word for 'challenge' is *skora*, of which the literal meaning is 'to cut', 'to mark out by cutting'.[4] Possibly the island was the last step in a long tradition going back to the marking out of a place for fighting such as is implied by the passage from Saxo discussed earlier.

A second problem is that of the method by which the *hólmganga* was used as a legal means of settling disputes. The duel was recognized as such among Teutonic peoples on the Continent in early times; Wagner points out that there are references to it in sixth-century Burgundian Law and in the early laws of the Ripuarian Franks, the Alamanni, Thuringians, Bavarians, and Saxons. There seems little doubt that it was intended in Iceland also to be a method not of evading justice but of serving it; this is emphasized in *Egils Saga* (lxv), which states that it was established

... by law and ancient custom, that anyone, whether he were defendant

---

[1] F. Wagner, 'L'Organisation du combat singulier au moyen âge dans les états scandinaves', *Revue de Synthèse*, XI (*Hist.*), vi, 1936, pp. 41 f.

[2] Gwyn Jones, 'Some Characteristics of the Icelandic *Hólmganga*', *J.E.G.P.* xxxii, 1933, pp. 203 f., and 'Religious Elements of the Icelandic *Hólmganga*', *M.L.R.* xxvii, 1932, pp. 307 f.   [3] Wagner, op. cit., p. 51.

[4] Jones, op. cit. ('Some Characteristics . . .'), p. 213.

or plaintiff, had the right to challenge the other party to *hólm-ganga*.

It was a custom, however, which laid itself open to obvious abuses, and after the Court of Appeal was set up in Iceland in A.D. 1004 the need for the *hólmganga* virtually disappeared.[1] Several stories are told of unsatisfactory duels which pleased neither side, and the abandonment of the custom is attributed to this. Some such incident may have hastened the end of a practice with which many no doubt were dissatisfied, but the true cause of its end was certainly more complicated, and was partly connected with the development of the legal system and partly with the giving up of the old heathen faith. Jones has rightly stressed the fact that the *hólmganga* is not to be looked on as a religious custom, the heathen equivalent of the Christian medieval trial by combat, by which the gods were called on to vindicate the innocence of a wronged individual. Nevertheless, the gods of the old religion were invoked as the protectors of law and order against anarchy and chaos, and if a man refused to accept a challenge to a duel, a 'scorn-pole' could be raised against him, proclaiming him a coward and calling on the land spirits to reject him,[2] so that he became as it were a moral outlaw from his community. It is said of such a man in *Vatnsdœla Saga* (xxxiii): 'He shall never be in the fellowship of good men, and he shall have the wrath of the gods and the name of a truce-breaker.' There are traces also of religious rites connected with the duel,[3] though by the end of the heathen period there is little doubt that they had lost most of their significance. Certainly the gods were held to support their worshippers, so that a duel or a battle might be seen as a test of the power and 'luck' of a man who claimed Thor, Odin, or the Christian God as his protector,[4] and there is

---

[1] K. Maurer, *Altisländischer Strafrecht und Gerichtswesen*, 1910, pp. 701 ff.

[2] For example, *Vatnsdœla Saga*, xxxiv, *Gísla Saga*, ii.

[3] See Magnússon's sensible comments on the rites of the *hólmganga*, *Saga Library*, vi (*Heimskringla*, iv), London, 1905, pp. 349 f. Cf. *Egils Saga*, lxv, and the appeal to the land spirits referred to above. Wagner notes that in the early days of the Settlement of Iceland, the duel was regarded as an authorized method of obtaining land, backed by the approval of the gods, and of Thor in particular. Cf. Dumézil, *Mythes et dieux des Germains*, 1939, pp. 80 f., for a different view of the berserks from that of ruthless bullies who profited by the *hólmganga*.

[4] For example, in the battle between Styrbiorn and King Eric, described in

little doubt that the idea of such a test of the strength and 'luck' of one side against another was still potent at the close of the heathen period, though the gods might no longer be involved.

Undoubtedly the practice of duelling in the Viking Age and earlier made the sword a most important and valued possession. It was the accepted weapon for the *hólmganga*, although an alternative weapon, such as the axe, was presumably allowed. Kormak is said to have intended to use an axe for his duel with Bersi, but he did not hesitate to use a sword instead when he had the chance of borrowing a good one (p. 166 above). It seems to have been customary to carry two swords when going to fight a duel; this practice is found in Saxo[1] and in the sagas. The reason usually given is that it is a safeguard against magic power possessed by an opponent which enables him to blunt the first weapons he looks upon. In *Gunnlaugs Saga* (vii), for instance, Gunnlaug had to fight a duel against a berserk, and was warned by the king to carry a second sword hung by a loop over his wrist, while he pretended he was going to use the one in his hand. When the berserk had blunted the first sword, he exchanged it for the other and slew him. In an account of a duel fought by Egill against Ljot, however,[2] Egill carried two swords, although there is here no suggestion that his opponent could blunt one by magic means.

Trials of strength between two companies of men were also known, and might be held in reply to a challenge. Olaf Tryggvason took part in one of these, described in *Heimskringla*;[3] he fought as one of a company of twelve, and his weapon was an axe. Here it would seem that the men fought in turn. A famous battle of this type was the fight on Samsø, when Hjalmar and Odd fought Angantyr and his eleven brothers; in one account of this Hjalmar and Angantyr slay one another and Odd kills the other brothers, one after the other. In *Egils Saga* (lii) there is a challenge to battle

---

Flateyjarbók, ii. 61, p. 72, one prayed to Thor for help and one to Odin. Thangbrand did not hesitate to fight a duel against a heathen opponent when he came to preach Christianity in Iceland (*Njáls Saga*, xcvii), while in the same saga he answers the taunt that Christ has been worsted in a duel by Thor.
[1] Saxo, vii. 223, p. 269.   [2] *Egils Saga*, lxiv.
[3] *Heimskringla*, *Óláfs S. Tryggvasonar*, xxxii.

of one army against another in a specially chosen field with hazel wands forming the boundaries. Magnússon pointed out that hazels do not grow in Iceland, and that therefore the hazelled field is not likely to have originated there. This episode may possibly preserve memories of earlier Teutonic customs connected with the marking out of the place of battle.

There is certainly some connexion between the challenge to a duel and the weapon oath. Grundtvig makes this clear when he quotes the curse of Sigrun from the poem *Helgakviða Hundings-bana* (ii. 35):

> May that sword pierce thee
> which thou dost draw!
> May it sing only
> round thine own head.

He refers to this in his study of the weapon oath among the early Teutonic peoples, to which allusion has already been made (p. 185 above). The point of such an oath is that should a man break the solemn pledge he has made upon his sword, then that sword itself will turn against him in battle, for the wrath of the gods will be brought upon him. Similarly, the man who will not accept the challenge to battle is viewed as more than a coward: he is rejected by both gods and men, and his own sword will play him false. Some such conviction as this seems apparent behind the conception of the duel among the Teutonic peoples in early times, when, as Tacitus tells us, *Deum adesse bellantibus credunt*. It continued until the close of the heathen period in the north, when the *hólmganga* was still an accepted means of settling quarrels.

CONCLUSION

THIS survey has shown how closely the archaeological and the literary material fit together, and how at many points the one supplements the other to build up a richer and truer picture of the subject as a whole. The pattern-welded blade and the hilt ornamented with gold, the runes on the sword and the cross on the scabbard, the ring on the hilt and the sword in the grave-mound—on these matters and many others we need the evidence from both archaeology and literature if we are to discover what they meant to Anglo-Saxon and Viking warriors. Before we can decide how the sword was forged, we need the practical knowledge which only archaeologists and metallurgists can give us; but we need also to know what poets and saga-tellers and chroniclers have said concerning the qualities of the finest blades, while a contemporary allusion to a particular sword of Wessex or Iceland or the court of Charlemagne gives a breath of new life to theories and generalizations. The axe, the spear, and the bow were useful and valuable weapons also, about which much can be discovered, but they had none of the richness of association possessed by the sword. The reason is largely because the sword was essentially the weapon of the leader, a personal treasure which was also a necessity for the man who would keep his precarious place at the head of others in a world of conflict and uncertainty. Though it was a practical weapon of great efficiency, it remained also a ceremonial object; while poets invested it with mystery and imaginative significance as the weapon of gods and heroes of the past.

The extent of the evidence which survives about the sword brings home to us its importance in the life of a man of high rank. It is worth while to consider briefly here how large a part it played for him, from childhood to the hour of death, for this is clearly established in the literature, and confirmed at many points by archaeology. Sometimes, like Olaf the Holy's sword Hneitir, the sword was a gift to a child at birth, when his name was given to him (p. 174 above); such a custom was evidently known among the Scandinavian Vikings on the Volga, since one of the Arab writers[1] says of them:

If a son be born to one of them, he casts a sword before him, saying, 'All shall be yours that you can win with your sword.'

There can be little doubt that boys played with toy swords in childhood, and certain small, light swords, like the one from Lough Gur (p. 40 above) may well have been made for lads of good family who would begin their training in sword-play before they had grown to manhood.

It would seem that the sword was frequently a gift to a youth when he first attained man's estate. He might receive a sword which had been a family treasure, as Sigurd received the fragments of his father's shattered weapon (p. 162 above), and Grettir when he left home was given by his mother the sword Ættartangi, passed down among the men of Ingimund's line in Vatnsdale (p. 171 above). It might be won by some deed of prowess away from home; thus Beowulf received a splendid sword from Hrothgar for his achievements at the Danish court, and later presented this to his own lord, Hygelac, to be given in return a gift of land and a sword which was among the treasures of the Geatish royal family.[2] According to Paul the Deacon (i. 33), it was a tradition among the Langobards that

. . . a son shall not eat with his father unless he first receives arms from the king of a foreign nation,

and he illustrates this by the story of young Alboin, who journeyed to Thrasamund, King of the Gepidae, and boldly demanded the arms of the king's son, whom he had slain in battle; he was granted this as his due, in spite of hostility at the court, and returned home to be welcomed by his father as a proved warrior. A young man might also receive a sword from the lord whom he pledged himself to serve as poet or warrior; thus Hallfred took a sword from King Olaf Tryggvason (p. 187 above) and Sigvat a sword from

---

[1] C. M. Frähn, *Ibn Foszlan's und anderer araber Berichte über die Russen älterer Zeit*, p. 3. [2] *Beow.* 1020 f.; 2190 f.

King Olaf the Holy. We know from one of Sigvat's own poems[1]
what this gift meant to him:

I received thy sword with pleasure, O Njord of battle, nor have I
reviled it since, for it is my joy. This is a glorious way of life, O Tree of
Gold; we have both done well. Thou didst get a loyal housecarle, and
I a good liege lord.

But whether the young man won his sword through a deed of
valour, received it as a family heirloom or as a gift from a powerful king, or whether, like the swords Skofnung and Hneitir, it was
a sword taken from a burial mound (p. 174 above), the implication
is clear: it was held to bear the 'luck' of former warriors, who had
used it well in past days. To the youth who received it, it must have
been an ever present symbol of continuity, binding him to the past
and spurring him on to emulate former glories.

The king himself had a special sword, perhaps made for his
coronation (p. 64 above). This would be worn by him on all
ceremonial occasions, and in the Norwegian court it was the
weapon which men touched as they swore the oath of allegiance
(p. 76 above). It is probable that this was the sword buried with
him at his death, as we know from Snorri that King Hakon the
Good's sword was laid in the grave with the king.[2] In a poem composed soon after his death, Hakon is pictured riding to Valhalla
with his sword in his hand,[3] and it is evident that no kinsman
inherited that good blade. Such a custom would account for the
number of outstanding swords of fine workmanship taken from
rich graves in Anglo-Saxon England, Scandinavia, and the Continent, of which the beautiful gold-hilted sword from Sutton Hoo is
one of the latest examples. In medieval times the sword of a king
would be hung over his tomb.

The sword might be used for the swearing of a solemn oath
(p. 210 above), and it was the customary weapon with which a
man would be prepared to defend himself if challenged to a duel.
He would fight for his life with it if suddenly attacked, and he
would use it against his enemies when he met them at close

---

[1] *N.I.S.*, B1, p. 243, 3.
[2] *Heimskringla, Hákonar S. Góða*, xxxii.   [3] *Hákonarmál*, 9.

quarters on the battle-field. At his death, if it did not rest in the grave with him, he would hope to hand it on to his son or near kinsman. This desire is something which inspires many moving scenes in heroic literature. The widow of Sigmund the Volsung gathered up the fragments of his broken sword, in hopes that they would one day be needed by his unborn child. Beowulf's lament when he felt death coming to him was that he had no heir to receive his war-gear before his life ended, so that he left it to Wiglaf, a distant kinsman, but one who stood by him loyally when others fled.[1] When Offa at last proved himself to be valiant, his old blind father rejoiced to be able to fetch him an ancient sword, which he had hidden away (in a tumulus, according to Sweyn Aageson's account)[2] thinking that he had no son worthy to receive it. In *Hervarar Saga* the resolute girl Hervor visited the haunted burial mound of her father to claim the family sword, Tyrfing, and was finally granted it without hostility by the dead man himself, after he had tried vainly to warn her of the curse laid on its blade.

Thus the sword was closely associated with much of what was most significant in a man's life—family ties, loyalty to his lord, the duties of a king, the excitement of battle, the attainment of manhood, and the last funeral rites. It was something from which its owner was never parted throughout his life, from the moment that he received it and had the right to wear it. He carried it in the king's hall and at law meetings, although on such occasions it was forbidden to draw it, and it might be fastened down in the scabbard (p. 184 above). At night it hung above his bed, as we know from *Beowulf* 1288–9 and the Icelandic Sagas (p. 185 above). A sudden attack often came at night, and to lose hold of one's sword, as King Æthelstan discovered (p. 111 above), was a terrifying experience. If it had to be sent away to be resharpened, it was necessary to find another sword to take its place, and even this temporary substitution might cost a man dear (p. 165 above). It was indeed, as is said in one of the Anglo-Saxon riddles, the prince's 'shoulder-

---

[1] *Beow.* 2729 f.
[2] 'He asked to be led to a tumulus (*ad tumulum*) in which formerly he had hidden a sword of great renown.' See Chambers, p. 213.

companion', his close friend ever at his side, and 'the warrior's comrade' (p. 155 above). Small wonder that Bersi the Dueller, famous swordsman and poet of the tenth century, declared that if he could no longer wield his sword, life held nothing more for him:[1]

The trolls may have my life indeed, when I can no more redden keen Laufi. Then you may carry the destroyer of the mailcoat's wand into the howe, without delay.

For a man who could no longer rely upon his sword had become a nonentity, a helpless figure relying on others for the protection of life, property, and reputation. The time had come to hand over the guardianship of the family, with the sword, to his descendants.

We now know that the finest swords of the period were splendid weapons indeed, capable of inflicting great injuries, and of outlasting several generations of men. We know too that they could not have been easy to obtain, and thus can understand better the value placed upon such weapons in the literature. We can see why the history of a good sword in Iceland was carefully chronicled. Nor is it surprising, from what we know of the difficulties of its making, that a certain mystery hung over the creation of a good sword, and that poets associated such weapons with gods and giants and long-dead heroes of the past. From what we know also of the complex ritual of duelling and the skill of good swordsmanship, it is only to be expected that a vast body of sword-lore—part technicalities and part superstition—grew up, a small portion of which has survived, and an even smaller portion of which is comprehensible to us now.

The conditions of society changed in time, and a more settled existence replaced the old heroic way of life of the warrior lord and his band of followers. Still the value of the sword as a weapon remained of sufficient importance to keep its reputation alive. Heroic tales continued to be told, based on a world of adventure in which the sword in the hero's hand was the key to achievement. In medieval times it gained fresh glories as the weapon of the Christian knight, and for a long while duelling customs kept up

[1] *N.I.S.* B1, p. 88.

the necessity for swordsmanship. Now it is obsolete, and we can catch only the reflection of its former splendour in the literature of the past. There is no single object among the possessions of a modern man which may be compared to it. It demands, therefore, a determined effort of study and imagination if we are to realize the significance of the sword, so powerful a weapon in men's hands and so potent a symbol in men's minds for hundreds of years. But such an effort is indeed worth while, for much of the life and vigour of our early literature must be lost for ever when the memory of the sword has faded.

APPENDIX A

The Forging of a Pattern-welded Sword

THIS account was prepared from a fuller description given by J. W. Anstee and L. Biek, which is to appear shortly. I am most grateful to them for their co-operation and help and also for permission to use the two diagrams. The work was done by J. W. Anstee at the Museum of English Rural Life, Reading.

In 1955 experiments were carried out on the special methods used

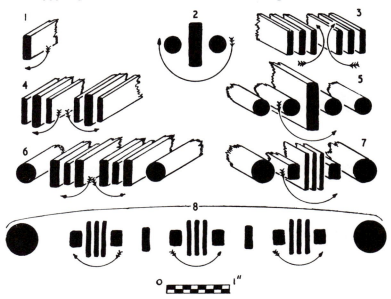

FIG. 1. Diagram by John Anstee showing the components used in the eight experiments, numbered as in the text. The arrows show which rods and/or bars were twist-welded together, and the direction of twisting.

to forge a 'pattern-welded' sword. The same simple equipment was used throughout: a blacksmith's hearth, with a continuous air-blast supplied by a hand-powered box-bellows of Chinese type; a cast-iron cheese-press weight, which served as an anvil; a small vice; a three-pound hammer; a pair of tongs. At first home-made charcoal was used as fuel, but owing to the large quantities required, coke was employed for the later work. High-grade Victorian wrought iron was used as raw material. Eight experiments were carried out, as illustrated in the diagrams in Fig. 1.

Experiment 1. Twisting a single strip

When a strip is twisted it forms a screw with a double start thread. Attempts were made to twist single strips of iron averaging 0·365 by 0·135 inch until a solid rod was formed. This was found to be impossible. A great deal of pulling strain was needed to prevent the spiral from buckling sideways, and the work always sheared before successive ridges of the spiral met and could join by welding.

Experiment 2. Twisting a strip with filler rods

Two iron rods of circular cross-section were placed one along each flat side of a strip, in order to fill grooves between successive turns of the spiral and facilitate the formation of a solid rod by twisting. Filler rods and strip were welded together at one end. This end was held in the tongs and the other in the vice, and the whole was then easily twisted at yellow heat to give a tight rod, the heating and twisting being performed in successive overlapping sections. There was no tendency to buckle, as the bars supported each other. Scale was forced from the surfaces by the twisting stress and fell off on light tapping with a hammer. The whole could then be screwed right up to form good scale-free seams. The rod was hammer-welded to a rectangular section at full welding heat. One face of the forging was ground to four step levels, which were polished and etched to show the changes in pattern. All internal welds appeared to be perfect except at one or two points where lumpy particles had been trapped. The loosening of the scale by the twisting appeared to be a major advantage of this process.

Experiment 3. Twisting of three equal strips

Two bundles of strips were each tack-welded at one end and bound with iron wire. They were then twisted in opposite directions in sections, to give two rods. As the twisting of a section was completed, the rods were welded together longitudinally for that length, and at the same time welding automatically took place between the individual strips. The finished bar measured 0·75 by 0·18 inch in section. The welds were as good as in the previous experiment, and the product appeared to be better in quality than its constituent parts. At the point where the six strips had not been twisted, they gave the etched, 'watered-silk' pattern typical of iron weapons built up from laminations. This effect is noticeable on most pattern-welded swords at the point where the strips have been gripped by the tongs and have remained untwisted.

Experiment 4. One main strip and two filler strips

The patterns seen on some swords suggest that thin filler strips were used, and that these became folded on themselves during the twisting. An attempt to simulate this was made by twisting together one main strip and two thinner and narrower filler strips. Lengths from each end were twisted in opposite directions and forged down to a rectangular section. The rod was then folded in half, and the two twisted ends welded together to form the core of a lance-head. After grinding, etching and polishing, this showed typical chevron patterns, but there appeared to be no directly recognizable relation between these patterns and the original tripartite rods. This shows the danger of hasty speculation about the details of manufacture on the basis of surface patterns alone.

Experiment 5. Forging a twisted rod to close spiral grooves, and addition of cutting edges

A strip and two filler rods were twisted to give a composite rod as in Experiment 2. The filler rods were deeply embedded in the spiral grooves formed. The projecting ridges of the main strip were forged down so that they tended to spread over the filler rods in a dove-tail form; the effect of this could be seen in the pattern of the final etched surface, and a resemblance to some existing sword patterns was recognized.

The rod was then forged to a bar with one sharply-tapered end. Cutting edges were welded to this as follows: a rod 0·27 inch in diameter was bent nearly double and secured round the tapered core by iron wire. It was welded to both sides of the core at the same moment to avoid excessive elongation.

Experiment 6. Small central strip and larger filler strips

A strip 0·35 by 0·11 inch in section was sandwiched between two larger strips. The bundle was twisted for some of its length at both ends and forged to a tight round rod. This was doubled back and welded to itself. Cutting edges were welded on as before. The pattern produced was so characteristic that it would be easily recognized on a sword of early times.

Experiment 7. Attempted carburization of central strips

One explanation of the patterns on sword-blades which has been put forward is that they are due to alternate layers of low-carbon and carburized iron. An attempt was made to surface-carburize three thin strips by allowing them to lie on edge for ten minutes in a reducing (i.e. non-oxidizing) fire made by shutting off the air blast. They were then wire-brushed, laid together in a bundle with two filler rods, and twist-welded and surface-forged to give a tight rod with only a faintly spiralled surface. Groups of triple strip edges formed spirals on this surface alternating with those due to the filler rods. Cutting edges were welded on as before.

A sloping face was cut at a low angle through half the thickness of the forging in the manner of a taper section. This when polished and etched showed varying types of pattern which merged into one another, and all the types appeared to duplicate those found on existing sword-blades both in shape and size, the light and dark zones being remarkably clear.

A report produced by the National Physical Laboratory after examination of this specimen showed that the patterns were due entirely to the characteristic structure of a series of welded pieces of wrought iron, and not to carburization, there having been no significant increase in carbon content. The assumption that alternate layers of high and low carbon iron are always necessary for the production of the patterns is therefore not justifiable.

Experiment 8. Forging a sword-blade (see Fig. 2)

The experience gained by this time was considered sufficient for an attempt to be made at a complete sword-blade. A special heat treatment with substances traditionally used by early armourers was included.

A composite rod was made as in the previous experiment. A stiff paste was made up as follows:

Pigeon droppings	.	.	39·5	(percentage by weight)
Plain flour	.	.	21·5	
Honey	.	.	14·5	
Olive oil	.	.	2·0	
Milk	.	.	22·5	
			100·0	

Total quantity used: 3 lb. 8 oz.

The components of two more rods (three strips and two square filler rods in each) were smeared and packed with the paste, wrapped in cloth and tied with string. The package was enclosed in sand in a gutter trough with a second trough inverted on top. The whole was heated at a red-orange heat for 90 minutes in a wood fire and then allowed to cool. When the strips were twisted up into rods as usual, greater twisting force was needed than for untreated strips.

The three composite rods were laid side by side, the untreated rod between the two others but separated from them by straight packing strips. The pieces were held by a sliding iron clip while they were welded together to form the sword core. A bent rod was then welded on to give the cutting edges. This was difficult because of the distance (1·4 inches) between welds which had to form at the same moment; and the solution lay in the exact siting of the forging at a critical point in the fire, and in the slow increase of temperature. There was no second chance if seams failed to weld.

A cold chisel was used to deepen the grooves left on both surfaces of the core down to a plane where the composite rods were firmly welded together. Final forging bouts were needed to thin out the blade. The

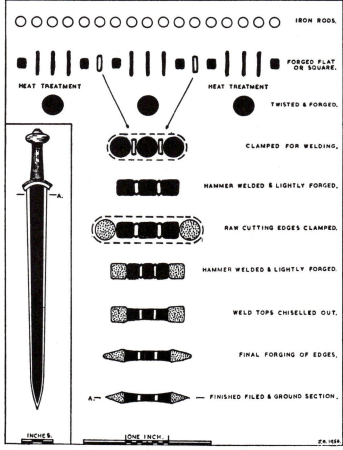

FIG. 2. Diagram by John Anstee showing the successive stages of manufacture of his pattern-welded sword, as described in Experiment 8.

chiselled grooves were roughed out into fullers, using a wet sandstone wheel and completing the work with a modern fine carborundum wheel. The cutting edges were filed and the whole polished. A hilt and pommel were added and a scabbard and belt made.

During manufacture stretching and grinding reduced the total cross-sectional area of the original by 70 per cent.; 1 lb. 3 oz. of metal was removed by abrasion, leaving 1 lb. 10 oz. for the blade. The 90-minute heat treatment was certainly responsible for a small but significant increase in hardness in the parts treated, although no carburization could be detected under the microscope. This hardening was additional to the general increase in hardness due to forging.

The time taken over the forging of the complete sword and fittings was as follows. In the number of heats given, " means that more than one strip or rod was in the fire at the same moment.

Stage	Description	No. of heats	Time (hours)
1	Forging 5 strips for central twisted rod . .	12"	2
2	Twisting 5 strips into central rod	24	3
3	Forging 10 strips for outer twists . . .	12"	2½
4	Mixing and packing compound for heat treatment	—	2
5	Preparing open hearth and fuel . . .	—	2
6	Heat treatment of 10 strips	1	2
7	Twisting outer composite rods	28"	3½
8	Forging two packing strips	5"	¼
9	Welding the core	15	2¾
10	Welding the edges	16	3
11	Chiselling out surface of core	—	2
12	Forming the tang	—	½
13	Rough forging of edges	15	1½
14	Rough filing of edges	—	1
15	Grinding the fullers	—	5
16	Fine filing of edges	—	2
17	Rough polishing of blade	—	6
18	Final polishing of blade	—	2
	Total for blade	128	43
19	Brass quillons made	—	3
20	Door-knob pommel trimmed and weighted .	—	1½
21	Boxwood grips	—	2½
22	Grip binding	—	½
23	Stone setting made	—	2
24	Wooden scabbard in two halves . . .	—	3½
25	Canvas cover sewn on	—	1½
26	Chape made	—	3½
27	Top scabbard mount	—	3½
28	Rough cutting of flint pebble	—	2½
29	Polishing and setting flint pebble 'en cabochon' .	—	2
30	Finishing the scabbard seam	—	½
31	Belt and buckle fittings	—	4
	Total time:		73½

Conclusions

The experiments have shown that any of the known chevron or allied and derived patterns can be produced by twisting and grinding piled strips of normal wrought iron. There is little doubt that the technique of carburization of individual strips was well known in all its complexity in early times, but it is highly probable that an unintentional decarburizing process, involving chemical reduction of oxide scale, occurred in many cases. No evidence was found during this series of experiments to support the time-honoured suggestion that iron can be heavily carburized by working it hot in the presence of carbon dust on the anvil.

The patterns on existing swords may be approximately copied by twisting rods or bars of pile-forged (laminated) iron. If, however, loose strips are twist-welded, the patterns are more accurately reproduced. But it must be noted that they can only be copied by a process of trial and error involving many experiments with strips varying in number, size, sectional ratio, material, and treatment. Even the intimate knowledge gained by making a composite rod does not always help when the operator tries to analyse the resulting pattern.

It is unlikely that composite rods were ever split longitudinally and welded together with their cut faces outwards, as has been suggested, since this—besides being pointless—would be very difficult to achieve without a modern hacksaw. Nor is it probable that the patterns were formed by welding the folds in a laminated bundle sharply corrugated across its length. Such a process would necessitate clamping in a vice immediately after removal from the fire, and by the time the bundle had been secured the metal would have cooled too much. All welding must be complete within seconds of removal from the fire.

The best time to apply any general pack-carburizing treatment would be when the blade was finished except for fine abrasive and polishing work. After the hardening and tempering stages the cutting edges could be honed up.

The twist-welding process was probably adopted in consequence of the type of raw material available to the smith. The raw iron was obtained in small heterogeneous units, and to remove the slag heavy forging was necessary, which would tend to produce thin strips or bars. The simplest way of getting thin strips (which would burn if treated singly) into a condition suitable for welding is precisely the type of operation which produces the composite twisted rod. The great advantage of the twisting lies in the reduction of the amount of slag inclusion and the even distribution of what remains, so that the chance of planes of weakness occurring in the blade is greatly reduced. The quality of a sword-blade would improve with the amount of forging, i.e. with the thinness and number of component strips and small rods used in its construction. The patterned surface of a sword therefore provided the customer with a guarantee of quality, but the pattern should be regarded as a by-product of the method of manufacture forced upon the smith.

APPENDIX B

The Shifford Sword

by R. E. OAKESHOTT

(THE Shifford Sword, now in the Museum at Reading, is the property of the Thames Conservancy Board, and it is with their permission, as also with that of the Curator of the Museum, that this note is published.)

Ever since its recovery from the River Thames in 1936 at Shifford, above Tenfoot Bridge, the sword illustrated in Fig. 25 has been known to have a blade bearing an inscription inlaid in iron letters, traces of which have always been visible in the black patinated surface. It was not until an X-ray photograph of the blade was taken by the Ancient Monuments Laboratory at the Ministry of Works on 26 July 1956, however, that it became possible to decipher the meaning of the letters.

The purpose of the X-ray was to determine whether or not this blade was pattern-welded; no trace of pattern-welding was shown by the photograph. But by a fortunate chance in June 1958 Mr. Leo Biek, of the Ancient Monuments Laboratory, showed the photograph to me. I was immediately struck by the patterns apparent on the blade; they consisted of rather blurred letters, an H followed by a Greek cross and a T: H+T. Further examination under magnification showed a B, an E, and an R preceding these: BERH+T as above. There are undoubtedly letters in front of the B; only the lower edges of the upright strokes can be seen, but one of the uprights is clearly visible on the surface of the blade itself. There seems to be little possibility of doubt that the completed inscription would read ULFBERH+T. The final five letters with the cross interposed can be applied to no other known inscription, while the crooked form of the letters and the way the last three dwindle in size has a similarity to many known and clearly visible ULFBERH+T signatures which might be called the characteristic handwriting of one of the smiths working in the Ulfberht foundry.

Thus the Shifford sword becomes the first example from England positively identified as an ULFBERHT, in the same way as the sword from the Thames at the Temple in London (p. 45 above and Fig. 30) was the first INGELRII when I was able to identify it in 1950.

INDEX

FURTHER REFERENCES

Relevant articles which have appeared since the first edition of this book are given below. A number are included in *Weapons and Warfare in Anglo-Saxon England*, Sonia Chadwick Hawkes ed., Monograph 21, Oxford Univ. Com. for Archaeology, 1989, listed as *Weapons and Warfare*.

I. THE MAKING OF THE SWORD

Adams, B.D. 1974: 'A Sword of the Viking Period from the R. Lea at Hertford', *Medieval Archaeology* 18, 154–8.

Bone, P. 1989: 'The Development of Anglo-Saxon Swords from the Fifth to the Eleventh Century', *Weapons and Warfare*, 63–70.

Briggs, C.S. 1985: 'A Neglected Viking Burial with Beads from Kilmainham, Dublin, Discovered in 1847', *Medieval Archaeology* 29, 94–108.

Davidson, H.R.E. and Webster, L. 1967: 'The Anglo-Saxon Burial at Coombe (Woodnesborough) Kent', *Medieval Archaeology* 11, 1–41.

Dunning, G.C. and Evison, V.I. 1961: 'The Palace of Westminster Sword', *Archaeologia* 98, 123–58.

East, K. 1986: 'A Lead Model and a Rediscovered Sword, both with Gripping Beast Decoration', *Medieval Archaeology* 30, 1–7.

Evison, V.I. 1967: 'A Sword from the Thames at Wallingford Bridge', *Archaeological Journal* 124, 160–89.

————1967: 'The Dover Ring-sword and Other Sword-rings and Beads', *Archaeologia* 101, 63–118.

————1975: 'Sword Rings and Beads', *Archaeologia* 105, 303–15.

Gale, D.A. 1989: 'The Seax', *Weapons and Warfare*, 71–84.

Hall, R.A. 1978: 'A Viking-Age Grave at Donnybrook, Co. Dublin', *Medieval Archaeology* 22, 64–83.

Härke, H. 1989: 'Early Saxon Weapon Burials: frequencies, distributions and weapon combinations', *Weapons and Warfare*, 49–61.

Hawkes, S.C. and Page, R.I. 1967: 'Swords and Runes in South-East England', *Antiquaries Journal* 47, 1–26.

Lang, J. and Ager, B. 1989: 'Swords of the Anglo-Saxon and Viking Periods in the British Museum: a Radiographic Study', *Weapons and Warfare*, 85–122.

Pirling, R. 1964: 'Ein fränkisches Fürstengrab aus Krefeld-Gellup', *Germania* 42, 188–216.

Watkin, J.R. 1986: 'A Late Anglo-Saxon Sword from Gilling West, North Yorkshire', *Medieval Archaeology* 30, 93–8.

Willems, W.J.H. and Ypey, J. 1985: 'Ein Angelsächsisches Schwert aus der Maas bei Wessem, Provinz Limburg (Niederlande)', *Archäologisches Korrespondenzblatt* 15, 103–13.

Wilson, D.M. 1965: 'Some Neglected Late Anglo-Saxon Swords', *Medieval Archaeology* 9, 33–54.

Ypey, J. 1982: 'Europäische Waffen mit Damaszierung', *Archäologisches Korrespondenzblatt* 12, 381–8.

————1983: 'Rekonstruktionsversuch der Schwertklinge von Sutton Hoo', *Archäologisches Korrespondenzblatt* 13, 495–8.

II. THE TELLING OF THE SWORD

Brady, C. 1979: 'Weapons in *Beowulf*: an analysis of the nominal compounds and an evaluation of the poet's use of them', *Anglo-Saxon England* 8, 79–141.

III. THE USING OF THE SWORD

Davidson, H.E. 1989: 'The Training of Warriors', *Weapons and Warfare*, 11–23.

Davis, R.H.C. 1989: 'Did the Anglo-Saxons have Warhorses?', *Weapons and Warfare*, 191–202.

Hooper, N. 1989: ' The Anglo-Saxons at War', *Weapons and Warfare,* 191–202.

Wenham, S.J. 1989: 'Anatomical Interpretations of Anglo-Saxon Weapon Injuries', *Weapons and Warfare,* 123–39.

PLATE I

a. Damascened Blade with 'Mohammed's Ladder' Pattern
b. Blade from Nydam
c. Sword from Kragehul
d. Blade from Ely Fields
e. Pattern-welded blade made by John Anstee

PLATE II

a. Pommel with runic inscription Gilton, Kent

b. Inscribed Guard of Viking Sword from Ballinderry, Ireland

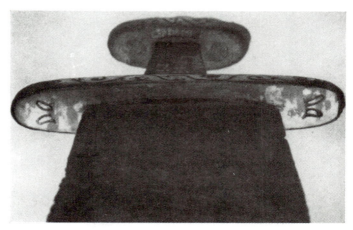

c. Reverse of Inscribed Guard from Ballinderry

PLATE III

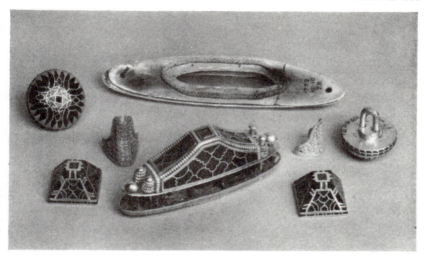

a. Hilt and Fittings from Sutton Hoo Sword

b and *c.* Pommel from Fetter Lane (both sides)

PLATE IV

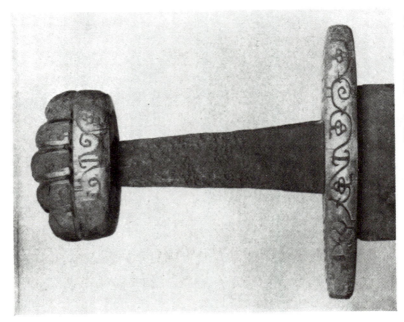

a. Hilt from Viking Sword from Ballinderry

b. Hilt from Viking Sword from Kilmainham cemetery, Dublin

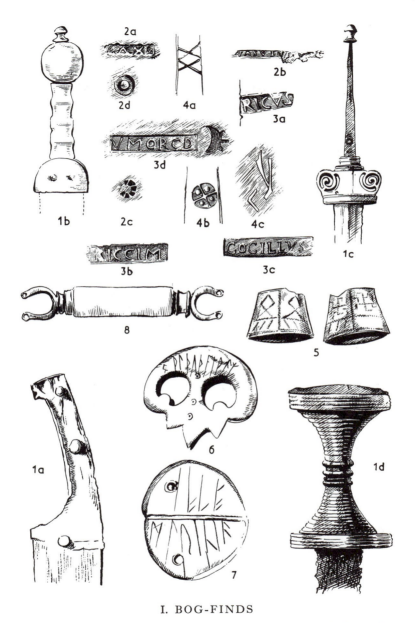

I. BOG-FINDS

1a–d. Early Danish Sword Types; 2a–d. Vimose Stamps; 3a–d. Nydam Inscriptions; 4a–c. Nydam Stamps; 5. Thorsbjerg Mount; 6. Thorsbjerg Chape;
7. Vimose Chape; 8. Vimose Mount

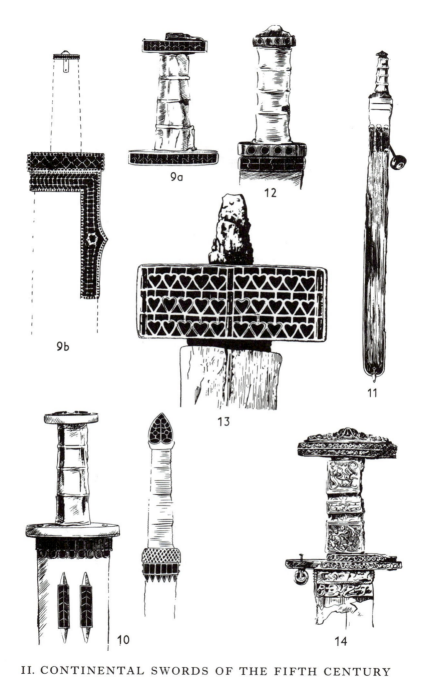

II. CONTINENTAL SWORDS OF THE FIFTH CENTURY

9a, b. Childeric's Sword and Sax; 10. Pouan Sword and Sax; 11. Klein Hüningen
Sword; 12. Lavoye Sword; 13. Altlussheim Hilt; 14. Snartemo Hilt

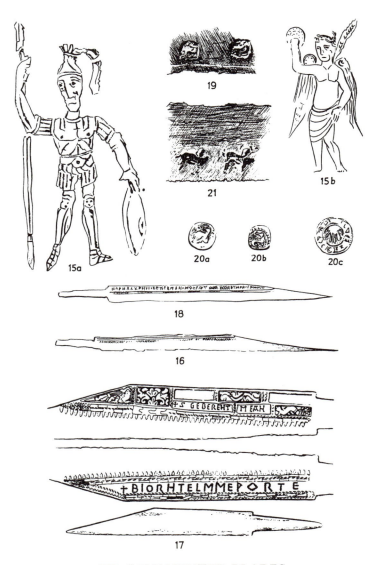

III. ORNAMENTED BLADES

15a, b. Figures on Roman Blades; 16. Little Bealings Sax; 17. Sittingbourne
Sax; 18. Thames Runic Sax; 19. Thames Sword with Coin Stamps;
20a–c. Sceatta designs; 21. Sword from River Lark with Boar Stamps

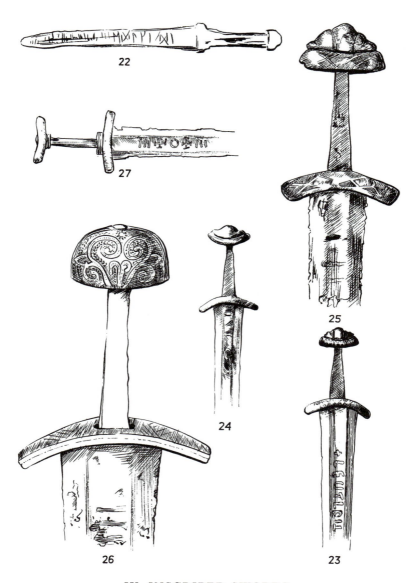

IV. INSCRIBED SWORDS

22. Arum Wooden Sword; 23. *Leutlrit* Sword from River Witham; 24. Tullie House Sword; 25. Shifford Sword; 26. Battersea Sword; 27. Lough Gur Sword

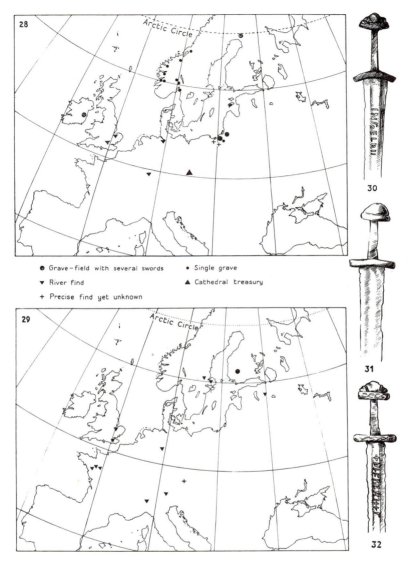

Key:

● Grave-field with several swords   • Single grave

▼ River find   ▲ Cathedral treasury

+ Precise find yet unknown

V. ULFBERHT/INGELRII GROUP

28. *Ulfberht* Distribution Map; 29. *Ingelrii* Distribution Map; 30. *Ingelrii* Sword from the Temple; 31. Wisbech Sword; 32. *Ulfberht* Inscription

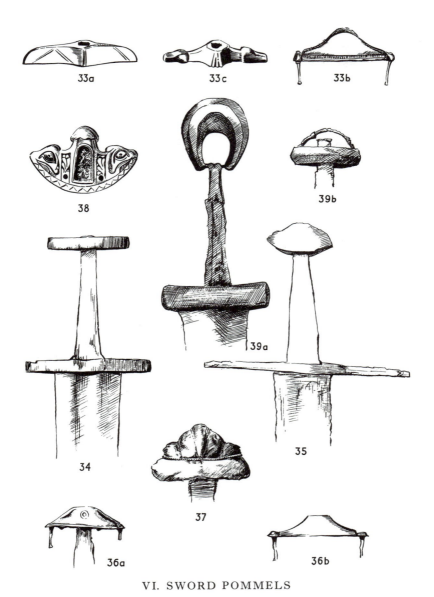

VI. SWORD POMMELS

33a–c. Pommel Forms; 34. Straight Pommel; 35. Brazil Nut Pommel; 36a, b.
Petersfinger Pommels; 37. Pommel from 'Earl of Pembroke's' Sword; 38. Seine
Pommel; 39a, b. Pommel support

VII. ENGLISH DECORATED POMMELS

40. Norwich Pommel; 41*a*, *b*. Dolven and Grønneberg Pommels; 42. Høven Pommel; 43. Grove Ferry Pommel; 44. Sarre Pommel (with Garnet); 45*a*, *b*. Lower Shorne Pommel; 46. Ingleton Pommel; 47. Tullie House Pommel-Bar; 48. Windsor Pommel

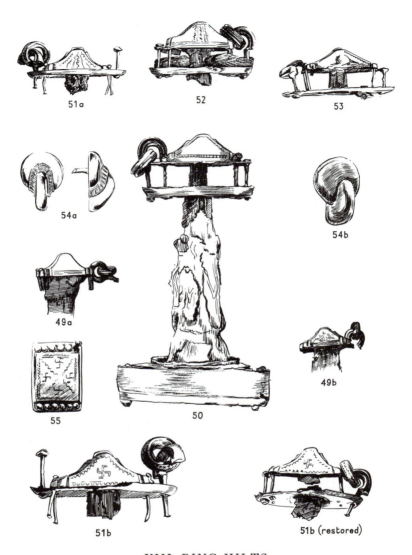

VIII. RING-HILTS

49*a*, *b*. Faversham Pommels; 50. Gilton Hilt; 51*a*, *b*. Bifrons Pommel I;
52. Bifrons Pommel II; 53. Sarre Ring-Knob; 54*a*. Sutton Hoo Knob;
b. Valsgärde Knob; 55. Bifrons Belt Plaque.

IX. RING-HILTS OUTSIDE ENGLAND

56a, b. Hilts from Chaouilly and Mainz Kastel; 57. Schretzheim Hilt; 58. Orsøy Pommel;
59. Vendel I Hilt; 60a, b. Nocera Umbra Hilts; 61. Väsby Pommel; 62. Valsgärde 8 Hilt

X. ENGLISH HILTS

63. Cumberland Hilt; 64. Crundale Down Hilt; 65. Combe Hilt; 66. Witham Hilt; 67. Abingdon Hilt; 68. Westminster Hilt

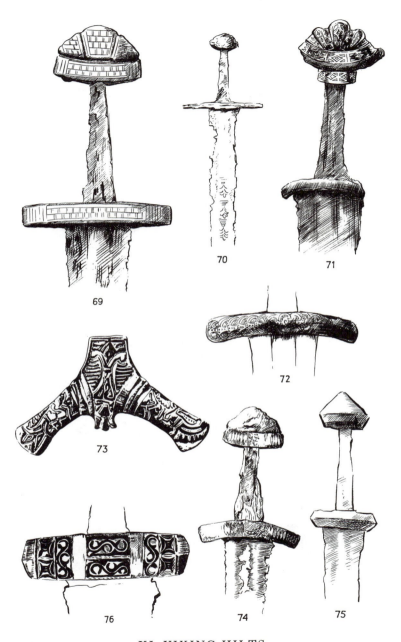

XI. VIKING HILTS

69. Edmonton Hilt; 70. Sword from River Bann; 71. Wensley Hilt; 72.
Hesketh Guard; 73. Guard, London Museum; 74. Wareham Hilt; 75. Enfield
Hilt; 76. Guard from the Palace, Westminster

XII. VIKING HILTS

77. Silver Hilt, Dublin; 78. Grip, Dublin; 79. Chequer-work Hilt, Dublin;
80. Ophus Hilt; 81. Sydow Hilt; 82. Askeaton Hilt; 83. Sändersø Hilt

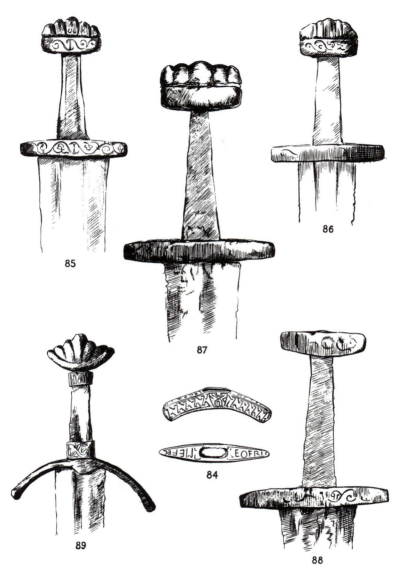

XIII. INSCRIBED HILTS

84. Exeter Pommel-Bar; 85. Kilmainham Hilt; 86. Malhus Hilt; 87. Hilt from Wallace Collection; 88. Hilt from Berlin; 89. Hilt from Korsøygarde

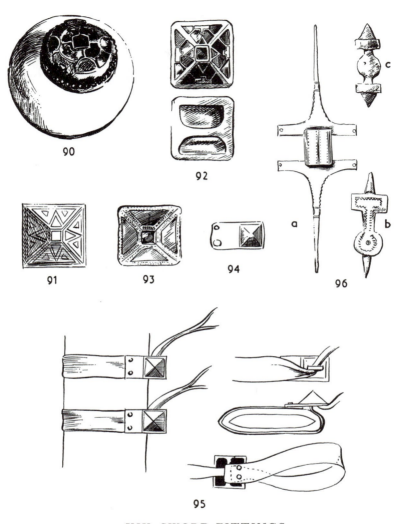

XIV. SWORD FITTINGS

90. Meerschaum Ball, Cologne; 91. Metal Pyramids, Faversham; 92. Sarre
Pyramid; 93. Broomfield Pyramid; 94. Bülach Pyramid; 95. Werner's Diagram;
96a–c. Strapholders

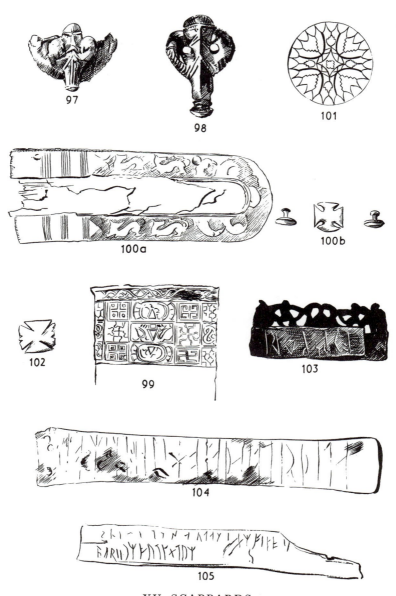

XV. SCABBARDS

97. Abingdon Chape; 98. Krefeld Gellup Chape; 99. Seine Scabbard;
100a, b. Brighthampton Scabbard and Cross; 101. Sutton Hoo Button;
102. Bülach Cross; 103. Chessel Down Runic Inscription; 104. Greenmount
Runic Inscription; 105. Lund Runic Inscription

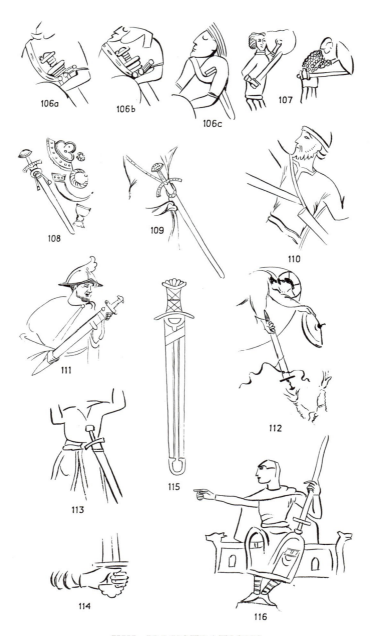

XVI. ILLUSTRATIONS

106a–c. Swedish Helmet Plates; 107a, b. Franks Casket; 108. Anglo-Saxon
Sword Fittings; 109. Anglo-Saxon Goliath I; 110. Anglo-Saxon Goliath II;
111. Lothair Gospels; 112. Utrecht Psalter; 113. Bayeux Tapestry; 114. Hand
with Pommel; 115. Ebberston Carving; 116. King with Sword